National Cycle Network

Nick Cotton and John Grimshaw

2 Cathedral Square
College Green
Bristol
BS1 5DD

First published by Sustrans in 2000
Second edition published 2002
Third edition published 2005

Copyright © Sustrans 2005

ISBN 1-901389-51-0

Printed in Italy by G. Canale & C. Turin

Sustrans is continually improving and refining its routes, so some of the routes may vary from the information currently in this book.

CONTENTS

National
Cycle
Network

This completely new edition sets out to introduce you to the 10,000 miles of the National Cycle Network. It is an impossible mission really, because each and every cyclist and walker will use different sections, follow different routes and find their own individual favourite fragments and useful bits. Even my own highlights, after years of working on creating the Network, vary so enormously and change so frequently that they are hard to choose.

My greatest satisfaction is seeing people using the routes, and knowing that without that path, bridge or link, a walking or cycling trip would have been impossible and we would all have been the poorer for it.

Another more obscure pleasure is seeing the fruits of a particularly difficult land negotiation, the signing of a long sought agreement, or the careful construction of a demanding detail. Even the exact positioning of a seat, to give the best view or add to the interest along the path, is a detail which gives pleasure and improves, imperceptibly maybe, the value and popularity of a route. Whilst an unsatisfactory entrance or an awkward ramp is a perpetual irritant!

The highlights I have assembled in this edition cover none of these, although you will see plenty of cyclists and walkers in the photographs, and you will find the details if you wish. Rather I have tried to select sections around the Network which tend to stick in one's memory.

Although these are often the extensive views, the beautiful bridges or the different perspectives of Britain as seen from the Network, they are really the flavour and essence of a journey. A journey which may be just across the local park, or to work along the riverside rather than down the main road, or across the breadth of the country on holiday.

Your journeys, of course, will have their own highlights. Enjoy the ride!

John Grimshaw

Chief Executive, Sustrans

FOREWORD

I've travelled all my life using every imaginable form of transport but nothing will ever surpass my love of the bicycle. Perhaps it is in my Danish genes to prefer the open road on two self-powered wheels as the best way, both in the UK and abroad, to get around and really engage with a place.

This book is a great introduction to the award-winning National Cycle Network, a comprehensive network of accessible, clearly signed routes for cyclists and walkers around the UK. About a third of the Network is traffic-free, making it as suitable for safe recreational and family journeys as it is inspirational for children getting to school, or adults going to work.

On my travels I've witnessed the reality of worsening traffic congestion and pollution. I would love to see us all using our bikes or walking more for short journeys, and I'm delighted to see that the National Cycle Network now makes this a realistic option in the UK for the majority of the population. It really can change our lives.

Work on creating the National Cycle Network has been co-ordinated by the UK's leading sustainable transport charity, Sustrans, and I urge you to get out on your bike and explore your local routes. In the process, you'll rediscover what a brilliant, practical, fun and exhilarating form of transport cycling is.

Sandi Toksvig

Sandi Toksvig

The National Cycle Network routes open 2005

National Cycle Network

SHETLAND ISLANDS

Stromness Kirkwall

John o'Groats

Scalloway Lerwick

Sumburgh

Inverness

Elgin

Aviemore Aberdeen

Fort William Pitlochry

Dundee

Oban Callander

Edinburgh

Glasgow Livingston

Hamilton Berwick-upon-Tweed

Irvine

Ayr

Ballycastle

Coleraine

Derry

Stranraer Dumfries Lockerbie

Antrim Newcastle

Ballyshannon Omagh Carlisle Sunderland

Belfast Keswick Durham Middlesbrough

Enniskillen Workington Penrith

Newry Whitehaven Kendal

Scarborough

Carrick-on-Shannon

Lancaster York

Blackpool Preston Leeds Kingston-upon-Hull

Holyhead Conwy Southport Manchester Barnsley Doncaster

Dublin Liverpool Sheffield

Caernarfon Chester Macclesfield Lincoln

Derby Nottingham Fakenham

Shrewsbury Stafford King's Lynn

Machynlleth Telford Peterborough Norwich

Aberystwyth Birmingham Leicester

Coventry Northampton Ely Ipswich

Builth Worcester Warwick Cambridge Harwich

Wells Milton Keynes

Fishguard Hertford

Chepstow Gloucester Oxford Luton Chelmsford

Newport Swindon Didcot London

Swansea Bristol Canterbury

Cardiff Bath Newbury Reading Richmond Ashford

Ilfracombe Winchester Guildford Gatwick Dover

Taunton Salisbury Folkestone

Chard Southampton Brighton Hastings

Exeter Portsmouth Newhaven

Padstow Okehampton Dorchester Bournemouth Newport

Exmouth

Land's End St Austell Plymouth

Legend

— On road section

— Traffic-free sections

— Further planned sections

○ Towns with railway stations

6

INTRODUCTION

Welcome to the Official Guide to the UK's National Cycle Network, a massive network of signed cycling and walking routes linking communities to schools, stations and city centres, as well as to beautiful countryside.

Well over 10,000 miles of route are already open and ready for you to use and enjoy, with thousands more miles under development. Every kind of journey is possible, whether cycling to work or to school, making local shopping trips, going on family leisure rides or undertaking long-distance tours. So, if you're reading this because you're wondering whether to rescue your long neglected bike from the back of the garage, or you're already a regular cyclist, this book's for you!

Routes for you
This guide will help you find and use the nearest, most useful routes for you. Cycling is a brilliant way to get around, and with over one third of the Network on traffic-free routes (often on former railway tracks, riversides and forest paths), it's ideal for newcomers wanting safety from traffic, as well as for more experienced cyclists. Increasingly, walkers are discovering the joys of the Network and many routes feature public sculptures to further enhance the experience.

▼ *Cyclists explore the Samphire Tower on the Chalk and Channel Way between Dover and Folkestone.*

Key to Day Ride map symbols (except London maps):

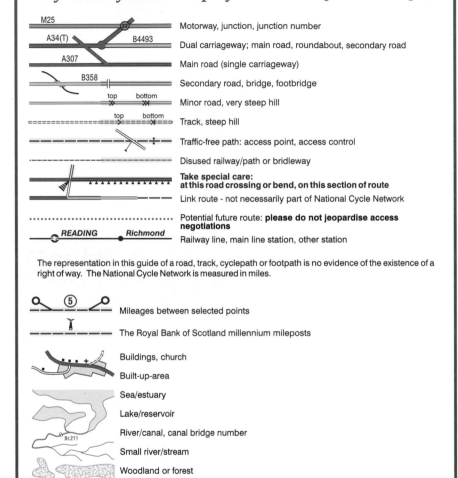

Motorway, junction, junction number

Dual carriageway; main road, roundabout, secondary road

Main road (single carriageway)

Secondary road, bridge, footbridge

Minor road, very steep hill

Track, steep hill

Traffic-free path: access point, access control

Disused railway/path or bridleway

Take special care:
at this road crossing or bend, on this section of route

Link route - not necessarily part of National Cycle Network

Potential future route: **please do not jeopardise access negotiations**

Railway line, main line station, other station

The representation in this guide of a road, track, cyclepath or footpath is no evidence of the existence of a right of way. The National Cycle Network is measured in miles.

Mileages between selected points

The Royal Bank of Scotland millennium mileposts

Buildings, church

Built-up-area

Sea/estuary

Lake/reservoir

River/canal, canal bridge number

Small river/stream

Woodland or forest

Major cliff or quarry

🄸	Tourist information centre (open all year)	☕ 🍴	Cafe, hotel or public house
🄸	Tourist information centre (seasonal)	♟ 🚲	Grocery shop, cycle shop or hire
♦♦ ✉	Public toilets, post office	▲	Campsite
▲	Youth hostel (YHA)/independent hostel	Abbey (NT)	National Trust property
✆	Public telephone (in rural areas only)	Nature Reserve	Selected places of tourist interest

The map sections in this guide cover a wide area; however it is only in the vicinity of the route that they have been surveyed in detail. Outside this area only major features have been mapped. If you wish to travel further afield we recommend the relevant Ordnance Survey Landranger maps. Neither Sustrans nor Stirling Surveys shall be responsible or liable for any loss or damage whatsoever arising from the use of the National Cycle Network or this map.

◄ *The riverside path from Bristol to Pill which goes under the Clifton Suspension Bridge.*

If you're wondering if the National Cycle Network runs anywhere near where you live, the answer is almost certainly, 'Yes'! It passes within two miles of over 75% of UK residents, and a continuous programme of development is creating links to reach more and more railway stations, schools, offices and shops, as well as famous sites and huge swathes of beautiful countryside. In the process, it gives countless historic landmarks like old railways, canals, bridges and viaducts a new lease of life.

Breathing free

Using a bike is great for your health, whatever your age. The Network is completely free and open to all, giving you a real alternative to using a car and making cycling the natural way to get about – just as it is in many neighbouring countries.

As use of the National Cycle Network grows, the impact that switching to walking or cycling can have in reducing car journeys is becoming clear. In 2003, 126 million trips were made on the National Cycle Network, and nearly one third of those replaced a car trip, meaning that 38 million car trips were avoided.

The National Cycle Network has been pioneered by the charity, Sustrans, working with hundreds of partners throughout the country. To find out more about Sustrans' work, see page 296.

We very much hope you discover the joys of the National Cycle Network. Please respect other users and follow the advice in this book.

thank you

▼ *Listening Ear on the Chalk and Channel Way between Dover and Folkestone.*

HOW TO USE THIS GUIDE

This guide helps you to discover and explore the delights of the National Cycle Network. Since it already comprises 10,000 miles of signed routes (and is growing rapidly), it would be impossible in a book of this size to provide comprehensive instructions/directions for you to follow. Instead, the aim of this book is to serve as an introduction to the sheer number and diversity of routes which are out there, and hopefully to inspire you to dust off your bike and give it a go. Routes are well signed, and if you require more detailed instructions on an individual route, you can easily obtain them from the National Cycle Network Information Service or from www.sustrans.org.uk.

Give it a try

Perhaps you'd like to try out a section of the Network close to home, with your family in tow? Maybe you're interested in planning a longer ride and would like to see which of the long distance routes most appeals. Might the Network offer a safe and attractive way for you to cycle to work - or for your children to get to school? Perhaps it will act as a catalyst for you to visit a nearby friend: cycle there and catch the train back or vice versa (check which way the wind is blowing!). Use your bike on the Network to explore nearby villages, towns and cities, canals, forests and country parks, ancient monuments and historic homes. From the vantage point of a bike saddle, visit Britain's rich industrial past and see how the National Cycle Network has helped regenerate derelict wasteland into corridors of greenery, dotted with specially commissioned sculptures.

The Network near you

In this guide the United Kingdom has been divided into nine areas, each of which starts with a map showing the Network in the area. Each route of the Network has been given a number (you may have already seen numbers on local signposts). The map will show you how close you are to the nearest part of the Network and where it links to. As an introduction to the Network you may simply wish to go for a there-and-back ride on the nearest section of traffic-free trail, before exploring other parts of the Network which follow quiet minor lanes.

Family rides

The National Cycle Network is for everyone, and the many traffic-free trails make for great family outings. Within each area you'll find a brief description of rides which have been specially selected with families in mind - in all, there are over 100 in this book. In most cases these are straightforward there-and-back rides along old railway paths or canal towpaths - just get yourselves to the starting point, and you're off! If you want the reassurance of full route details before setting off, have a look at the National Cycle Network website - it has a fantastic mapping facility - or call the National Cycle Network Information Service.

Day rides

The 43 day rides in the book offer a tremendous variety of bike rides for you to enjoy. Some go right through cities, including one which runs alongside the River Thames in West London, others explore some of the more rugged and remote scenery of Scotland, Wales and Northern Ireland.

Planning longer trips

You may wish to start from home and make a trip to visit a friend or relative who lives on or close to the Network, or perhaps you would like to explore a different part of the country altogether whilst on holiday. You have plenty of choice! The Network runs from Land's End to the Shetlands, from the spectacular coastline of West Wales to the channel ports of Dover and Ramsgate. Many of the long distance routes are covered by maps which enable you to complete a satisfying section of the Network. The best known of these is the C2C (Sea to Sea Route) from Whitehaven or Workington to Tynemouth or Sunderland but there are many others, the easiest being the Hull to Harwich route down the East Coast of the country. The hardest is probably Lôn Las Cymru (the Welsh National Route), crossing three ranges of mountains on its way from Holyhead to Cardiff. The range of award-winning long distance route maps published by Sustrans is detailed on page 266.

National Cycle Network Information Service

Based at the National Cycle Network Centre in Bristol, the Sustrans Information Service offers a range of free information sheets on the National Cycle Network, Safe Routes to Schools and other Sustrans projects, plus a full selection of cycling literature (some available for free). Goods for sale include a range of National Cycle Network maps, packs of leaflets produced by local authorities, and cycle guidebooks describing rides in many regions of the country.

The Information Service has an on-line mail order service so you can place a credit card order 24 hours a day, from anywhere in the world, via the website. The website also offers you a really useful on-line mapping facility covering Network routes.

National and Regional Routes

The National Cycle Network is made up of National and Regional Routes, signed with red and blue patches respectively. National Routes form the backbone of the Network - high quality linear routes linking major towns and cities across the UK. Regional Routes are also built to a high standard, and tend to link up smaller urban centres, often as a network of circular routes. In this guide, the routes featured are National Routes unless otherwise specified.

Canal towpaths

Please note that on many canal towpaths, cyclists must carry a cycling permit, downloaded from www.waterscape.com/cycling/permit.html or obtained from British Waterways on 01923 201 120.

National Cycle Network Information Service
National Cycle Network Centre
PO Box 21, Bristol BS99 2HA
Telephone: 0845 113 0065
9.00am-5.00pm Monday to Friday
excluding Bank Holidays.
www.sustrans.org.uk

▼ *A view of the 15 spans of the 17th century Berwick bridge, between Tweedmouth and the old walled town of Berwick-upon-Tweed.*

The West Country

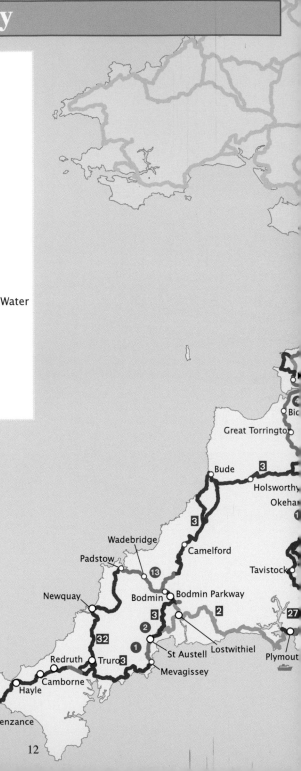

Tewkesbury
45
Cinderford
Cheltenham
48
Gloucester
16
Stroud
9
Berkeley
45
41
Nailsworth
Cirencester
48
Cricklade
Bristol
10
Swindon
Avebury
45
Clevedon
8
Chippenham
Calne
11
15
12
Marlborough
26
4
Weston-super-Mare
3
10
Melksham
Bath
33
Cheddar
10
Trowbridge
Devizes
4
Burnham-on-Sea
24
Radstock
45
Wells
Frome
Warminster
Bridgwater
Glastonbury
24
Salisbury
3
30
Castle
Cary
Gillingham
rnstaple
3
26
Taunton
33
Woodbridge
Tiverton
Yeovil
Ilminster
Sherbourne
herleigh
Tiverton Parkway
6
30
41
Chard
25
27
Wimborne Minster
Blandford Forum
Exeter
52
Axminster
Poole
5
52
2
Bridport
7
17
52
Seaton
Dorchester
Christchurch
rtmoor
28
Sidmouth
Lyme Regis
Wareham
Bournemouth
Dawlish
Budleigh Salterton
2
Newton Abbot
Exmouth
Weymouth
2
Teignmouth
Torquay
Totnes
Paignton
Ivybridge
28
Salcombe

Exmoor

New Forest

	National Cycle Network traffic-free routes
	National Cycle Network on road routes
	National Cycle Network future routes
3	National Route Numbers
10	Regional route numbers
○	Towns with railway stations
○	Towns without railway stations
12	Regional ride numbers

13

THE WEST COUNTRY

The West Country is home to a wide range of exceptional National Cycle Network routes, offering cyclists exciting opportunities to explore the coastline, national parks and beautiful towns and cities of the south west peninsula. For families, there are many leisurely traffic-free stretches on which to improve skills, confidence and stamina; local urban routes provide quick access to the countryside; whilst those ready for longer rides will find the area brimming with highlights.

The region is rural in nature, so is perfect for cycling and the sense of freedom that goes with it. Of the many outstanding routes here, Route 3 (incorporating the Cornish Way and West Country Way) runs from the tip of the mainland at Land's End to Bristol (or Bath), taking in Cornwall, Exmoor, the Somerset Levels and the Mendip Hills in the process. Many routes interlink with Route 3, including the stunning and in places challenging Devon Coast to Coast ride. This connects Plymouth on the south coast with Ilfracombe on the north, tackling some steep Dartmoor slopes as well as the much gentler Tarka Trail along the estuary to Barnstaple.

The largest city in the area is Bristol, home to the very first section of the National Cycle Network to be completed - the Bristol & Bath Railway Path - as well as to Sustrans, the charity behind the Network. Bristol stands at the junction of two routes - 3 and 4. Travelling westwards, Route 4 takes riders across the old Severn Bridge and along the Celtic Trail through South Wales, whilst to the east of Bristol the route links to Bath, Chippenham, Newbury, Reading and London.

There are many other superb routes criss-crossing this picturesque region - just take a look at the map, then read on for some ideas on where to get started. Whether you want to take your family on an introductory pootle along the Camel Trail, explore the prehistoric stone circles of Wiltshire, or admire sweeping views of Dartmoor along The Granite Way from Okehampton, you'll find more guidance on the following pages.

▼ *Foxgloves line Route 27 near Meldon Viaduct.*

John Grimshaw's
HIGHLIGHTS

Saltford
This is where it all began, where the local cycling group, Cyclebag, started the construction of the Bristol and Bath Railway Path in 1979. This was the birthplace of the Network!

Miller's Crossing, Exeter
A good example of the many wonderful new bridges built to give pedestrians and cyclists easy and direct journeys.

The Bournemouth and Poole promenade
The decision to open the promenade to cyclists for much of the year was a most unexpected surprises. Every visitor who has had the pleasure of cycling this route should drop a card to the Council expressing their appreciation. Without this link there would be no South Coast route.

Meldon Viaduct
The centrepiece of Devon's determined programme to open up long and beautiful railway paths for visitors.

The Eden Project
The goal of many journeys. You have arrived. You have made the effort. It's been worth it!

The Blue Bridge at Chippenham
No less than three, specially commissioned, iconic bridges between Chippenham and Calne give us a memorable route and remind us of what local authority vision at its best can achieve.

▼ *The National Cycle Network can take you all the way to the Eden Project.*

WEST COUNTRY FAMILY RIDES

St. Austell to Mevagissey/ Heligan (and link to Pentewan). 6 miles (+ 1 mile link). Route 3

Enjoy wild flowers, a wooded riverside and fine views on this mostly traffic-free route, starting in the picturesque town of St. Austell. The route takes you through woods and along the flat former railway line to the beach at Pentewan, a lovely spot to take a break and watch the waves roll in. A link across the river takes you up the former carriage drive to the wonderful Lost Gardens of Heligan, which are well worth a look (though be aware that there is a long climb between Pentewan and Heligan). The descent into Mevagissey is steep, so those with small children may prefer to push. Refreshments and toilet facilities are available at St. Austell, Heligan, Mevagissey and Pentewan.

The Clay Trails to the Eden Project.

What better way to reach the magnificent Eden Project than by bike? The Clay Trails are a series of mostly traffic-free routes that will help you to reach this popular attraction - and beat the traffic queues into Eden as well! Your ride follows former mineral tramways

▶ *Taking a breather.*

▲ *Mevagissey on the Cornish Way with the spectacular view down to the harbour and the town.*

which are remnants of Cornwall's industrial heritage, as well as specially created paths. You pass through a unique landscape which is almost lunar in appearance, and includes old flooded quarries such as Ruddle Pit. Follow the Clay Trails to the Eden Project, and your journey will be as memorable as your final destination! The Eden Project offers discounted entry for cyclists and walkers who pay on arrival.

Plym Valley Trail. 10 miles. Routes 27 & 2

This lovely, mostly traffic-free family route takes you from the seashore to open moorland. Starting from the National Marine Aquarium in Plymouth, you take in two National Trust properties: the magnificent 18th century mansion Saltram House, and the sanctuary of Plymbridge Woods. Following the course of the

◀ *The Plym Valley Trail, an ideal route for children.*

Taw rivers, crossing Isley Marsh nature reserve to reach Barnstaple. Finally, you pedal along the north bank of the River Taw to Braunton and the unique Braunton Burrows nature reserve.

Exeter South to Turf Lock. 5.5 miles. Route 2
What are you waiting for! This excellent family friendly cycle

old Great Western Railway up the Plym valley, the route features four spectacular viaducts and offers much to explore, making for an exciting and fun day out. There are refreshments and facilities aplenty in Plymouth, and a pub at the end of the ride in Clearbrook.

Tarka Trail - Meeth to Braunton. 31 miles. Route 27
Whether you tackle the whole 31 miles of this topnotch family ride in one go, or ride it in stages, you're in for a treat! This traffic-free route follows a disused railway line, is pretty flat and includes fantastic countryside and estuary views.

The inland section from Meeth follows the River Torridge to Bideford and its fabulous Long Bridge, then skirts the estuary of the Torridge and

▲ *Miller's Crossing near Exeter, a landmark of the area.*

path takes you from Exeter city centre, along the River Exe to the glorious expanse of the Exe Estuary and a beautiful wildlife reserve. The marshes here are a year-round haven for thousands of birds. In the spring you can see breeding lapwings and redshanks, whilst winter high tides are perfect for spotting roosting and feeding curlews, lapwings and wigeons. Exeter offers you plenty of refreshments, and there are two handy pubs, one half way along and one at the ride's end at Turf Lock.

◀ *Wave Shelter by Geoff Stainthorpe on the Tarka Trail near Barnstaple.*

17

▲ *Avon towpath on the way to Pill.*

Ilminster to Chard.
6.5 miles. Route 33

Visit two attractive market towns with a popular cycle ride in between – what a great day out! This largely traffic-free route provides great family cycling, taking you along a disused railway line through the South Somerset countryside. Already a favoured ride for locals as well as visitors, there is much to experience along the way – from poignant reminders of the Second World War (the Taunton stop line defences) to a bird watching haven at Chard Reservoir. There are plenty of refreshments available at either end of the route, too. Go on – give it a try!

Dorchester to Maiden Newton. 8 miles. Route 26

Passing close to the River Frome, this lovely, level ride provides an attractive journey through the Dorset countryside. Starting in Dorchester at the statue of its most famous son, Thomas Hardy, you follow paths until Stratton, where the route then meanders gently on to Maiden Newton. The village's fine medieval parish church has a Norman door - thought to be the oldest in England. You can explore the nearby watermeadows of the River Frome - a wildlife haven for water birds and traditional meadow flowers. You'll find plenty of refreshments at either end of the journey.

Bristol to Pill and Portishead. 10.5 miles (6 miles to Pill). Routes 41 and 33

This mostly traffic-free route has proved a hit with families as well as commuters, taking riders on a riverside path through the spectacular Avon Gorge. From Bristol's docks you pass underneath Brunel's amazing Clifton Suspension Bridge, along a wooded riverside path through the Avon Gorge and on to Pill. A new path alongside the railway then takes you safely underneath the M5 and links via quiet lanes to Portishead, an attractive seaside town with great views across to Wales. There are plenty of refreshments available in Bristol, Pill and Portishead (which also has an open air swimming pool and public toilet facilities).

◀ *Sustrans Rangers on the Dorchester to Maiden Newton route.*

Stonehouse to Nailsworth.
6.5 miles. Route 45

This delightful, traffic-free ride follows the line of the old Midland railway, providing easy riding and a wonderful alternative to busy local roads. You begin in Stonehouse in the Stroud Valley, picking up the railway path at Ryeford. You're treated to wonderful views of the Cotswolds as you pedal along, and you're never far from water in the form of the River Frome, the Stroudwater Canal or the Nailsworth Stream. Water mills and other buildings add further interest along the way until the ride concludes at Nailsworth, a friendly little town complete with cafes and independent shops.

Bath to Devizes. 21 miles. Route 4

This ride along the Kennet & Avon Canal towpath is perfect for a longer family outing, with a good, mainly level surface and lots to look at. It's also a popular walking route, so be careful! The ride starts close to Bath's Sydney Gardens, continuing into the Avon Valley to explore a world of locks, woodland and aqueducts. There are many marvellous places to stop for refreshment, not least at Bradford-on-Avon, which features a wonderful medieval bridge and tithe barn. Finally, at Devizes, you will pass a staggering flight of 16 locks.
Chippenham to Calne.

6.5 miles. Route 4

This is a largely flat and traffic-free route, ideal for novice cyclists, or for those with young children. The ride follows an old railway path and passes through a diverse country landscape near to monuments, sites of historic interest, industrial archaeology, public art and other attractions. Along the way you'll pass over a number of prize-winning new bridges, including the outstanding Calne Millennium Bridge. There are plenty of refreshments at both ends of the route, and those with spare energy can continue to the neolithic stone circles at Avebury.

Marlborough to Chiseldon and Coates Water Park. 8 miles. Route 45

This superb ride, which is mainly traffic-free, whisks you from the old coaching

▲ *Calne Millennium Bridge.*

town of Marlborough to the family friendly Coate Water Park. You start in the fascinating and historic town of Marlborough, heading north along a disused railway line through open Wiltshire countryside, an area steeped in neolithic history. An extension to this route now takes you safely over the motorway and into Coates Water Park, home to more trails, a 56-acre lake, walks, orchids, fishing and boat hire, as well as play areas. Reward yourself with a spot of relaxation before riding back, or take the new Queen's Avenue cycle route to the centre of Swindon.

▼ *By the Kennet & Avon Canal near Bradford-on-Avon.*

CAMEL TRAIL – BODMIN TO PADSTOW

One of the most popular traffic-free routes in the country, attracting around 500,000 visitors a year, the Camel Trail is one of Cornwall's major attractions. The Trail takes you along a railway path through the shade of beautiful woodland and alongside the River Camel. From Wadebridge you cycle beside the sandy shores of the Camel Estuary to the attractive harbour town of Padstow, where there are plenty of restaurants, cafes and shops.

You don't even need your own bike for this one as there are plenty of options for cycle hire in Bodmin, Wadebridge and Padstow.

This is a multi-use trail, so expect to meet horseriders and wheelchairs, and note the Camel Trail code which is posted at the main access points.

The Camel Trail forms part of both the West Country Way which continues beyond Bodmin all the way to Bristol and Bath, and the Cornish Way which extends to Land's End.

Starting point
Bodmin Parkway railway station, five miles south east of Bodmin.
Bodmin Jail, town centre.
Wadebridge town centre.
Padstow harbour.

Distance
The Camel Trail runs for 17 miles from Padstow to Poley's Bridge (situated between St Tudy and Blisland) - 34 miles there and back. You have a variety of options:
The most popular is Wadebridge-Padstow-Wadebridge (12 miles round trip).
The longest would be Padstow-Bodmin-Poley's Bridge-

Bodmin-Padstow (34 miles). You may wish to devise your own lane routes from the ends of the trail back to Bodmin. Be warned that it is hilly around here!
The Forest Enterprise managed woodland which adjoins part of the trail is open for cyclists and walkers.

Grade
The Camel Trail itself is easy, running along the course of an old railway line. The link from Bodmin Parkway to the start of the trail is fairly strenuous.

Surface
Variable mainly gravel surface suitable for mountain and hybrid bikes.

Roads, traffic, suitability for young children
The Camel Trail is ideal for young children, with lots to see along the way and superb cycle hire facilities in Wadebridge and Padstow which cater for all requirements.
You have to go through the centre of Wadebridge on streets but there are so many cyclists that traffic does not pose the normal threats.
The (hilly) route from Bodmin

◄ *One of the signs on the Camel Trail.*

► *Wadebridge Bike Hire - one of several useful hire outlets on the Camel Trail.*

Parkway to the Camel Trail is mostly on-road, and includes the new Millennium bridge over the A30. Care should be taken crossing the A389 in Bodmin.

Hills
The section between Bodmin and Padstow is flat. There is a gentle 200ft climb from Bodmin north east along the Camel Trail to Poley's Bridge. The route between Bodmin Parkway station and the start of the Camel Trail is hilly with one particularly steep climb.

Refreshments
Lots of choice in Bodmin, Wadebridge and Padstow. Tea shop near Boscarne Junction.
Wine tastings at Camel Valley Vineyard.

Nearest railway stations
Bodmin Parkway is linked to Route 3 via the A30 Millennium Bridge. The Bodmin and Wenford Railway tourist line runs infrequently between Bodmin Parkway, Bodmin and Boscarne Junction and carries bikes free of charge.

The National Cycle Network in the area
The Camel Trail is part of Route 32 and is used as part of both the West Country Way and the Cornish Way which run from Land's End to Bristol and Bath. Route 2 runs from Bodmin to Looe and Plymouth and will eventually go on to Dover.

Other nearby rides (waymarked or traffic-free)
There are forest trails in Cardinham Woods, east of Bodmin.

The Camel Trail starts in Bodmin, the former County town, where attractions include a steam railway, the old Gaol

▼ *The Camel Trail is a good place for children to practice their cycling skills.*

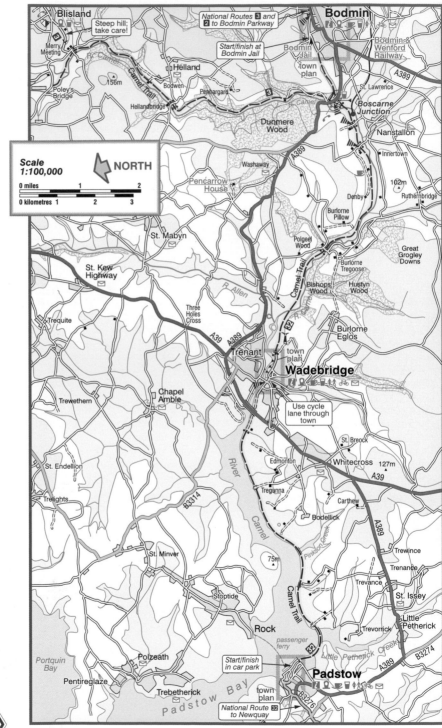

The Camel Trail – Bodmin to Padstow

Blisland

Steep hill; take care!

National Routes **3** and **2** to Bodmin Parkway

Bodmin

Merry Meeting

Bodmin & Wenford Railway

Start/finish at Bodmin Jail

Bodmin Jail

town plan

Poley's Bridge

R. Camel

Camel Trail

156m

Helland

Bodwen

Penhargard

Hellandbridge

St. Lawrence

Boscarne Junction

Nanstallon

Innertown

Dunmere Wood

Washaway

A389

102m

Ruthernbridge

Scale
1:100,000

0 miles 1 2
0 kilometres 1 2 3

NORTH

Pencarrow House

Denby

Burlorne Pillow

Polgeel Wood

Great Grogley Downs

St. Mabyn

R. Allen

Burlorne Tregoose

Bishops Wood

Hustyn Wood

St. Kew Highway

Three Holes Cross

Camel Trail

Burlorne Eglos

Trequite

A39 A389

Trenant

town plan

Wadebridge

Trewethern

Chapel Amble

Use cycle lane through town

St. Endellion

St. Breock

Whitecross 127m

A39

River Camel

Edmonton

Trelights

Tregunna

Carthew

B3314

Bodellick

Trewince

Trenance

Pinkson Creek

75m

Trevance

St. Issey

St. Minver

Stoptide

Camel Trail

Trevorrick

Little Petherick

Rock

passenger ferry

Little Petherick Creek

A389 B3274

Portquin Bay

Polzeath

Start/finish in car park

Padstow

town plan

Pentireglaze

Trebetherick

P a d s t o w   B a y

National Route **32** to Newquay

B3276

32

22

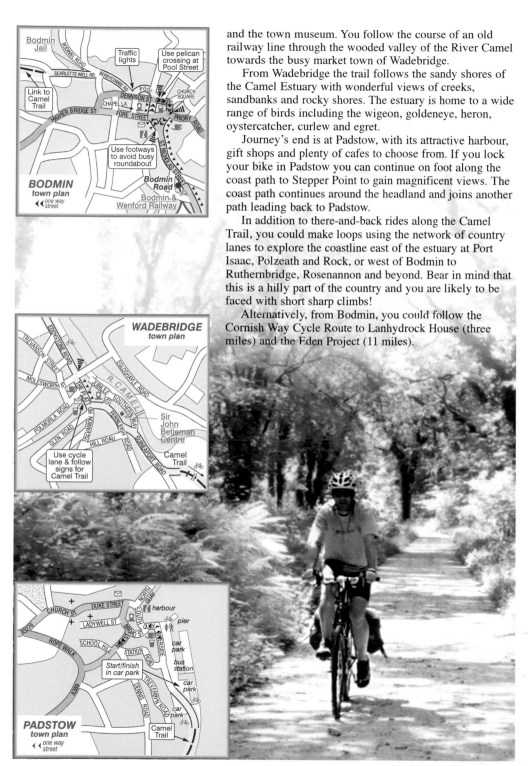

and the town museum. You follow the course of an old railway line through the wooded valley of the River Camel towards the busy market town of Wadebridge.

From Wadebridge the trail follows the sandy shores of the Camel Estuary with wonderful views of creeks, sandbanks and rocky shores. The estuary is home to a wide range of birds including the wigeon, goldeneye, heron, oystercatcher, curlew and egret.

Journey's end is at Padstow, with its attractive harbour, gift shops and plenty of cafes to choose from. If you lock your bike in Padstow you can continue on foot along the coast path to Stepper Point to gain magnificent views. The coast path continues around the headland and joins another path leading back to Padstow.

In addition to there-and-back rides along the Camel Trail, you could make loops using the network of country lanes to explore the coastline east of the estuary at Port Isaac, Polzeath and Rock, or west of Bodmin to Ruthernbridge, Rosenannon and beyond. Bear in mind that this is a hilly part of the country and you are likely to be faced with short sharp climbs!

Alternatively, from Bodmin, you could follow the Cornish Way Cycle Route to Lanhydrock House (three miles) and the Eden Project (11 miles).

23

THE GRANITE WAY: OKEHAMPTON STATION TO MELDON, LAKE VIADUCT AND LYDFORD

Forming part of the Devon Coast to Coast Cycle Route, this long stretch of railway path offers wide views into the heart of Dartmoor and out over the rolling Devon countryside lying to the north of Okehampton. The ride starts from the beautifully restored railway station at Okehampton (the highest railway station in southern England), runs alongside the railway line as far as the spectacular Meldon Viaduct, then continues along the course of the old railway line itself past Sourton Church and over a second vast viaduct at Lake. Beyond here there is a section of the old railway land still in private ownership so you will need to use the road network to bypass this if you choose to go to Lydford. You have four options: stay on the railway path and stop for a picnic at Lake Viaduct or just beyond, retracing your steps back to Okehampton; drop down from Lake Viaduct on a track to the pub at Lake then come back up to the railway path; use the waymarked route on (hilly) minor lanes via Bridestowe to rejoin the railway path and continue on to Lydford; finally, if you are experienced cyclists, use a one-mile section of the busy A386 to access the southernmost section of railway path into Lydford. The village of Lydford has a good pub, the ruins of a castle and atmospheric walks along Lydford Gorge.

Starting point
Okehampton railway station which is located up the steep hill to the south of town.

Distance
10 miles.

Grade
Easy on the railway path. The lane section from Lake to Lydford is more strenuous.

▼ *The magnificent Lake Viaduct, where trains used to thunder across - now it is a superb cycle path.*

Surface
Excellent surface throughout, almost all tarmac. The descent from Lake Viaduct to the main road (to visit the pub there or to join the lane to Bridestowe) is on a rougher track.

Roads, traffic, suitability for young children
No roads as far as Lake Viaduct. On the road section towards Lydford there is a tricky crossing of the A386 by the Bearslake Inn (Lake) where great care is needed. The lane network through Bridestowe is relatively quiet. The A386 alternative between the end of the railway path and Shortacombe (approx. one mile) should only be undertaken by experienced cyclists.

Hills
Gentle climb towards the centre of the ride (the highpoint is between Meldon Viaduct and Sourton church) from both ends. If you choose to go on to Lydford by lane there is a steep climb south of Bridestowe.

the route uses lanes through Hatherleigh and Sheepwash to reach the Tarka Trail near Petrockstowe, where it links with Route 3, the West Country Way.

Beyond Lydford, Route 27 heads for Tavistock and Plymouth.

Other nearby rides (waymarked or traffic-free)

1. The traffic-free Tarka Trail starts at Meeth, on the A386 about 10 miles north of Okehampton.
2. There are forest trails in Abbeyford Woods, just north of Okehampton.
3. To the south of Okehampton Camp, the Military Road is a tough but spectacular 10-mile loop on mainly tarmac roads into the very heart of Dartmoor.

Refreshments

Cafe at Okehampton railway station. Cafe at Okehampton YHA (on the other side of the tracks).
Buffet car at Meldon Viaduct.
Highwayman Inn down off the route in Sourton.
Bearslake Inn, Lake (also does cream teas).
White Hart Inn, Bridestowe
Castle Inn, Lydford.

Nearest railway stations

Five trains a day run on Sundays only from spring to autumn between Exeter and Okehampton. Phone 01837 55637 for details.
The Dartmoor Railway runs steam trains between Okehampton and Meldon Viaduct station and takes bikes free of charge.

The National Cycle Network in the area

This ride is part of Route 27, the Devon Coast to Coast Cycle Route. North of Okehampton

To find out about other cycle routes in this area visit www.sustrans.org.uk

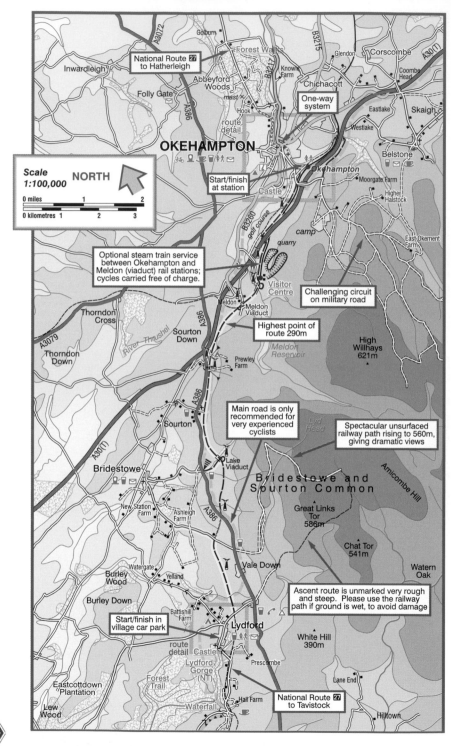

The Granite Way

Scale
1:100,000   NORTH

0 miles · 1 · 2
0 kilometres 1 · 2 · 3

National Route 27 to Hatherleigh

One-way system

OKEHAMPTON

Start/finish at station

Optional steam train service between Okehampton and Meldon (viaduct) rail stations; cycles carried free of charge.

Challenging circuit on military road

Highest point of route 290m

Main road is only recommended for very experienced cyclists

Spectacular unsurfaced railway path rising to 560m, giving dramatic views

Ascent route is unmarked very rough and steep. Please use the railway path if ground is wet, to avoid damage

Start/finish in village car park

National Route 27 to Tavistock

Inwardleigh
Folly Gate
Abbeyford Woods
Forest Walks
Golburn
Knowle Farm
Chichacott
Glendon
Corscombe
Coombe Head
Eastlake
Skaigh
Westlake
Belstone
mast
Hook
route detail
Castle
Okehampton
Moorgate Farm
Higher Halstock
golf course
camp
quarry
East Okement Farm
Visitor Centre
Meldon
Meldon Viaduct
Thorndon Cross
Sourton Down
River Thrushel
Meldon Reservoir
High Willhays 621m
Thorndon Down
Prewley Farm
Sourton
Lyd Head
Bridestowe
Lake Viaduct
Bridestowe and Sourton Common
Amicombe Hill
New Station Farm
Ashleigh Farm
Great Links Tor 586m
Chat Tor 541m
Watern Oak
Watergate
Yelland
Vale Down
Burley Wood
Burley Down
Battishill Farm
White Hill 390m
Lydford
route detail
Castle
Lydford Gorge (NT)
Prescombe
Lane End
Eastcottdown Plantation
Forest Trail
Hilltown
Lew Wood
Waterfall
Hall Farm

27

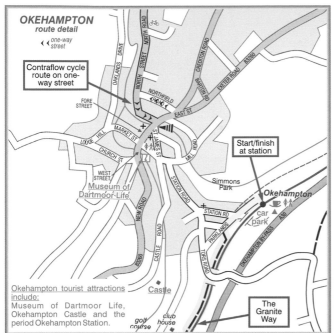

OKEHAMPTON
route detail

‹‹ *one-way street*

Contraflow cycle route on one-way street

FORE STREET

OAKLANDS DRIVE
NORTH STREET
KEITH ROAD
CREDITON ROAD
B3260
EXETER ROAD
BARTON RD
NORTHFIELD ROAD
EAST ST

MARKET ST
ST JAMES ST
MILL ROAD

LODGE HILL
CHURCH ST
WEST STREET
NEW ROAD

Museum of Dartmoor Life

STATION ROAD

Simmons Park

Start/finish at station

Okehampton

STATION RD

car park

A30

CASTLE ROAD
B3260
PARKLANDS
TORS ROAD
OKEHAMPTON BYPASS

Castle

golf course
club house

Okehampton tourist attractions include:
Museum of Dartmoor Life, Okehampton Castle and the period Okehampton Station.

The Granite Way

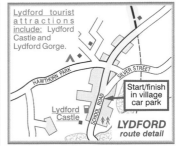

Lydford tourist attractions include: Lydford Castle and Lydford Gorge.

HAWTHORN PARK
SILVER STREET
SCHOOL ROAD

Start/finish in village car park

Lydford Castle

LYDFORD
route detail

Use the on-line mapping at www.sustrans.org.uk to find other National Cycle Network routes near you.

▼ *Lydford Castle.*

27

BRISTOL & BATH RAILWAY PATH

The Bristol & Bath Railway Path offers a complete escape from the urban hearts of Bristol and Bath into the countryside between.

The route was the first path on the National Cycle Network to be built and has happily and proudly stood the test of time. Now one of the most popular sections in the country, it's used by walkers and cyclists alike for school trips, commuting, shopping errands and days out.

With slight gradients and tarmac surfaces this is an easy route. The attractions, restaurants and cafes in both Bath and Bristol give you something to aim for and there are teashops and pubs at points along the route which make good turnaround points.

Whilst in Bristol, why not visit the National Cycle Network Centre, home to Sustrans' head office, and where you can find out about routes throughout the country, pick up maps and leaflets and search on-line mapping at free computer terminals.

Starting point
National Cycle Network Centre, by the cathedral in Bristol, or Castle Park.
The Riverside Path, just off the A4 Upper Bristol Road in Bath.

Distance
16 miles one way, 32 miles return. If you start in Bristol, good turnaround/refreshment points are at Warmley (12 miles round trip), Bitton (17 miles round trip) and Saltford (22 miles round trip).

Grade
Easy.

Surface
Excellent surface throughout, all tarmac.

Roads, traffic, suitability for young children
The path is traffic-free, ideal for beginners. The signposted approach roads from both Bristol and Bath city centres carry some traffic.

Hills
None.

Refreshments
Lots of choice in Bristol.
Cafes on the railway path at Warmley (seasonal) and at Bitton Station (at the weekend, all year round).
Stationmaster PH, Warmley; Bird in Hand PH, Jolly Sailor PH, Saltford.
Lots of choice in Bath.

▼ *Bath Abbey and Pump Rooms*

Nearest railway stations
Bristol Temple Meads, Bath Spa.

The National Cycle Network in the area
Route 4 runs from South Wales to London and uses the whole of the railway path. Routes 4 and 41 together form the Severn & Thames Cycle Route from Gloucester to Newbury. Route 3, the West Country Way and the Cornish Way, heads south west from Bristol to the furthest tip of mainland Britain at Land's End.

Other nearby rides (waymarked or traffic-free)
1. A section of the railway path (between Saltford and

▲ Brief Encounter by Steve Joyce at Warmley Station.

Mangotsfield) is used by the Avon Cycleway, an 85-mile signposted route using the network of quiet lanes around Bristol.
2. The five-mile, traffic-free Pill Riverside Path runs from the Bristol Harbourside along Cumberland Road, then alongside the River Avon to Pill, passing beneath the Clifton Suspension Bridge. There is also a link to this path through Leigh Woods.
3. The Kennet & Avon Canal Towpath offers a beautiful route from Bath to Devizes.

◄ Trailers offer an ideal way to carry young children on traffic-free paths.

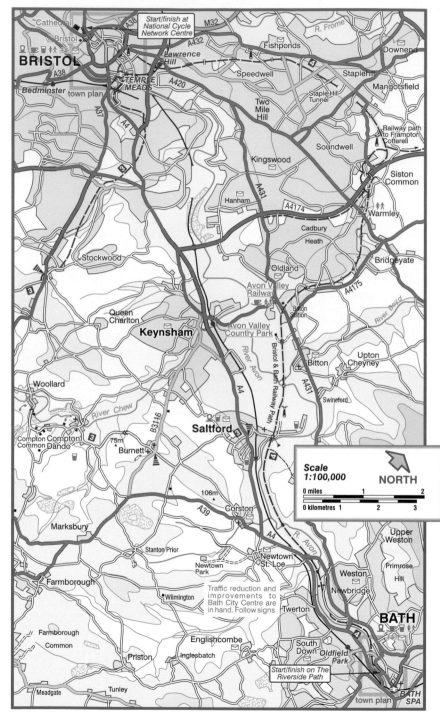

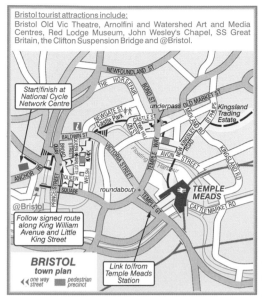

Bristol tourist attractions include:
Bristol Old Vic Theatre, Arnolfini and Watershed Art and Media Centres, Red Lodge Museum, John Wesley's Chapel, SS Great Britain, the Clifton Suspension Bridge and @Bristol.

Start/finish at National Cycle Network Centre

underpass

Kingsland Trading Estate

TEMPLE MEADS

Follow signed route along King William Avenue and Little King Street

roundabout

CATTLE MARKET RD

BRISTOL
town plan
one way street   pedestrian precinct

Link to/from Temple Meads Station

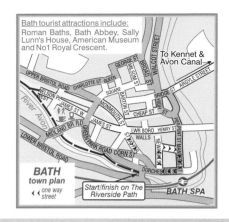

Bath tourist attractions include:
Roman Baths, Bath Abbey, Sally Lunn's House, American Museum and No1 Royal Crescent.

To Kennet & Avon Canal

BATH
town plan
one way street

Start/finish on The Riverside Path

BATH SPA

The railway path starts half a mile from Temple Meads station. You can pick up the route in Bristol city centre from the National Cycle Network Centre which is next to the cathedral. Visit the Centre to get maps and guides and information about routes throughout the country. It is also the head office of Sustrans.

The railway path travels through the east of Bristol and even this inner city section has a green and rural feeling to it, passing through wooded cuttings with a plethora of wildflowers along the verges in the spring and early summer.

You'll find a feast of attractions as you make your way along the route: sculptures of wood, metal and stone (keep an eye out for the upside-down fish and the drinking giant!); a ¼-mile tunnel at Staple Hill; and the old train station at Bitton complete with real, working steam engines.

You'll also make several crossings of the meandering, peaceful River Avon; pass glades of broadleaf woodland carpeted with bluebells in late spring in Kelston Woods; and finally follow a riverside stretch from the end of the railway path into the heart of the historic city of Bath.

The steam railway and teashop at Bitton or the riverside pubs at Saltford make great turnaround points for shorter rides.

▶ *The Bristol and Bath railway path offers a green corridor right into the city centre.*

ROUTES OUT OF GLOUCESTER: TO MAISEMORE, HIGHNAM AND FRAMPTON ON SEVERN

This ride explores three exits from the cathedral city of Gloucester, two of which lead to extensive networks of quiet lanes, giving you the opportunity to plan longer rides. To the west the route passes beneath the railway, over the river on Telford's old hump-backed stone bridge then under the A40 to link to the attractive new path to the village of Highnam (Highnam Court is open the first Sunday in every month, and serves teas). The route to Maisemore starts as described above but then follows a riverside path to the pub in the village. Beyond here quiet lanes could be followed north towards Tewkesbury. To the south of the city the Gloucester & Sharpness Canal offers an excellent escape route into the countryside, with the Cotswold Hills running parallel away to the east. Opened in 1827 to bypass a treacherous and winding stretch of the River Severn, the canal was at the time the widest and deepest in the country. The towpath is well-surfaced for about three miles, as far as Rea Bridge, after which you have a choice of using the waymarked Route 41 on quiet lanes or, if you are on a mountain bike, continuing along the canal towpath, which can be rough at times. Please show consideration to other users when on the towpath. Both options take you to the lovely village of Frampton on Severn with its vast green, attractive old houses, pubs and stores. If you are experienced cyclists you can continue south for a further 6 miles

▲ *Along the canal between Frampton upon Severn and Gloucester.*

(mainly on Route 41) to access Cam & Dursley railway station and catch a train back to Gloucester (alternatively, catch the train first and cycle back).

NB. It is worth checking with the Gloucester Tourist Information Centre (01452 421188) about times of the natural phenomenon known as the Severn Bore. This is a form of tidal wave, caused by each incoming tide funnelling into shallower water, and can result in a bore up to two metres high. The road at Stonebench is an excellent site to see the Bore at its most impressive.

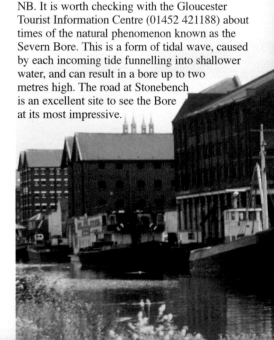

Starting point
Gloucester Docks (Llanthony
Road) in the heart of the city.

Distance
2½ miles from Gloucester
Docks west to Highnam.
2½ miles from Gloucester
Docks northwest to Maisemore.
10 miles from Gloucester
Docks south to Frampton on
Severn.

Grade
Easy, but see below under
'Surface'.

Surface
Fine gravel path from
Gloucester to Maisemore or
Highnam. South of Gloucester
the towpath to Rea Bridge is
good quality but beyond here it
is at times quite rough (best to
use mountain bikes) although
very beautiful. The alternative
is to use the waymarked Route
41 on quiet lanes to Frampton
on Severn.

▼ *Gloucester Docks.*

**Roads, traffic, suitability for
young children**
A short section along Llanthony
Road in the centre of
Gloucester leads to the traffic-
free path that takes you all the
way to Highnam or Maisemore.
To the south of the city, the
towpath section from the centre
of Gloucester to Rea Bridge is
good quality and traffic-free.
The lanes south from here to
Frampton on Severn are quiet.
The towpath is traffic-free but
rough south of Rea Bridge.

Hills
None.

Refreshments
Lots of choice in the centre of
Gloucester.

Heading west
Toby Carvery PH, on
the A40 on the way
to Highnam.
Delicatessen at

Over Garden Stores.
Village stores in Highnam.
White Hart PH, Maisemore.

Heading south
Anchor Inn, Epney.
Ship Inn, Upper Framilode.
Bell Inn, village stores,
Frampton on Severn.

Nearest railway stations
Gloucester, Cam & Dursley.

**The National Cycle Network
in the area**
This route is mostly on Route
45 which runs from Salisbury
to Chester. Between Saul and
Gloucester this coincides with
Route 41 from Bristol to
Stratford-upon-Avon and
Rugby.

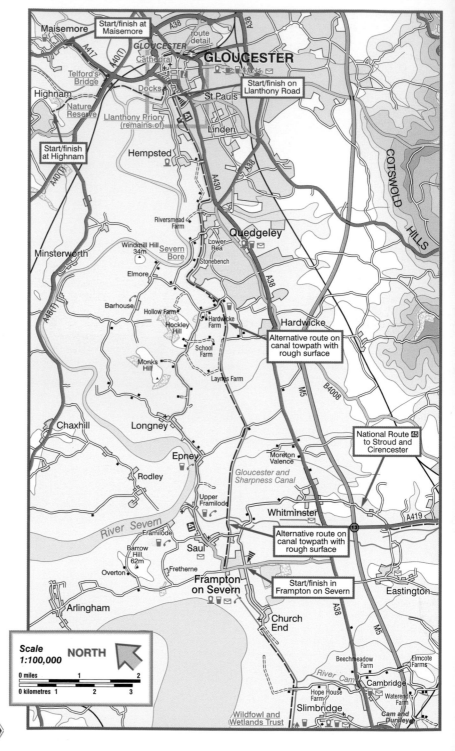

ROUTES OUT OF GLOUCESTER

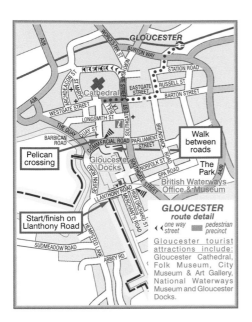

Gloucester tourist attractions include: Gloucester Cathedral, Folk Museum, City Museum & Art Gallery, National Waterways Museum and Gloucester Docks.

▲ *Over Farm Market is a farm shop situated a mile west of Gloucester.*

Other nearby rides (waymarked or traffic-free)
1. There is a waymarked, traffic-free circuit in the Forest of Dean about 15 miles southwest of Gloucester. A link from Highnam to the Forest of Dean is planned.
2. The Stroud Valleys Cycle Trail is a five-mile railway path running north from Nailsworth and is part of Route 45 to Cirencester, beyond which there are several traffic-free trails in Cotswold Water Park, to the south of Cirencester.

▼ *The link from Gloucester to Highnam.*

BOURNEMOUTH PROMENADE BETWEEN HENGISTBURY HEAD AND POOLE HEAD

From mid September to mid June (excluding the peak summer months) the wide sweep of Poole Bay offers a wonderful flat ride alongside mile after mile of fine sandy beaches, with views west to the outcrop of Ballard Down above Studland Bay and east to the sandy hill of Hengistbury Head. This is an out-and-out seaside ride and if it is a hot day, travelling by bike is the perfect way to find an uncrowded section of the 10-mile long beach. Crowds tend to gather where there is easiest access by car, so 5-10 minutes on a bike whisk you away from these busier places to quieter areas. Be warned that even outside the peak season the whole promenade does become crowded on hot days so it is best to choose a time when there are fewer people around - early morning or evening or mid-week. Hengistbury Head has an abundance of traditional beach huts, brightly coloured dinghies in Christchurch

Harbour and a ferry across to Christchurch itself. A short stretch through woodland leads on to the only road section of the whole 10-mile ride, linking to the eastern end of Bournemouth promenade. From here on the ride is a gentle glide alongside the sandy beaches with plenty of chances to stop for refreshments. The prevailing wind is from the west, so if you have started at the eastern end of the ride you are likely to be blown back to Hengistbury Head from wherever you decide to turn around.

NB. Cycling is not allowed from 1000 - 1900 hrs from mid June to mid September. Please also note that there is a 10mph speed limit for cyclists and you should always give way to pedestrians. Be particularly aware of young children who may suddenly run out in front of you.

▲ Holidaymakers can hire bikes to enjoy the local route.

Starting points
Hengistbury Head.
Bournemouth Tourist Information Centre just west of the pier by the aquarium and International Centre.
Poole Head.

Distance
10 miles.

Grade
Easy.

Surface
All tarmac, although parts of this may be covered in sand at the Hengistbury Head end of the ride.

Roads, traffic, suitability for young children
There is a one-mile road section between the Hungry Hiker Cafe

near to Hengistbury Head as far as Pointhouse Cafe at the eastern end of Bournemouth promenade. There is also one short section in the middle which is a car parking area so there will be some traffic, although it is travelling slowly.

Hills
None.

Refreshments
Beach House Cafe, Hungry Hiker Cafe in Hengistbury Head.
Lots of cafes and tea stalls all along Bournemouth promenade.

Nearest railway station
Bournemouth, about ½ mile from the seafront.

▼ *Bournemouth promenade.*

The National Cycle Network in the area
This ride is part of Route 2 which will run all the way from Dover to Cornwall, largely along the coast. Route 25 goes north from Poole to Bath via Blandford Forum and Frome.

Other nearby rides (waymarked or traffic-free)
1. The Bourne Valley Greenway is a recently opened route linking Canford Heath (on the northwest edge of Bournemouth) through Bourne Bottom, Talbot Heath, Coy Pond and Bournemouth Upper Gardens to Bournemouth Square.
2. There are many miles of traffic-free trails in the New Forest, east of Christchurch.
3. The Poole Heritage Cycle Route is also nearby.

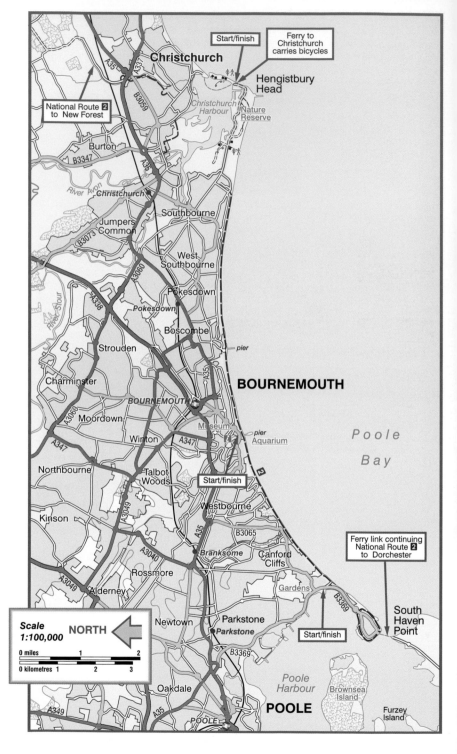

BOURNEMOUTH PROMENADE

Start/finish

Ferry to Christchurch carries bicycles

Christchurch

Hengistbury Head

National Route **2** to New Forest

Christchurch Harbour

Nature Reserve

Burton

B3347

River Avon

Christchurch

Jumpers Common

Southbourne

B3073

West Southbourne

A3060

Pokesdown

Pokesdown

A3338

River Stour

Boscombe

Strouden

pier

Charminster

BOURNEMOUTH

BOURNEMOUTH

A3060

Moordown

A347

Museum

pier
Aquarium

Poole Bay

Winton

A347

Northbourne

Talbot Woods

Start/finish

Kinson

A3049

Westbourne

B3065

Ferry link continuing National Route **2** to Dorchester

Branksome

Canford Cliffs

A3040

Rossmore

Gardens

B3369

South Haven Point

Alderney

A3049

Newtown

Parkstone

Parkstone

Start/finish

Scale
1:100,000

NORTH

0 miles   1   2

0 kilometres   1   2   3

B3369

Poole Harbour

Oakdale

Brownsea Island

A349

A35

POOLE

POOLE

Furzey Island

38

▼ *Poole's bay is a great place to cool off after the ride.*

POOLE BEACHES
SHORE ROAD

NO INFLATABLES

Poole's Beaches – *naturally beautiful*

The South East

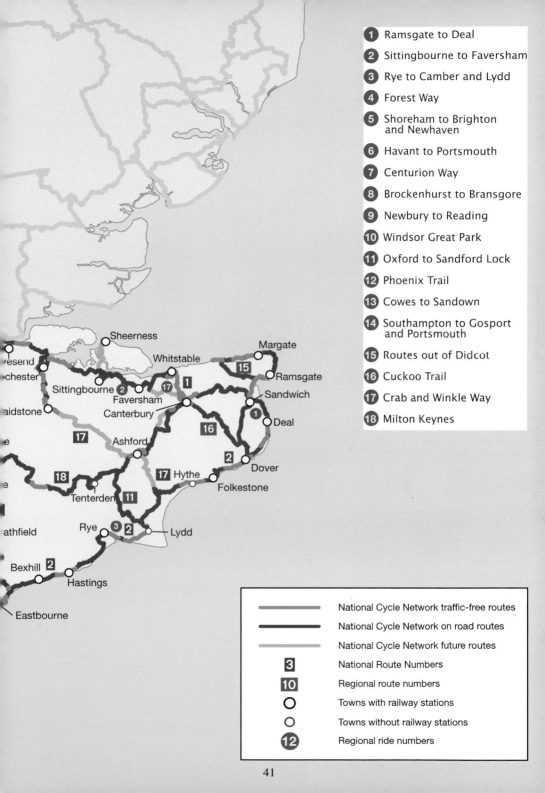

1. Ramsgate to Deal
2. Sittingbourne to Faversham
3. Rye to Camber and Lydd
4. Forest Way
5. Shoreham to Brighton and Newhaven
6. Havant to Portsmouth
7. Centurion Way
8. Brockenhurst to Bransgore
9. Newbury to Reading
10. Windsor Great Park
11. Oxford to Sandford Lock
12. Phoenix Trail
13. Cowes to Sandown
14. Southampton to Gosport and Portsmouth
15. Routes out of Didcot
16. Cuckoo Trail
17. Crab and Winkle Way
18. Milton Keynes

National Cycle Network traffic-free routes

National Cycle Network on road routes

National Cycle Network future routes

3 National Route Numbers

10 Regional route numbers

O Towns with railway stations

O Towns without railway stations

12 Regional ride numbers

41

THE SOUTH EAST

The National Cycle Network provides some wonderful routes in the South East, giving every incentive to discover this densely populated area by bike. Using the Network, it's easy to escape from the busier roads and experience numerous historic sites, fascinating old villages and towns, and the tranquility of unique and enchanting countryside. Whether you're seeking leisure rides away from the city, or a better way to make short daily journeys, the National Cycle Network is the place to be.

Major routes in the South East include two routes from London to the south coast. Route 1 runs eastwards through Faversham to reach the cathedral city of Canterbury, passing through Kent's 'Garden of England' before following the coast from Deal to Dover. The second route travels south from London through the chalk hills of the North Downs, linking with the superb and traffic-free Cuckoo Trail, and on to Eastbourne.

Route 2 will eventually span the entire stretch along the south coast from Dover to Plymouth. Extensive stretches in the South East are already in place, with much of the remainder of the route due for completion in 2005. On a smaller scale, the bicycle-friendly Isle of Wight is a great spot, with Route 22 providing an easy and beautiful traverse of the island.

Finally, to the west, Route 4 leads out from London, past Hampton Court to Windsor, Maidenhead and Reading, where Route 5 starts its way to Oxford.

The following pages provide plenty of inspiration on the miles of great routes just waiting for you and your bike in the South East. From the dreaming spires of Oxford to the glories of Hampton Court and Windsor Great Park, the wooded delights of the Chiltern Hills to the white cliffs of Dover, there's no shortage of ideas for you and your family.

▼*Newbury to Marsh Benham on Route 4.*

John Grimshaw's

HIGHLIGHTS

The Sea & Promenades
Thanet, Deal, Dover, Hythe, Hastings, Brighton and Portsmouth have all opened up the sea to cyclists. If you live in a seaside town the promenade is level, direct and traffic-free, and when I'm on these routes it's the highlight of my journey.

Ferries
Hayling Island, Gosport, Hamble and Hythe ferries take only pedestrians and cyclists, so make the South Coast route from Havant to the New Forest particularly memorable.

The Thames
When you are cycling down the Thames, at Oxford, Reading, and most particularly from Staines to Kingston, you feel as though you are on an ancient route which still remains intact, separate and continuous through the urban sprawl that has covered much of the South East.

Oxford
There are cyclists everywhere. You feel normal and welcome. It's a relief.

Milton Keynes
Is another world - a brave vision of space, of boulevards, of traffic-free routes where you can chose to be citizens of tomorrow's world.

Guildford High Street
Preserved in aspic, Guildford's high street is a poignant reminder of a less trafficked age and all we have to do for a sustainable future.

▼ *Ferries provide useful links in the National Cycle Network.*

SOUTH EAST FAMILY RIDES

**Ramsgate to Deal. 13 miles.
Route 1 and Regional Route 15**
This is a very attractive and flat
coastal ride with lots for all the
family to enjoy. Ramsgate
marina is a fabulous place to
start the route, as you take in
all the moored boats and
interesting goings-on. You
follow a bike path adjacent to
the road, passing through the
bird sanctuary. Sandwich is an
attractive town, and you
continue on a marvellous
traffic-free path through the
golf links to wind up at Deal.
It's a great spot for a well-
deserved ice cream as you
explore the picturesque town or
watch people fishing from the
pier. From here you could
continue on to Walmer Castle.

▲ *Brighton Promenade.*

▼ *Causeway on the Sittingbourne
to Canterbury route.*

**Sittingbourne to Faversham.
10 miles. Route 1**
This ride takes you on a
journey of discovery across
Kent's hidden flatland of
marshes and creeks.
Situated just across the
Swale from the Isle of
Sheppey, your route takes
advantage of traffic-free
paths and minor roads
linking these towns.

Setting out from Sittingbourne
railway station, you follow the
cycle path alongside Eurolink
Way, then the Route 1 signs
eastwards. Meandering country
lanes and a traffic-free path
lead you into the centre of
Faversham. From here, you can
return by train, or head for the
village of Oare to visit the
nature reserve there.

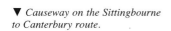

◄ *The Forest Way Country Park, situated in the heart of the East Sussex countryside.*

Rye to Camber and Lydd. 9 miles. Route 2

This completely flat and mainly traffic-free ride starts from the medieval town of Rye, a port given privileged status in the 13th century to ensure the defence of this stretch of coast. From Rye station, follow signs for Route 2 through this beautiful and historic town. Soon you cross the River Rother, continuing past small lakes populated by herons. On the outskirts of Camber and its long sandy beach, the ride takes you onto the sea wall before turning inland to Lydd, past bird sanctuaries popular with wetland fowl and seabirds.

Forest Way (East Grinstead to Groombridge). 9.5 miles. Route 21

This idyllic ride makes a wonderful family outing. The ride is traffic-free, following a disused railway line which is now a level, tree-lined track winding through peaceful fields and scattered farmsteads among rolling, wooded hills. The route passes Hartfield, which was the setting for the much loved AA Milne tale

'Winnie the Pooh'. The rural scenery may remind you of the quintessential English countryside AA Milne described, whilst younger Pooh fans should keep their eyes peeled for Tigger, or even Kanga and Roo! There are plenty of amenities and great spots to picnic along the way.

Shoreham to Brighton and Newhaven. 15 miles. Route 2

Enjoy a great day out on this coastal ride – it's full of variety! Starting at Shoreham Station follow the on-road route around the busy harbour of Shoreham-by-Sea until you join the traffic-free route at Hove, packed with imposing Regency architecture. At Brighton, the atmosphere and pace change from the sedate to the cosmopolitan, and you pass by the Palace Pier and near the Royal Pavilion, complete with Indian domes and minarets. Your ride continues on a traffic-free section to Rottingdean and Saltdean, and ends with a climb (and

▼ *Wide open promenades offer space for cyclists away from traffic and beside the sea.*

◀ *Sunlight streaming through the trees in the New Forest.*

passes through open farmland and woodland, leading to the edge of the South Downs. Your path is dotted with interesting sculptures, including a Roman work gang, devised with local schools. If you want to dine like Romans, you'll have no problem – refreshments are plentiful in Chichester, and in the pubs at Mid Lavant and West Dean. From here you can carry on to the open air museum at Singleton or the top of the South Downs.

The New Forest: Brockenhurst to Bransgore 9 miles. Route 2

A beautiful ride that takes you from the heart of the New Forest out to the village of Bransgore. The ride is mainly traffic-free, with the rest on quiet roads and takes you through typical New Forest countryside with a mixture of heathers and brackens. You will get fine views northwest towards Burley, and of the hills on the Isle of Wight to the south. You may even spot some of the famous New Forest ponies. There are refreshments

▼ *Rye to Camber Bridge.*

marvellous views!) up to Newhaven's Harbour Heights before dropping to the busy fishing port.

Havant to Portsmouth via the Hayling Billy Trail. 6.5 miles. Route 2

Offering lovely birdlife and coastal views, this ride makes a great family outing. From Havant station, you follow the Hayling Billy railway path southwards until the busy Langstone Bridge, where we suggest you walk your bike along the pavement (though we hope there will be a continuous cycle route in the future). At the end of the trail you can either return directly to Havant, or catch the Portsmouth ferry. In Portsmouth, ride along the Esplanade to the Sea Life Centre, and on to Portsmouth & Southsea railway station, where you can catch a train back.

Centurion Way – Chichester to West Dean. 5.5 miles. Regional Route 88

This short, traffic-free ride from the Cathedral City of Chichester to West Dean takes you along the course of an old railway to Midhurst. The ride

and toilets at each end, with Holmsley tearooms providing a good stopping point halfway.

Newbury to Reading on the Kennet and Avon Canal.
19 miles. Route 4

With its gentle gradients and close-up view of canal side life, this mainly traffic-free route is a great way for families to explore the area. From the modern centre of Reading, riders follow the canal towpath, enjoying the scenery, wildlife and brightly coloured canal boats that typify the Kennet and Avon Canal. The Nature Discovery Centre and reed beds at Thatcham provide an interesting and popular resting point on the route, and there are many other opportunities to take a break and find refreshments and facilities.

Windsor Great Park.
4 miles. Route 4

The estate surrounding Windsor Castle is a terrific place for families to explore by bike, as the winding estate roads are largely traffic-free. Established by William the Conqueror, Windsor Castle is the largest inhabited castle in the world. As well as views of this great castle and its magnificent tower, you'll enjoy the tranquility of this beautiful estate and surrounding countryside. You can follow Route 4 or simply roam the permitted areas as you please, perhaps enjoying a picnic, or a treat from the village shop! Route 4 also links the park with Windsor town centre and the railway stations.

Oxford to Sandford Lock. 3 miles. Route 5

This is the perfect family excursion to enjoy Oxford's waterways and famed 'dreaming spires' – an easy and entirely traffic-free path to Sandford Lock, with plenty of refreshments at either end to reward yourself! Starting at the point where Marlborough Road crosses the river take the towpath to the railway bridge then a path beside the railway to Sandford Lock. Please note that the path is popular with walkers too, so do go carefully, use your bell, and give way to pedestrians whenever necessary.

The Phoenix Trail - Princes Risborough to Thame.
7 miles. Route 57

The Phoenix Trail is a useful link between two attractive market towns, providing an ideal traffic-free ride for individuals and families with young children. Signposted from Princes Risborough station, the route allows you to enjoy the countryside without tackling hills or long distances. Rich in wildlife, the trail is particularly renowned for red kites, impressive birds of prey that thrive in the area, and it also features some great artworks, some of which reflect the route's railway heritage. The Chiltern hills make a fantastic backdrop, and the trail intersects with some enticing-looking lanes inviting further exploration. Alternatively continue past Lord Williams' School for a signposted route to Oxford.

▼ *On the beach at Deal.*

COWES TO SANDOWN, COAST TO COAST ACROSS THE ISLE OF WIGHT

This ride might be considered the easiest 'coast to coast' ride in the country, crossing the Isle of Wight from one side to the other, from Cowes to Sandown. There are two long sections of railway path, the first starts just south of Cowes, runs parallel with the yacht-filled River Medina and finishes on the northern outskirts of Newport. After threading your way through the streets of Newport, the second, much longer railway path is joined at Shide and takes you through a lovely countryside of wildflowers, pasture and woodland to the outskirts of Sandown, a popular seaside resort with miles of fine sandy beaches.

The Isle of Wight has adopted a very positive attitude towards cycling and is a great place to explore by bike. It is well connected to the mainland via ferries from Portsmouth, Southampton and Lymington.

The ferry from Portsmouth connects directly to the railway at Ryde Pier, so a clear option would be to catch the train south to Sandown (note that this train service carries a maximum of four bikes only). From there, travel west along the railway path to Newport then, if you have the energy, continue on to Cowes.

Alternatively, the ferry from Southampton brings you to East Cowes where you can take the chain ferry (cycles free of charge) to West Cowes and follow the signs to the beginning of the railway path to Newport.

If you plan to spend a weekend on the island and are riding a mountain bike there are plenty of fine chalk byways and bridleways on the western half of the island, including the spectacular Tennyson Trail with views out to the English Channel and back over the Solent to the mainland.

Starting points
The chain link ferry terminal in West Cowes.
Sandown railway station.

Distance
11 miles.

Grade
Easy.

Surface
Good quality gravel path.

Roads, traffic, suitability for young children
The traffic-free path from the western edge of Sandown to the southern edge of Newport is ideal for families, as is the much shorter section from the north of Newport to the south of Cowes. Care should be taken on the streets in Sandown, Newport and Cowes, particularly with the abundance of one-way systems.

Hills
None.

Refreshments
Lots of choice in Cowes, Newport and Sandown.
Pointer Inn just off the route in Newchurch (this involves a steep climb).

Nearest railway stations / ferry terminal
1. Sandown railway station is connected to Ryde and the ferries and hovercraft to Portsmouth.
2. The ferry from Southampton goes to East Cowes which is connected by a chain link ferry to West Cowes, close to the start of the traffic-free path to Newport.

The National Cycle Network in the area
The Cowes to Sandown route is the southernmost section of Route 23 which goes all the way to Reading.
Route 22 runs across the island from east to west from Ryde to Yarmouth and Freshwater Bay. It is possible to make a circular trip using the Isle of Wight Steam Railway from Wootton to Smallbrook Junction. Cycle from Sandown to Newport then take Route 22 beside the main road to Wootton and back by steam train and the Island line.

Other nearby rides (waymarked or traffic-free)
1. There are two other short railway paths on the Isle of Wight: Shanklin to Wroxall and Yarmouth to Freshwater Bay.
2. The Tennyson Trail is a chalk and stone bridleway from Freshwater Bay to Newport, excellent for mountain bikes in the summer months.

▼ *The beach at Sandown.*

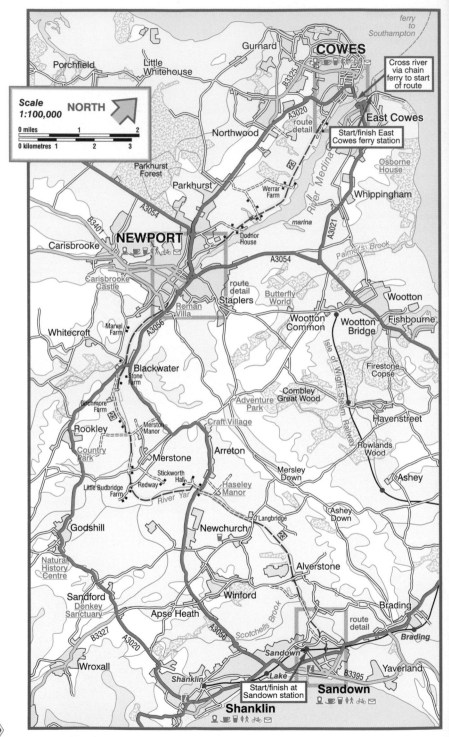

Scale
1:100,000

NORTH

0 miles   1   2
0 kilometres 1   2   3

Cross river via chain ferry to start of route

ferry to Southampton

COWES

Gurnard

Porchfield

Little Whitehouse

East Cowes

Start/finish East Cowes ferry station

Northwood

Osborne House

Whippingham

Parkhurst Forest

Werrar Farm

River Medina

Parkhurst

A3054

A3020

route detail

A3021

marina

Palmer's Brook

Carisbrooke

NEWPORT

Dodnor House

B3401

A3054

Wootton

Carisbrooke Castle

Roman Villa

Staplers

route detail

Butterfly World

Wootton Common

Wootton Bridge

Fishbourne

Whitecroft

Marvel Farm

A3056

Firestone Copse

Blackwater

Stone Farm

Adventure Park

Combley Great Wood

Isle of Wight Steam Railway

Havenstreet

Birchmore Farm

Craft Village

Rookley

Merston Manor

Arreton

Rowlands Wood

Country Park

Merstone

Mersley Down

Ashey

Little Budbridge Farm

Stickworth Hall

Redway

Haseley Manor

River Yar

Ashey Down

Godshill

Langbridge

Newchurch

Alverstone

Brading

Natural History Centre

Sandford

Donkey Sanctuary

Winford

Scotchells Brook

route detail

Brading

Apse Heath

A3056

Sandown

Yaverland

B3327

A3020

Wroxall

Shanklin

Lake

Start/finish at Sandown station

B3395

Sandown

Shanklin

23

Use the on-line mapping at www.sustrans.org.uk to find other National Cycle Network routes near you.

NEWPORT
route detail

Newport tourist attractions include: Guildhall Museum and Classic Boat Museum

Roman Villa

SANDOWN
route detail

Sandown tourist attractions include: Dinosaur Isle and Amazon World

Start/finish at Sandown station

COWES
route detail

East Cowes

Cowes tourist attractions include: Cowes Maritime Museum

SOUTHAMPTON TO GOSPORT AND THE PORTSMOUTH FERRY (TO PORTSEA)

Linking two of the most famous maritime cities on the south coast of England, this ride has some surprisingly quiet rural sections, together with long stretches with views over the Solent. This is one of the most popular sailing areas in the country, and you will often see yacht races with brightly coloured sails speeding across the water. Heading east from Southampton, cycle lanes on the Itchen Bridge take you high above the River Itchen as it joins Southampton Water. Beyond Woolston you soon join the first traffic-free waterside section. Royal Victoria Country Park with its handsome red-brick Heritage Centre is the next highlight, soon followed by the winding narrow streets, tea shops and pubs of the pretty marina at Hamble-le-Rice. An unusually pink ferry takes you and your bikes to the other side of the River Hamble towards the most rural part of the ride, through the Chilling estate on gravel tracks through woodland and past fields.

Titchfield Haven represents the start of the built-up area through Hill Head, Lee-on-the-Solent and Gosport, much of which is on wide shared-use pavements with views out to sea. A short railway path brings you to the final urban cycle lanes and the regular ferry across Portsmouth Harbour to the historic naval city of Portsmouth, home of HMS Victory, Nelson's flagship; HMS Warrior, the world's first iron-clad warship; and the recovered remains of the Mary Rose.

Starting points
Itchen Toll Bridge on the east side of Southampton.
Gosport Ferry Terminal (connected to Portsmouth Harbour railway station).

Distance
21 miles.

Grade
Easy.

Surface
Tarmac, good gravel paths.

Roads, traffic, suitability for young children
The whole ride is a mixture of shared-use pavements, cyclepaths and minor roads.

Hills
None.

Refreshments
Prince Consort PH, shops, Netley.
Lots of pubs, tearooms in Hamble.
Emma's Tea Shop, Osborne View PH, east of Titchfield Haven.
Lots of choice in Gosport.

Information
Hamble Ferry - 023 8045 4512.

Nearest railway stations
Southampton, Netley, Hamble, Fareham, Portsmouth Harbour.

The National Cycle Network in the area
This ride forms part of Route 2 which will run along the length of the South Coast from Dover to Plymouth. From Southampton, Route 24 heads northwest to Salisbury and Route 23 northeast to Winchester.

Other nearby rides (waymarked or traffic-free)
1. The Meon Valley Trail is a railway path running north from Wickham (north of Fareham) to West Meon.
2. There is a waymarked woodland trail in West Walk Forest, north of Fareham.
3. There are plenty of trails in the New Forest, west of Southampton.

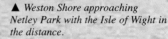

▲ *Weston Shore approaching Netley Park with the Isle of Wight in the distance.*

◄ *Portsmouth Ferry at Gosport.*

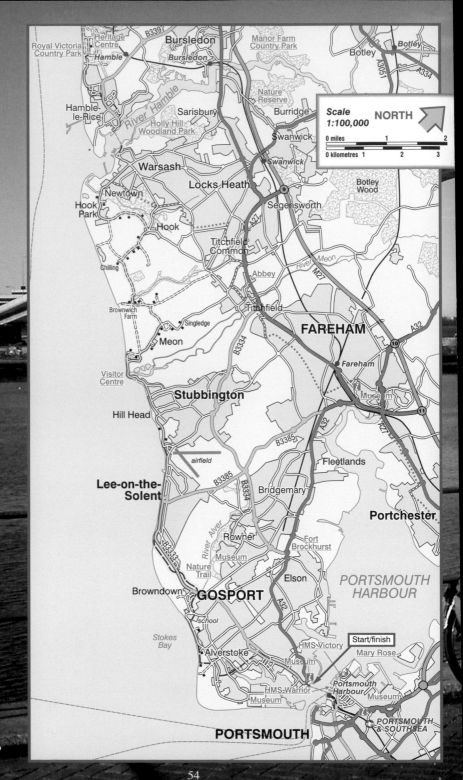

▼ *The Itchen bridge to Southampton.*

The map shows:

SOUTHAMPTON

Museum
Museum
Museum
docks
River Itchen
Bitterne
Bitterne
Start/finish
Woolston
Itchen
Woolston
Harefield
Hatch Bottom
M27
Horton Heath
West End
B3342
Sholing
Weston
Sholing
Thornhill
A334
7
Hedge End
Wildern
B3354
A3025
B3033
A3024
A27
B3036
Butlocks Heath
8
Windmill
Hedge End
Botley
Netley
Botley
Heritage Centre
B3397
Bursledon
Manor Farm Country Park
Royal Victoria Country Park
Hamble

SOUTHAMPTON WATER

Itchen Valley Country Park

55

ROUTES OUT OF DIDCOT

Didcot lies at the heart of an extensive network of cycleways built by Sustrans that enable you to leave the town safely on traffic-free paths linking to the delightful lane network of Oxfordshire with its myriad attractive villages. Three short there-and-back rides to Upton, Long Wittenham and Abingdon are described here. Didcot is dominated by the huge power station cooling towers and the ride to Abingdon passes right beneath them, giving you a true appreciation of their scale. Didcot is also famous for its Railway Centre where there are working steam engines from the Great Western Railway and a reconstructed Victorian station. The route to the attractive village of Long Wittenham, with

its two pubs, takes you right past Pendon Museum, open on weekend afternoons, with a model-sized display of the Vale of the White Horse and its railway as it was in the 1930s. To the south of Didcot, a section of railway path takes you between fields with views ahead towards the Ridgeway. In Upton, follow Prospect Road for access to the pub and take care crossing the busy A417. The final (and longest) of the three routes out of Didcot passes through the attractive village of Sutton Courtenay then goes past the Abingdon Marina before entering the handsome town of Abingdon with its Saxon gateway, 15th century almshouses and 17th-century Town Hall.

Starting points
Didcot railway station.
Abingdon Tourist Information Centre.
Upton.
Long Wittenham.

Distance
3½ miles from Didcot to Long Wittenham.
3 miles from Didcot to Upton
5 miles from Didcot to Abingdon.

Grade
Easy.

Surface
Tarmac or good quality gravel paths.

Roads, traffic, suitability for young children
Almost all the routes in and around Didcot are on shared-use pavements or dedicated cyclepaths and the streets are crossed via toucan crossings. Quiet lanes are joined to visit the villages of Upton and Long Wittenham. The Abingdon ride is more on road than traffic-free and care should be taken through Sutton Courtenay, where there is extensive traffic-calming, and in the centre of Abingdon.

Hills
None.

Refreshments
Lots of choice in Didcot.
Upton ride
George & Dragon PH, Upton.
Horse & Harrow PH, West Hagbourne.
Fleur de Lys PH, East Hagbourne.
Long Wittenham ride
Plough Inn, Vine PH, Long Wittenham.
Abingdon ride
Stores, Plough PH, Sutton Courtenay.
Lots of choice in Abingdon.

Nearest railway station
Didcot.

The National Cycle Network in the area
This ride forms part of Route 5 which runs from Reading to Oxford and on to Birmingham (and eventually all the way to Holyhead on Anglesey!). From Abingdon you can continue on a traffic-free section of Route 5 to Radley. Regional Route 44 continues from Upton to Didcot.

Other nearby rides (waymarked or traffic-free)
1. The towpath along the Thames can be followed north from Cowley Rail Bridge into Oxford.
2. The Phoenix Trail is a railway path from Thame to Princes Risborough (see page 47).
3. Long sections of the Ridgeway (south of Didcot) offer challenging offroad riding on mountain bikes in the summer months.

▼ *Didcot Power Station provides a distinctive landmark.*

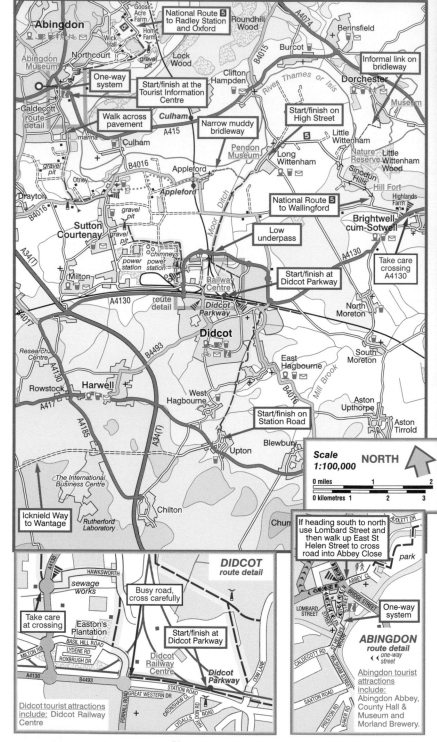

► *This seat by Andrew Osbourne has a slot for cycle parking.*

CUCKOO TRAIL

This is one of the most popular family cycle rides in the South East which gained its name from the Sussex tradition that the first cuckoo of spring was released at Heathfield Fair.

It offers superb traffic-free cycling, with only a few short road sections, and is ideal for children. There is a gentle climb of 400ft over 11 miles from Polegate to Heathfield which means a gravity-assisted return journey!

Along the way, you'll pass through a mixture of woodland, open grassland, farmland and pasture, with wildflowers in the verges. There are sculptures to look out for, carved wooden seats for resting points and views.

▼ *Hamish Black's gateway artwork prevents motor traffic from entering the path.*

Starting point
Hampden Park Station, two miles north of Eastbourne town centre.
Polegate Station, four miles north of Eastbourne in the centre of Polegate village.

Distance
13½ miles one way, 27 miles return.
The route can easily be shortened. Bear in mind that there is a 400ft climb from Polegate up to Heathfield so it is easier heading south than north!

Grade
Easy.

Surface
Tarmac and fine gravel path.

Roads, traffic, suitability for young children
The Cuckoo Trail is traffic-free and ideal for children. There are short sections on road at the start from the railway stations in Polegate and Hampden Park, and through Hailsham in the middle of the ride. There are several quiet lanes to cross. The three busy roads that need to be crossed have toucan crossings.

Hills
There is a gentle 400ft climb over 11 miles from Polegate up to Heathfield, and two short climbs at bridges over the railway and the A27.

Refreshments
Lots of choice in Hampden Park, Polegate, Hailsham and Heathfield. Cafe in Horam and a tea shop on the trail at the Old Loom Mill Craft Centre (two miles north of Polegate, just before crossing the B2104).

Nearest railway stations
Polegate or Hampden Park.

The National Cycle Network in the area
The Cuckoo Trail forms part of Route 21 which runs south from London through Redhill and East Grinstead to Eastbourne. From Polegate the South Coast Cycle Route (Route 2) runs east through Pevensey to Bexhill and west to Newhaven and Brighton.

Other nearby rides (waymarked or traffic-free)
The Forest Way and Worth Way are two railway paths starting in East Grinstead, running west to Crawley and east to Groombridge. There are cycle tracks along parts of the promenades in Eastbourne, Hastings, Brighton and Hove. The South Downs Way is suitable for fit cyclists on mountain bikes. There is also a route around Bewl Water, south

▼ *Artwork at Horam*

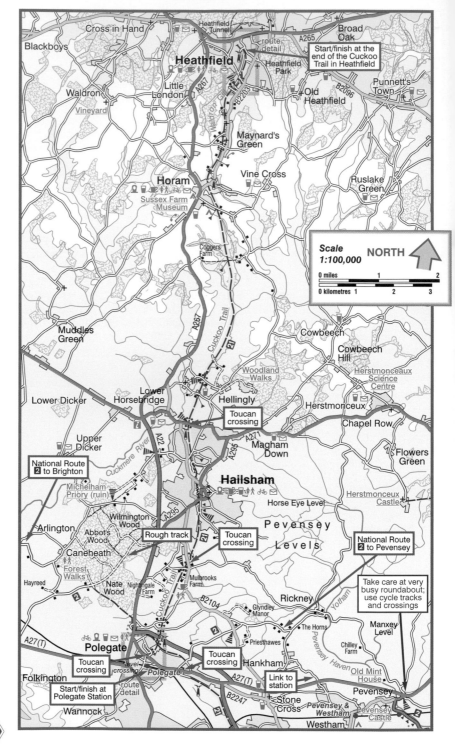

CUCKOO TRAIL

Scale 1:100,000

NORTH

0 miles   1   2
0 kilometres   1   2   3

Start/finish at the end of the Cuckoo Trail in Heathfield

National Route 2 to Brighton

Rough track

Toucan crossing

National Route 2 to Pevensey

Take care at very busy roundabout; use cycle tracks and crossings

Toucan crossing

Toucan crossing

Toucan crossing

Link to station

Start/finish at Polegate Station

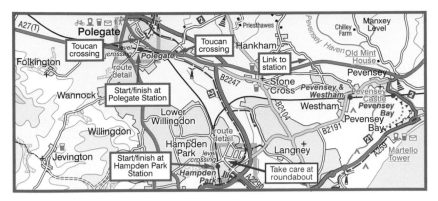

HEATHFIELD
route detail
Heathfield tourist
attractions include:
Heathfield Tunnel,
Millennium Green

east of Tunbridge Wells (summer-time only).

From Hampden Park in the north of Eastbourne you take the mostly traffic-free route to Polegate, with great views of the South Downs rising to the west. The section of route in Polegate follows the old railway line that used to run directly eastwards to Pevensey.

In several places where bridges have been dismantled and houses have been built on the course of the railway, the route continues on short

sections of estate roads through Hailsham and Horam to regain the railway path.

Along the way are metal sculptures by local artist Hamish Black which pick up on local heritage. There are also plenty of carved wooden seats with a variety of motifs made by the sculptor Steve Geliot from local oaks blown down in the Great Storm of 1987. The verges are thick with wildflowers such as willowherb and vetch.

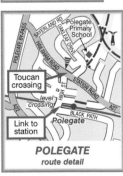

POLEGATE
route detail

HAMPDEN PARK
route detail

▲ *Sculpture at Hellingley*

CRAB & WINKLE WAY

This route from the cathedral city of Canterbury to the harbour town of Whitstable takes its name from the railway line that ran from 1830 until 1952.

It offers wide variety, taking you from the heart of a beautiful city, via quiet roads and cycle paths, and along the course of a dismantled railway, to an attractive seaside town. Along the way you'll go through woodland, past fruit farms and end up with great views over the estuary.

This is a short ride with a steady 200ft climb out of Canterbury followed by an undulating section before a drop into Whitstable.

Starting point
Westgate, Canterbury.
Whitstable town centre.

Distance
Canterbury to Whitstable - seven and a half miles one way, 15 miles return.
Canterbury to Fordwich - three miles one way, six miles return.

Grade
Easy.

Surface
Streets at the start and finish, a fine stone-based path between the university and South Street, on the edge of Whitstable.

Roads, traffic, suitability for young children
The route through Canterbury and Whitstable uses traffic-calmed streets or cycle paths.

The central section is on a newly-built traffic-free path through woodland partially using the old railway line.

Hills
There is a 200ft climb out of Canterbury and an undulating middle section before dropping down to the coast at Whitstable.

Refreshments
Lots of choice in Canterbury.
Lots of choice in Whitstable.

Nearby railway stations for longer linear rides
Starting from Whitstable you could follow Route 1 west to Faversham and Sittingbourne or east to Sandwich, Deal and Dover and catch the train back.

The National Cycle Network in the area
Canterbury lies at a crossroads of the Network. The east-west route from London to Dover is already in place (Route 1). To the south Routes 17 and 18 will go to Ashford whilst Regional Routes 16 and 17 are already in place to Dover and Hythe respectively. To the north Regional Route 15 will run along the North Kent Coast to Ramsgate.

Other nearby rides (waymarked or traffic-free)
The Cathedral to Coast Ride is a waymarked 50-mile circular route linking Canterbury, Folkestone and Dover. It is made up of Regional Routes 16 and 17.

▶ *Walkers on the Crab & Winkle Way.*

The ride starts in the beautiful, cathedral city of Canterbury which has over 2000 years of history. Now a UNESCO world heritage site, the city became a place of pilgrimage for many (including the characters in Geoffrey Chaucer's 'Canterbury Tales') after the murder of the Archbishop of Canterbury, Thomas à Becket, in the Cathedral in 1170. It's worth exploring the cathedral area, with its backways and delightful streets, before you start. However, this is best done on foot as there is a restriction on cycling here between 10.30am and 4pm.

You'll take a series of sections on traffic-calmed streets or cycle paths as the route climbs steadily out of the city with wonderful views opening up behind you. After passing close to the university the route soon joins a traffic-free section that runs for over four miles past fruit farms and woodland.

Blean Woods is one of the largest areas of broad-leaved woodland in the country, and in Clowes Wood listen out for woodpeckers, warblers and nightingales.

The route takes you to South Street on the edge of Whitstable. Cyclepaths and traffic-calmed streets lead right in the heart of this fine coastal town, famous for beautiful sunsets and oysters (you may even catch the oyster festival in July!).

Another option from the centre of Canterbury is to follow the path out to the east to Fordwich where you join a delightful network of lanes meandering across rich agricultural country eastwards to Sandwich and the coast.

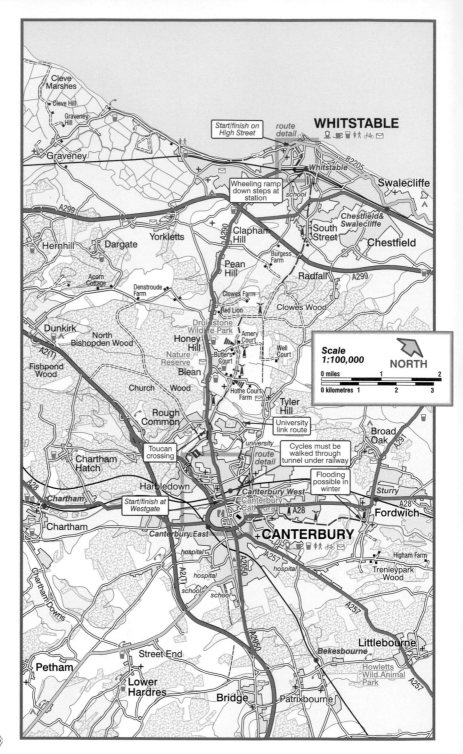

To find out about other cycle routes in this area visit www.sustrans.org.uk

CANTERBURY
route detail

━━ pedestrian precinct

Canterbury tourist attractions include: Canterbury Cathedral, Canterbury Heritage Museum, Roman Museum and The Canterbury Tales Visitor Attraction

WHITSTABLE
route detail

Whitstable tourist attractions include: The Oyster & Fisheries Exhibition and Whitstable Museum & Gallery

MILTON KEYNES

If you have never cycled in Milton Keynes you will be astonished when you explore the place for the first time. Cycle routes, including those that form part of the famous Redway Network, enable you to explore the city, from the centre to lakes, canals, and the Buddhist pagoda, all the while diving in and out of woodland. You'll also come across attractive villages, full of character, that are now part of urban Milton Keynes.

The parks along the route are ideal for young children, with picnic spots and adventure playgrounds. The ride uses parts of the National Cycle Network through Milton Keynes with two links, to give a circular route through the city. It has been signed as the Milton Keynes Millennium Circular Cycle Route.

Starting point
Milton Keynes Central railway station.

Distance
12-mile circuit.

Grade
Easy.

Surface
Red tarmac or gravel paths throughout.

Roads, traffic, suitability for young children
All busy roads are crossed via underpasses or bridges. Several quiet estate roads are crossed and some quiet roads are used.

Hills
The route follows the valleys, avoiding most of the hills in Milton Keynes.

Refreshments
Lots of choice in the square by the railway station and elsewhere in central Milton Keynes. Pub and shop in Woughton on the Green (just off the route). Tea shop at Bradwell Abbey. Nag's Head PH, Great Linford. Pub at Furzton Lake (just off the route).

Nearest railway stations
Milton Keynes Central,
Wolverton.

The National Cycle Network in the area
Milton Keynes is at a
crossroads of the National
Cycle Network. Route 6 passes
through Milton Keynes on its
way south from Leicester and
Northampton to St Albans and
London.

Route 51 runs from Oxford to
Bedford, Cambridge and the
east coast.

The circular route could be
adapted by following Route 6
to Castlethorpe, an attractive
village on the way to
Northampton. For the more
ambitious, Route 51 would take
you out into the

Buckinghamshire countryside
to Winslow, an attractive town
with a famous tea shop. If you
prefer to stay within Milton
Keynes, you could make for
Willen Lake and the Open
University on the course of
Route 51.

The route along the canal
towpath from Milton Keynes to
Leighton Buzzard is also being
developed.

**Other nearby rides
(waymarked or traffic-free)**
There is a comprehensive
network of traffic-free paths
and quiet roads with plenty of
adventure playgrounds and
picnic sports along the way.

The route is made up of gravel-
finished paths through parks,

red tarmac paths that form the
famous Redway Network and
many quiet roads.

The city was designed as a
whole series of individual
communities, and central
Milton Keynes is unlike any
other city centre in the country,
with its wide boulevards,
unusual architecture and
impressive sculptures.

The ride takes in paths
beside the Grand Union Canal,
Campbell Park, the beautiful
old stone buildings of Great
Linford, a section of dismantled
railway through a thickly
wooded cutting, and a leisure
route along the Loughton
Valley passing through a
curious little tunnel.

Last but not least there is a
chance to see the famous

▼ *Campbell Park, Milton Keynes.*

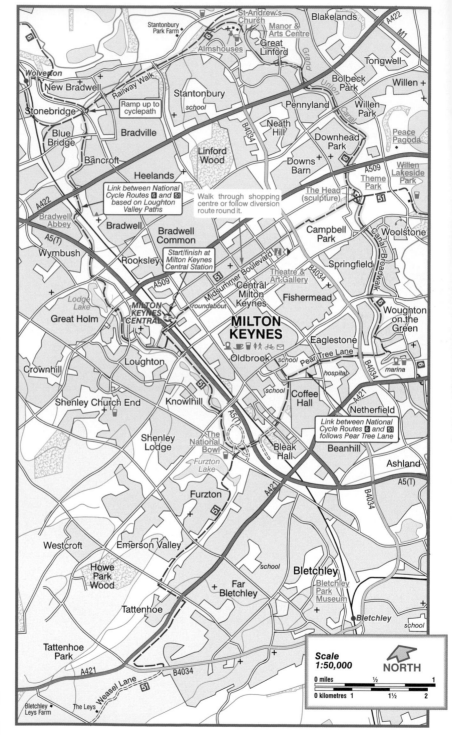

concrete cows of Milton Keynes and a whole host of other outdoor sculpture.

A slight detour to Willen Lake North offers a good picnic spot and chance to explore the first Peace Pagoda in the west with a frieze telling the life story of the Buddha. You'll also see the Circle of Hearts Medicine Wheel, a North American stone circle and symbol of peace; and Tim Minett and Neil Higson's turf maze with bronze roundels representing the four races of mankind.

The park by Furzton Lake where you can see Silhouetted Portals, created from railway sleepers, is ideal for very young cyclists.

For details of free cycling leaflets for this area visit www.sustrans.org.uk

▼ *Route 6 beside the Grand Union Canal at Willen.*

Rayners Lane

Sudbury Hill

61

Uxbridge

London
Paddington

6

3

2

Hammersmith

Hyde
Park

Kew
Gardens

Heathrow Airport

7

8

Richmond

Barnes

Wandswo

Hampton
Court

5

Putney

Earlsfield

11

Richmond
Park

Kingston

22

Hampton

4

Morden

Carshalton

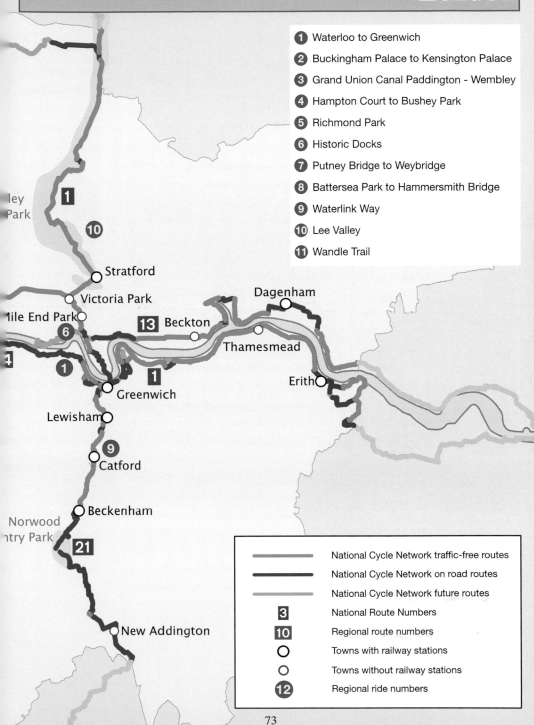

London

1. Waterloo to Greenwich
2. Buckingham Palace to Kensington Palace
3. Grand Union Canal Paddington - Wembley
4. Hampton Court to Bushey Park
5. Richmond Park
6. Historic Docks
7. Putney Bridge to Weybridge
8. Battersea Park to Hammersmith Bridge
9. Waterlink Way
10. Lee Valley
11. Wandle Trail

Map labels: ...ley Park, Stratford, Victoria Park, Mile End Park, Greenwich, Lewisham, Catford, Beckenham, Norwood ...try Park, New Addington, Beckton, Dagenham, Thamesmead, Erith

Legend:

National Cycle Network traffic-free routes
National Cycle Network on road routes
National Cycle Network future routes
3 National Route Numbers
10 Regional route numbers
○ Towns with railway stations
○ Towns without railway stations
12 Regional ride numbers

LONDON

If you've never tried cycling in London, the National Cycle Network offers a huge and very pleasant surprise, including numerous family-friendly routes. Great routes abound, providing not only a highly practical solution to navigating the nation's capital, but many delightful new perspectives on a city you may have thought you already knew well. The Network is a treasure trove of green corridors, watercourses, parks and commons, stringing together suburbs as well as many of London's best known landmarks.

Creating continuous, high quality routes in London has presented enormous challenges, and required major investment. As you ride around London on the National Cycle Network, you'll notice many special road crossings, traffic-calming measures and other features, installed to improve safety and access for cyclists and walkers. Major new provision for cyclists has been made at Millbank and at Lambeth Bridge, and completely new, dedicated bridges such as the one under Chelsea Bridge (taking you into Battersea Park) have been created too. The aim is to encourage you to cycle more, and to ensure

that one of the best ways to view and travel in the city is by bike.

In the pages that follow you'll find plenty to whet your appetite. Imagine taking your family on a bike tour of central London from Buckingham Palace to Kensington Palace, free of traffic... you can do exactly this on the National Cycle Network. Explore the South Bank or the industrial history of the city's canals, ride to Hampton Court Palace, Richmond Park or the Thames Barrier, or from east London along the Lee Valley - it's all there for you to enjoy.

The London Cycle Network

The London Cycle Network Plus (LCN+) is being developed by Transport for London in partnership with the boroughs. Due for completion by 2009, 900 kilometres of routes will provide direct access to railway stations and to every major centre of employment, education and leisure. Get hold of the 19 free London Cycle Guide maps from www.tfl.gov.uk/cycling or pick up them up from transport information offices.

London Cycling Campaign

The London Cycling Campaign provided much of the mapping information for the free cycle guides. It has local groups in every London borough, and members receive bike shop discounts and a regular magazine - to join, telephone 020 7928 7220 or visit www.lcc.org.uk

▼ *The National Cycle Network will give you a different view of London.*

HIGHLIGHTS

The Thames
Cycling through London besides the Thames is always a wonderful experience. The river is so large that the views are extensive. You are separate from traffic. You can stop. There is so much history, so much change. The river is never the same.

Hyde Park
Marble Arch to Hyde Park Corner follows the course of one of London's very first cycle routes and it remains a thrill to cycle down the long avenue of trees in the very heart of London.

Mile End Park
The route through Mile End Park to the Millennium Park and Victoria Park is a triumph of continuity, with the tree-lined and landscaped

park bridge over Mile End Road a real highlight of the Network.

The Wandle Trail through Morden Hall Park
The whole of this route is rather extraordinary, running through an informal riverside corridor, and unexpectedly rural. At Morden Hall, the path links past swampy marshlands with sight of the new Croydon tramway – a complete contrast in scale and technology.

▼ *Route 4 passes by the London Eye.*

LONDON FAMILY RIDES

Waterloo Station to Greenwich. 6 miles. Route 4

This urban ride is a brilliant way to enjoy London's regenerated South Bank (however, as it's partly on road and very busy with pedestrians at weekends, we don't recommend it for those with young children). Starting at Waterloo Station, the route follows close to the Thames, taking you on a memorable tour of some of London's favourite spots including the London Eye, National Theatre, Globe Theatre, Tate Modern and Tower Bridge. You then follow quiet roads, parks and waterfronts through historic Bermondsey until the finish point at the Cutty Sark in Greenwich, where there are plenty of pubs and cafes in which to recuperate.

Buckingham Palace to Kensington Palace. 2.5 miles. Route 6

From the Queen's grand London residence, through Green Park and down Constitution Hill, this traffic-free route leads you to

▲ Cycling beside the River Thames with a view of Canary Wharf.

Hyde Park where you can bask in the splendour of this corner of the West End. Thanks to a new crossing at Hyde Park Corner and the opening up of sections of the park for cyclists, this unusual London journey is a relaxing and pleasant experience. The route through the park links the royal memorials of Prince Albert and Princess Diana, and you can also stop and view contemporary art at the Serpentine Gallery.

Grand Union Canal - Paddington to Wembley. 7 miles. Route 6

This is an intriguing yet little known traffic-free towpath ride, taking you from the heart of London to its leafy suburbs via the Grand Union Canal. Starting at Paddington Station (Westbourne Terrace) you ride underneath the A40 until you reach the canal. Follow the towpath underneath arches and bridges to the unexpected swathe of countryside at Berkeley Fields and Horsenden Hill. Horsenden Hill is the highest point in North West London, providing a stunning panorama of the surrounding areas of Sudbury Hill and Harrow Hill. The towpath is narrow in places, so please show consideration to other users.

◄ The Tea Clipper Cutty Sark at Greenwich. Often seen during the London Marathon.

▲ *The beatifully ornate fencing of Hampton Court Palace, a true work of art.*

Hampton Court and Bushy Park. 5.5 miles. Route 4

Starting by the Thames at the sumptuous Hampton Court Palace, this route takes in one of the most tranquil and beautiful spaces in west London. Following the riverside path east until Kingston Bridge, just relax and take in the sights and sounds of riverside life. At Kingston Bridge follow the Hampton Court Road through the park, turning into Christopher Wren's beautiful Chestnut Avenue, and riding around the world famous Diana Fountain. Follow the Avenue up to Teddington Gate and look back to enjoy the striking view.

Richmond Park Circuit. 5.5 miles. Route 4

Richmond Park is London's largest open space, and a wonderful place to cycle. This Royal Park boasts an array of wildlife and an uninterrupted view of St Paul's Cathedral (12 miles distant) from the highest point. This ride is a circuit of the park, taking in some of the famous sites which include the deer park and Pembroke Lodge, a beautiful Georgian mansion set in landscaped grounds. There are places to stop for refreshments in the park, so you can just get out there and explore!

Historic Docks - Tower Bridge to Lee Valley. 2 miles. Regional Route 13

This short ride follows mainly traffic-free paths, taking you on a journey of discovery through the old docks and warehouses of East London. The route starts on the northern side of the River Thames at St Katharine's Dock, by Tower Bridge, and you follow an ornamental canal past Tobacco Dock to Shadwell Basin. Quiet riverside back streets then take you onwards to the Limehouse Basin and then Westferry. Refreshments can be found along the way, and if you're hungry for more cycling, follow the link to Route 1, which takes you north along the Lee Valley.

▼ *Richmond Park has a network of routes to explore, with wonderful views all round, a very historic place to visit.*

PUTNEY BRIDGE TO WEYBRIDGE

For anyone who believes that there is no escape for cyclists from London's traffic, this ride is the answer: enjoy cycling along the green corridor that lies right on the doorstep of the capital. The route takes a mixture of quiet roads and traffic-free paths with a wonderful nine-mile stretch of path alongside the River Thames from Kingston to Weybridge. You'll cycle through Richmond Park, where you could take a detour to see the deer, and get the chance to visit Hampton Court Palace along the way.

Starting points
The south side of Putney Bridge.
The riverside path (by the pedestrian ferry) in Weybridge.

Distance
18 miles one way, 36 miles return.
For a shorter trip, starting from Putney Bridge, there are good turnaround points at Richmond Park (12-mile round trip), Kingston upon Thames (18-mile round trip) or Hampton Court (24-mile round trip).

Grade
Easy.

Surface
Mixture of tarmac and good quality gravel paths.

Roads, traffic, suitability for young children
The route is a mixture of quiet streets and cyclepaths. The best traffic-free section alongside the river runs west from Kingston Bridge, crosses to the other side at Hampton Court then continues to Weybridge (a total of nine miles one way, 18 miles return).

Hills
Richmond Hill.

▼ *Traffic-free sections are ideal for trips with young children.*

78

Refreshments
All along the way.

Nearest railway stations
Putney, Barnes, Kingston upon Thames, Hampton Court.

The National Cycle Network in the area
The ride described here is the first section of the Thames Valley Cycle Route which runs from Putney Bridge to Oxford (Route 4 to Reading then Route 5 from Reading to Oxford). East from Putney Bridge the London Thames Cycle Route runs right through the heart of London to Greenwich and Dartford.

Other nearby rides (waymarked or traffic-free)
There is a traffic-free circular ride around Richmond Park. The National Cycle Network bears away from the river after a mile or so, past the Wetlands Centre at Barnes, then crossing Richmond Park (where you have the option of completing a totally traffic-free circuit of the park) before rejoining the river, threading its way through Kingston upon Thames and passing the majestic buildings of Hampton Court. The Thames is followed closely for the next six miles, passing Sunbury Lock and finishing at Weybridge. This route is part of the Thames Valley Cycle Route and if you wish you could follow the ride beyond Weybridge to Windsor, Reading and Oxford.

▼ *The best family outings have lots of breaks built in.*

79

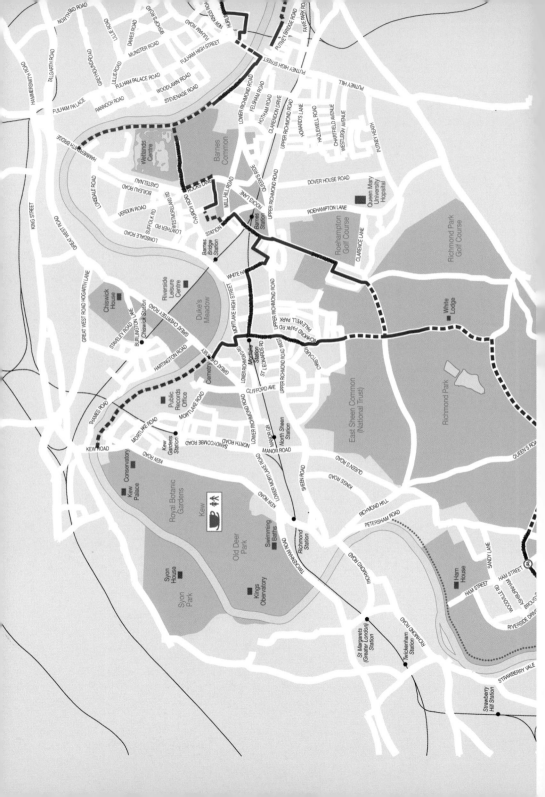

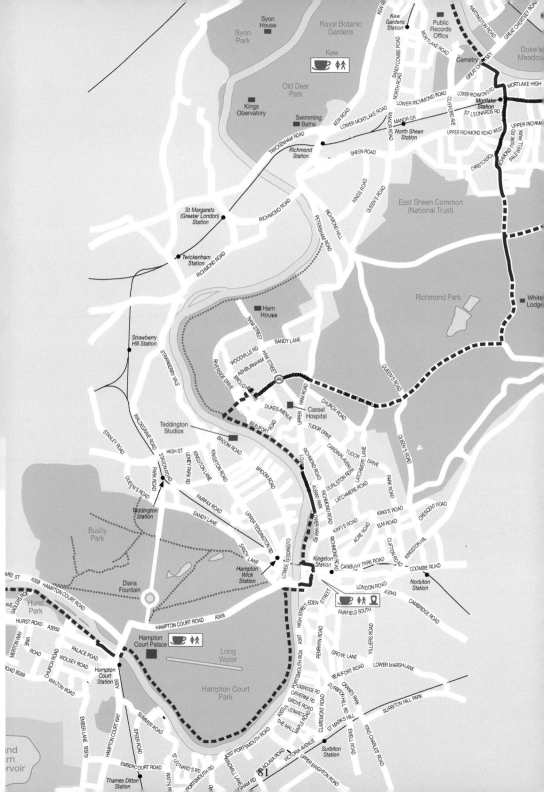

BATTERSEA PARK TO HAMMERSMITH

This short easy ride offers the perfect afternoon escape from the city without really leaving it at all. There's plenty to see along the way and the route is well served with lots of choice for refreshments. Alternatively, you may choose to use just part of the route to get to one of several parks that it links.

Before starting the ride it is worth exploring Battersea Park, with its fountains, lake (with boating in the summer), children's play area and zoo, or to wonder at the beautiful Peace Pagoda by the riverside. You could even do a warm-up on the traffic-free paths that circle the park.

The route mainly follows the river on traffic-free paths, occasionally cutting inland on short road sections, towards Wandsworth and Putney, where you'll find a variety of restaurants and cafes.

After Putney Bridge, you have two options. Follow the signs for Route 4 away from the river towards Barnes Common and you soon get to the London Wetlands Centre. When it was opened in 2000, it was the first project of its kind, creating 40 hectares of wetlands and the chance to see a wide variety of wildlife right in a capital city. The Wetlands Centre makes an interesting diversion and has some of the best cycle parking in London and free toilets to boot.

Alternatively continue along the Thames Cycle Route to your final destination, Hammersmith, which offers a wide range of refreshments stops and shops.

◀ *Cycling along Battersea Reach.*

Starting points
Battersea Park.
Hammersmith Bridge.

Distance
6 miles.

Grade
Easy.

Surface
Roads or riverside towpath.

Roads, traffic, suitability for young children
Much of it is traffic-free but some major junctions may need to be walked.

Hills
None.

Refreshments
Battersea Park, Wandsworth Town Centre, Putney, Hammersmith.

Nearest railway stations
Victoria Station (cross Chelsea Bridge from north of the river), Wandsworth Town, Putney.

The National Cycle Network in the area
This ride is largely on Route 4 which travels west to Richmond and on towards Reading, Bristol and South Wales.
Route 4 links with the Wandle Trail (Route 22) which runs south from Wandsworth.
To the east it links with Route 1 at Greenwich, towards Canterbury and Dover.

Other nearby rides (waymarked or traffic-free)
Richmond Park is accessible via Route 4 in Barnes.

▼ *The Peace Pagoda in Battersea Park*

84

85

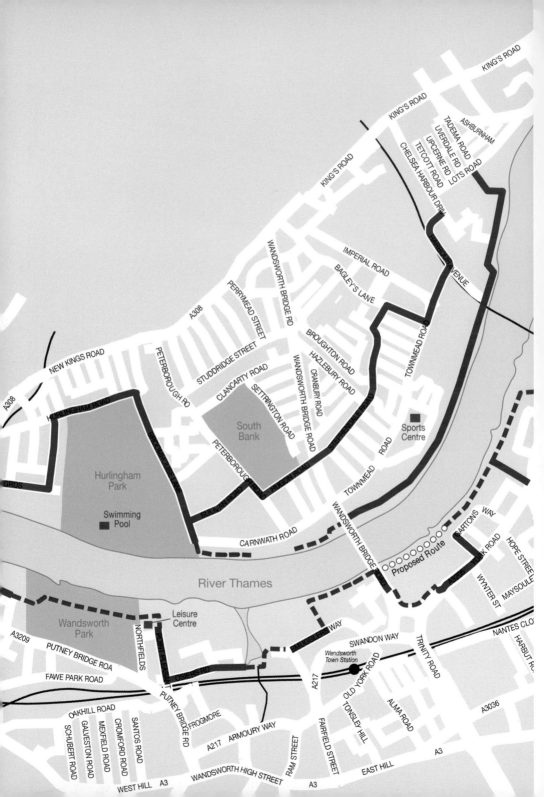

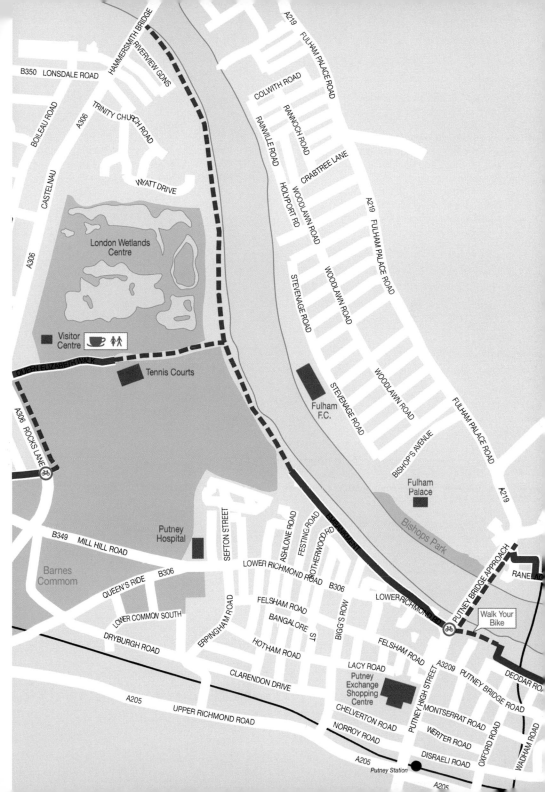

THE WATERLINK WAY
GREENWICH TO BECKENHAM

Starting on the banks of the Thames at Greenwich, under the bow of the Cutty Sark, the Waterlink Way makes its way south through Lewisham, Bromley and Croydon. It follows the valley of the little-known Ravensbourne River, journeying through an uncharacteristic area of London. Many new bridges and underpasses have been built for the route (as part of the new Docklands Light Railway works). There's even a suspended walkway through a tunnel over a river!

The route takes you through many delightful parklands, both new and rejuvenated, making at least half of the ride traffic-free.

At Catford, the route picks up the Pool River and follows it into Bromley. From park to park you hop before entering the borough of Croydon at Elmers End. Here, you can pick up a train back to London or head on south into South Norwood Country Park.

Starting Points
Greenwich (Cutty Sark).
Clockhouse Station, Beckenham Road, Beckenham or South Norwood Country Park.

Distance
Six miles one way, 12 miles return.

Grade
Easy.

Surface
All tarmac.

Roads, traffic, suitability for young children
Where the route passes though parkland it is ideal for young children. However, there are also several road sections which are only suitable for older children (10+).

Hills
None.

Refreshments
Lots of choice near the Cutty Sark. Various pubs near the route on the way south.

Nearest railway stations
Greenwich and Clockhouse at either end of the ride and several others in between (Lewisham, Ladywell, Catford, and Lower Sydenham).

The National Cycle Network in the area
1. The Waterlink Way is part of Route 21 (London to Hastings).
2. North of Greenwich, Route 1 runs across the Isle of Dogs and Victoria Park to join the Lee Valley.
3. Route 4 runs west through London to Putney Bridge to join the Thames Valley Cycle Route.
4. East of Greenwich, Route 1 runs past the Millennium Dome and the old Woolwich Arsenal on its way to Erith and Dartford.

▼ *Playgrounds are a good place for children to stretch their legs whilst you rest yours.*

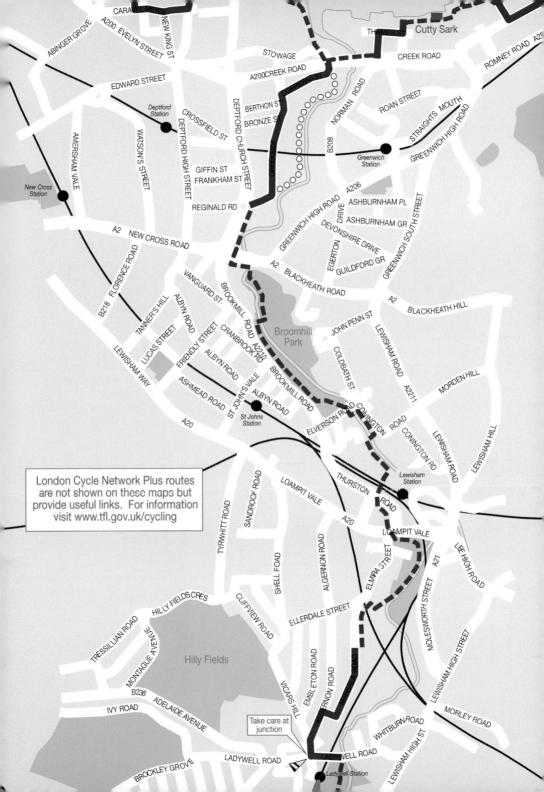

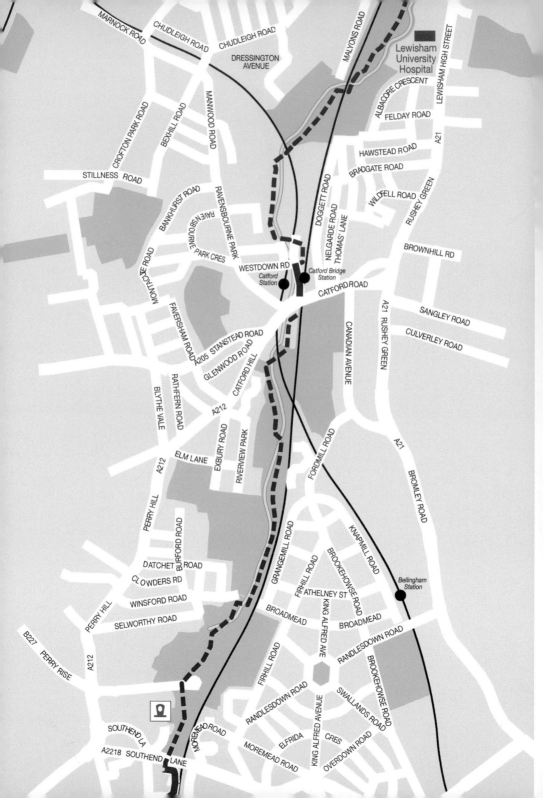

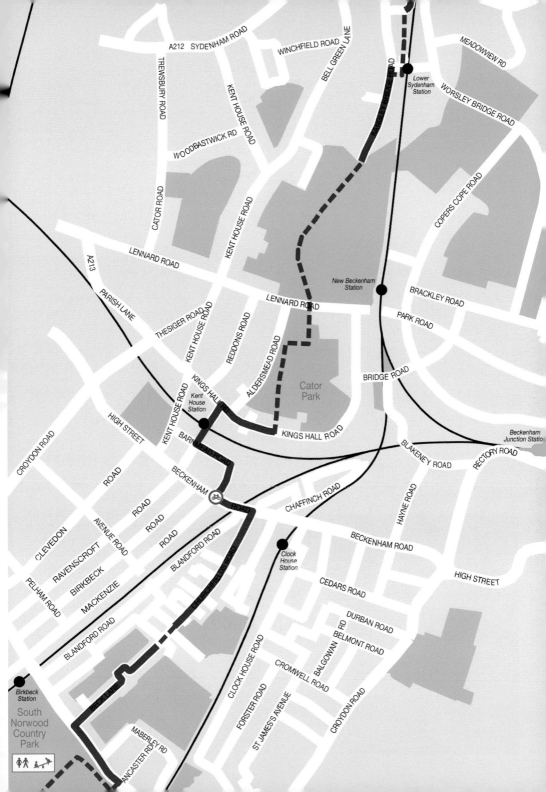

LEE VALLEY

This patchwork of parks, waterways and commons will give you a new perspective on east London. Starting in Greenwich - not far from the Cutty Sark - the route takes you under the Thames via the Greenwich Foot Tunnel. You emerge to find yourself on the Isle of Dogs, home to Canary Wharf and the Mudchute Park and Farm: Europe's largest City Farm. After crossing Millwall Dock and passing the edge of the Canary Wharf development, you soon join the path of Regents Canal, and on into the new Mile End eco-park, crossing the Mile End Road via a 'green' bridge covered with grass and lined with trees. You leave the Regents Canal to cross Victoria Park before joining the River Lee Navigation towards Hackney Marshes, home to Europe's largest collection of football fields. Depending on the day, you could be spectator to more than 100 football games! The route then continues through Walthamstow Marshes Nature Reserve, a Site of Special Scientific Interest and home to over 300 species of plants, towards Waltham Abbey. North of here the Lee Valley Park offers miles of traffic-free cycling.

Starting points
The Greenwich Foot Tunnel, next to the Cutty Sark.
Waltham Abbey.

Distance
13 miles.

Grade
Easy.

Surface
Tarmac, grit.

Roads, traffic, suitability for young children
This route is mainly traffic-free and suitable for young children. Once you join the Regents Canal, the route is entirely traffic free all the way to the North Circular Road.

Hills
None.

Refreshments
Lots of choice in Greenwich. Cafes at Mudchute Farm; at the Visitor Centre, Middlesex Filter Beds Nature Reserve; and at the Springfield Marina by Walthamstow Reservoirs.

Nearest railway stations
Greenwich, Limehouse, Hackney Wick, Clapton and Tottenham Hale.

The National Cycle Network in the area
1. To the east of the Thames Barrier, Route 1 continues along the Thames estuary as far as Gravesend, where it heads inland through Kent then on to Canterbury and Dover.
2. Route 21 links London with the South Coast via the Waterlink Way, running down through Deptford and Lewisham towards Croydon and Redhill.
3. Route 1 will eventually continue north to Roydon and Chelmsford.

Other nearby rides (waymarked or traffic-free)
1. There are miles of attractive traffic-free cycling in the Lee Valley Park, which continues north from the end of the route.
2. London Cycle Network Routes 54, 14 and 11 intersect with the route, providing good on-road options for onward journeys.

◄ *A park on a bridge! This 'green bridge' crosses the busy Mile End Road.*

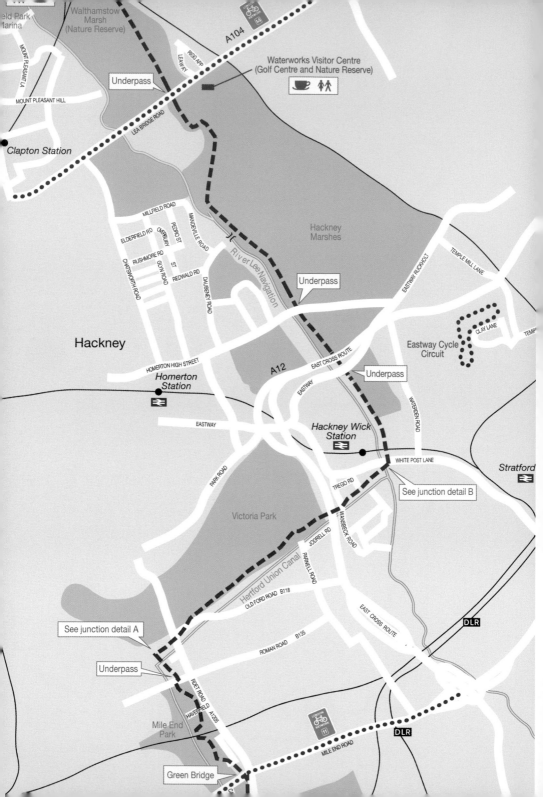

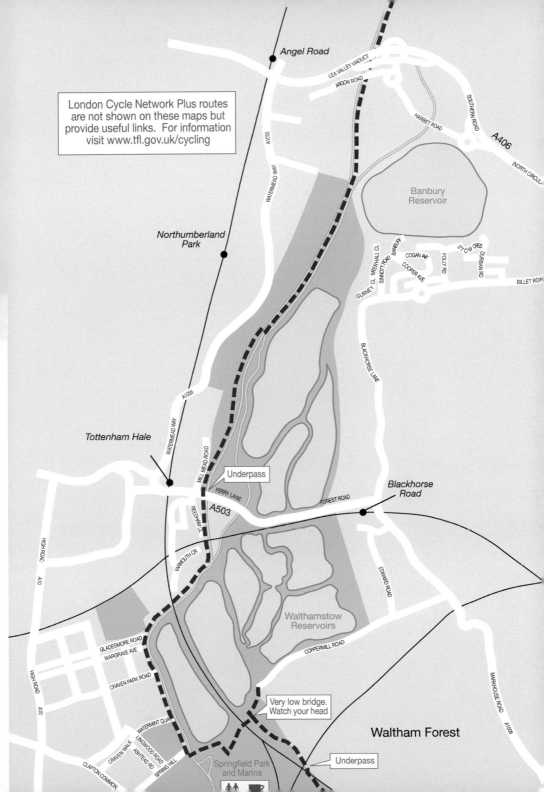

THE WANDLE TRAIL FROM WANDSWORTH TO CARSHALTON

London has several cycle routes which use the watercourses through the city as green corridors, most notably the Thames, but also the Grand Union Canal to the northwest, the Lee valley to the northeast and the Pool River / Ravensbourne River to the southeast, the latter used on the Waterlink Way. The Wandle Trail follows the River Wandle, from its junction with the Thames in Wandsworth through a series of small riverside parks south to Carshalton. In its industrial prime the River Wandle was Britain's 'hardest working river' with over 90 mills along its banks. It is one of those rides that improves each time you do it as you begin to memorize the sequences of left, right and straight on that link the green, traffic-free stretches. There is an excellent coffee / tea stop at the National Trust property in Morden Hall Park, a former deer park with a network of waterways including meadow, wetland and woodland habitats. The park also boasts a spectacular rose garden with over 2,000 roses, particularly fragrant from May to September. The historic mills and the 19th-century estate buildings house craft workshops including wood turning and furniture restoration.

NB. The Wandle Trail for cyclists does not always follow the Wandle Trail for walkers. There are three places where new proposed routes (in each case bringing the trail closer to the River Wandle) will significantly improve the quality of the overall route and it is hoped these will be in place in the near future. In the meantime please pay attention to the cycle signs.

Starting points
The junction of the River Wandle with the Thames, to the west of Wandsworth Bridge. Carshalton railway station.

Distance
11 miles.

Grade
Easy.

Surface
Tarmac or fine gravel and dust path.

Roads, traffic, suitability for young children
There are several traffic-free sections through parkland linked by short road sections, many of which have safe crossings via pelican crossings. The longest traffic-free stretch runs south from Merton High Street to Ravensbury Park, passing through Morden Hall Park.

Hills
None.

Refreshments
Lots of choice in the centre of Wandsworth.
Lots of choice on Merton High Street.
Cafe at Morden Hall.
Surrey Arms PH, Morden Road, just south of Morden Hall Park.
Lots of choice in the centre of Carshalton.

Nearest railway stations
Carshalton, Mitcham Junction, Haydons Road, Earlsfield and Wandsworth Town.

The National Cycle Network in the area
Route 4 of the National Cycle Network, joined at the northern end of the Wandle Trail, runs west from Wandsworth to Putney Bridge, the start of a long, mainly traffic-free section to Weybridge. Route 22 will continue south and west through Dorking, Guildford and Farnham down to the south coast at Portsmouth.

Other nearby rides (waymarked or traffic-free)
1. Putney Bridge to Weybridge is almost all traffic-free alongside the Thames.
2. The Tamsin Trail in Richmond Park is a traffic-free circuit around the perimeter of the park.

▼ *Visit parks and green spaces on the Wandle Trail.*

'Blue ceramic plaques' by Jemima Burrell.

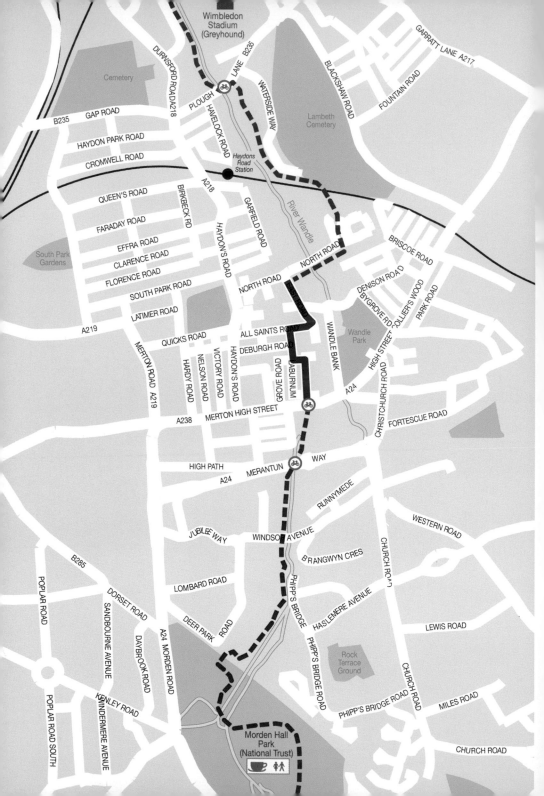

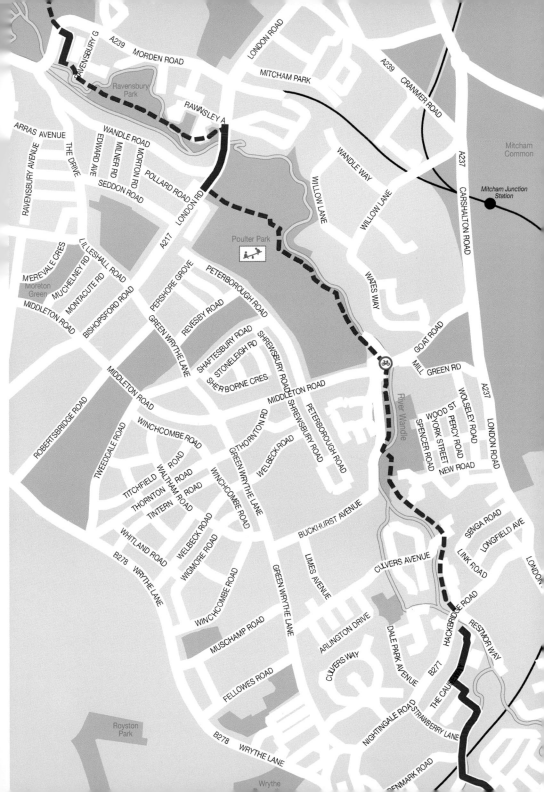

Wells-next-the-Sea

Hunstanton

Little Wals

Fakenhan

King's Lynn

Stamford

Wisbech

Castor

Dereha

14

Downham Market

7

March

63

13

Peterborough

11

12

Thetford

Ely

Huntingdon

Bury St Edmunds

51

51

51

Cambridge

Newmarket

St

8

51

Bedford

5

Sandy

13

51

9

Hadleigh

12

51

11

Saffron Walden

Leighton Buzzard

6

Bishop's Stortford

Colchester

Stevenage

Stansted

1

Dunstable

Luton

Welwyn Garden City

16

Braintree

1

Wi

Harpenden

Ware

Witham

57

13

Hertford

Hatfield

Harlow

1

Chelmsford

Tiptree

St Albans

12

2

Maldon

6

4

Watford

13

Basildon

16

3

100

Tilbury

Southend-on-sea

1. Wivenhoe Trail
2. Chelmsford to Writtle
3. Southend-on-Sea to Shoeburyness
4. Ebury Way
5. Bedford to Sandy
6. Harwich
7. March Station to Rings End Pocket Park
8. Cambridge Riverside to Bottisham
9. Sudbury Railway Path to Long Melford
10. Frinton to Clacton
11. Heart of Lowestoft
12. East Tilbury to Tilbury Fort
13. St Albans – Welwyn Garden City – Hertford – Ware
14. Peterborough Green Wheel
15. Marriotts Way
16. King's Lynn to Shepherd's Port

———	National Cycle Network traffic-free routes
———	National Cycle Network on road routes
———	National Cycle Network future routes
3	National Route Numbers
10	Regional route numbers
O	Towns with railway stations
O	Towns without railway stations
12	Regional ride numbers

EAST OF ENGLAND

This is the flattest and driest of all the regions of the National Cycle Network, which is music to the ears of many cyclists! Not only is the terrain predominantly flat, but many areas are relatively sparsely populated, making for some tranquil routes popular with those new or returning to cycling, and ideal for family rides. The area is characterised by magical rural fenland scenes, superb bird watching opportunities, interesting market towns and lively seafronts.

Route 1 is perhaps the most established and best used route in the region. Part of the North Sea Cycle Route, the section between Harwich and Hull follows a long arc around East Anglia, visiting King's Lynn via North Norfolk, before sweeping around the Wash and heading north again towards Lincoln and Hull. Linking international sea ports as it does, it's no surprise that the route is popular with continental visitors. Route 11 is another of the many notable routes in the region, running north through Saffron Walden and Cambridge to Ely and King's Lynn.

This section features many suggestions to help you experience the best of the National Cycle Network in the East of England. Ride to Southend-on-Sea for a taste of English seaside life, visit Peterborough's splendid Norman cathedral, Colchester's Roman remains and the bustling streets of King's Lynn. All this, plus miles of peaceful countryside, lies in store.

▼ *The award winning Shanks Millennium Bridge is a great place for a rest on the Peterborough Millennium Green Wheel and the National Cycle Network.*

Moulton
The centre of the region. Its ancient packhorse bridge has been a link for travellers throughout the centuries.

Cambridge
This is cycling city. You feel you have arrived, cyclists are everywhere, you are amongst friends and compatriots!

Kesgrave High School, near Ipswich
This has almost twice the number of cycling pupils of any other school in Britain. With 60% of its pupils cycling to school, it is the hope for our future.

The bridge over the A505 between Dunstable and Leighton Buzzard
A triumph of ingenuity and determination by our regional team that found ways of building this important crossing for a modest budget.

The A414 toucan crossing at Hertford
This is the vital link between the town centre and the Cole Green Way to Welwyn, and has finally made the walking and cycling journey simple, after years and years of perseverance.

Ely Cathedral
Rising up above the River Great Ouse, the cathedral signals the end of a journey from far away.

The Millennium Milepost at the Greenwich Meridian
Halfway between Peterborough and March – nowhere, and yet on that absolutely particular astronomical line which marks out time and distance around the whole world.

> Use the on-line mapping at www.sustrans.org.uk to find other National Cycle Network routes near you.

▼ *Cycle parking at Cambridge station - it seems to go on for ever, but finding a space is not easy.*

EAST OF ENGLAND FAMILY RIDES

attractive village green and duckpond, and refreshments are available from the nearby Writtle College garden centre and teashop, as well as in Chelmsford.

Southend-on-Sea to Shoeburyness.
3 miles. Route 16

Welcome to English seaside heaven! Southend and its surrounding areas have a lively seafront and some of the best estuaries and saltings for birds in the whole of the UK, so what better way to explore it all than by bike? There's lots to see on this ride at any time of year, but winter, when the popular seaside resort quietens down, is the best time for bird watching. This traffic-free route runs along the busy promenade, so whether you're into bird watching or whelks, chips and amusement arcades, this is the place to be.

Wivenhoe Trail. 4 miles. Route 51

This flat and largely traffic-free ride makes an ideal family day out, and provides excellent wildlife spotting opportunities along the River Colne. Colchester's Roman ruins make for a grand start to the ride, where bikers travel safely through the town on cycle paths, with a short section on road before rejoining the Wivenhoe Trail. The trail follows the River Colne, passing Wivenhoe station and going near the Saxon church at Wivenhoe, with its distinctive dome shaped roof. Wivenhoe itself is a picturesque harbour town full of quaint back streets to discover. Refreshments are available at both ends of the ride.

Chelmsford to Writtle. 3 miles. Route 1

This is an easy going, mainly traffic-free ride which makes a lovely family outing. The route includes plenty of riverside path and there are a number of places to stop and enjoy watching whatever's going on. Central Park and Admiral's Park feature a lake, golf course and riverside paths, whilst Old Chelmsfordians' sports field often hosts games of football and cricket. Writtle has an

▶ *Postal workers using the riverside path in Cambridge.*

Ebury Way. 3.5 miles. Route 6
Ebury Way is an easy and enjoyable traffic-free ride through a wonderful green space between Rickmansworth and Watford, offering some great family picnic spots. Keep your eyes peeled as you pass through Croxley Common Moor (a designated Site of Special Scientific Interest) and Withey Beds, where you might spot many different types of bird, including the green woodpecker. The route crosses three rivers and the Grand Union Canal, so there's plenty of riverside life on view along the way. Refreshments and toilet facilities are available at both ends of the ride.

**Bedford to Sandy.
8 miles. Routes 51 and 12**
This traffic-free route provides a useful link for everyday journeys between Bedford and Sandy, but is also fun to explore at a more leisurely pace. Beginning in Kempston, you follow the River Great Ouse, enjoying Bedford's Embankment Gardens and continuing into the wildlife haven of Priory Country Park. Further on you come to the Danish Camp, believed to have been used as a boatyard by the Vikings. The visitor centre here offers refreshments, bike hire, fishing and boat rides. Pedal on to Sandy where refreshments are available in the market place.

**Harwich - International Port to Leisure Centre.
4 miles. Route 51**
This easy ride across the Harwich peninsula is mostly traffic-free, with lots of sights and just one short climb. The ride starts at Harwich International railway station or the international port, and includes new parks at Harwich Parkeston Quay and the Hangings, plus Cliff Park in

▼ *Industry, heritage, wildlife, modern housing developments - all part of the dramatic views from Route 13 along the north bank of the Thames.*

Dovercourt, with fine sea views. From Cliff Park you can continue into Old Harwich, with its historical sites and narrow streets, or cycle along the promenade to the leisure centre. The Promenade is a popular choice for children, since it provides access to Dovercourt's sandy beach - the main focus of this seaside resort.

March Station to Rings End Pocket Park. 3 miles. Route 63

Starting at March station, this gentle circular route mixes quiet roads with traffic-free paths, giving a taste of the unique Cambridgeshire Fens and a chance to explore the Rings End Pocket Park. March, once an island surrounded by marshes, is now a pleasant market town. If you have time, don't miss the Church of St Wendreda, and especially its magnificent timber roof with 120 carved angels. The church was described by the late Poet Laureate, Sir John Betjeman as 'worth cycling 40 miles in a headwind to see'. We hope you won't have to!

Cambridge Riverside to Bottisham. 7 miles. Route 11

Almost totally traffic-free, this is an ideal family route for enjoying Cambridge's riverside and access to the nearby Fen countryside. Starting the route at Jesus Green, you head away from the city centre and the elegant buildings of the University colleges. You ride alongside the River Cam, passing through the city on the south side of the river, and continuing along the traffic-free path and through Newmarket Road Park and Ride before joining a roadside path that takes you out to the villages of Stow-cum-Quy and Bottisham. Refreshments are available here before your return journey - or you can continue on either to the National Trust property at Anglesey Abbey or along Route 51 towards Newmarket.

Sudbury Railway Path to Long Melford. 4.5 miles. Route 13

This short ride combines a traffic-free railway path with quiet roads, exploring beautiful rural scenes as depicted by John Constable, the landscape artist. The ride starts in Sudbury, an attractive town set in the Stour Valley, an area of outstanding natural beauty. If you're of a superstitious disposition, you may get shivers up your spine as you pass the site of the infamous Borley Rectory, reputably the most haunted house in England, which was destroyed by fire in

▼ *Bridge over the 20-Foot River near March - note the signals still visible on the former railway line.*

1939. You continue along country lanes to the National Trust's Melford Hall, a turreted Tudor mansion open to the public.

The Sunshine Coast - Frinton to Clacton. 5 miles. Route 51

Here's an easy, traffic-free seafront ride to blow away the cobwebs - it's generally flat, although you'll enjoy cliff-top as well as sea level views! Starting at the Greensward at the southern end of Frinton's esplanade, you're treated to extensive sea views and the contrast between the tranquil open space of the Greensward and the busy Clacton pier area. Your route follows the sea wall and promenade (mostly on tracks and paths behind the sea

▼ *The Wivenhoe Trail with views across the River Colne.*

defences), before dropping down to join the promenade through Clacton-on-Sea, finishing at the pier. Refreshments are widely available.

Heart of Lowestoft. 5 miles. Route 1

This rewarding, circular ride starts and finishes at Lowestoft Ness, mainland Britain's most easterly point. Parents with young children should note that although generally flat, the ride includes some steep hills, and that whilst 60% of the route is traffic-free, 40% is on quiet urban roads. The first bit of the ride offers good views, as you pedal along the sea wall heading north out of Lowestoft Ness, before quiet roads link you to a linear park along a disused railway line. The final (on-road) section brings you

back into the town centre, where refreshments are readily available.

East Tilbury to Tilbury Fort. 5 miles. Route 13

This level ride is mostly traffic-free and provides great contrasts and many points of interest. Starting out from East Tilbury railway station you are soon out in an open landscape, a haven for bird watching which also has much historical interest. Coalhouse Fort is a Victorian coastal defence fort, considered to be one of the finest examples of its kind. You head west along the estuary towards Tilbury Power Station and then Tilbury Fort, before reaching Tilbury itself. Refreshments are available before returning to your starting point by train.

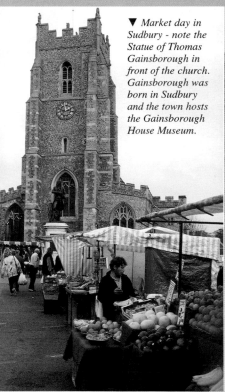

▼ *Market day in Sudbury - note the Statue of Thomas Gainsborough in front of the church. Gainsborough was born in Sudbury and the town hosts the Gainsborough House Museum.*

From St Albans to Ware via Welwyn Garden City and Hertford

Three traffic-free rides in Hertfordshire, two on railway paths and one along a canal towpath, are linked together here to create a 16-mile linear route running east from the attractive cathedral town of St Albans to Ware at the northern end of the Lee Valley. Leaving Abbey Station in St Albans, you soon join the railway path known as the Alban Way which runs through deep wooded cuttings with occasional glimpses back to the famous abbey and past a fine little lake, fringed with bulrushes. The Alban Way runs along the former route of the Hatfield to St Albans branch line of the Great Northern Railway, opened in 1865, and finally closed down in 1969. The Gallerias shopping mall at Hatfield seems to belong to a different world to cycle trails and green corridors. A complicated but well-signposted route around the fringe of Welwyn Garden City drops you at the start of the second long traffic-free section, at first open with views across fields but soon wooded. Hertford Town Football Club marks the end of the railway path and the start of the urban section through the attractive heart of Hertford with its many cafes and pubs. This time the link section between the two traffic-free rides is much shorter and before long you are on the lovely towpath of the Lee Navigation which can be followed from Ware (beyond the end of the ride described here) and all the way into London.

Starting points
St Albans Abbey railway station.
Ware railway station.

Distance
16 miles.

Grade
Easy.

Surface
Tarmac or fine gravel path.

▼ *The approach to the Cole Green Way, which forms part of this ride, from Hertford.*

Roads, traffic, suitability for young children
The two long sections of railway path, from St Albans to Hatfield and from Welwyn Garden City to Hertford, and the Hertford to Ware towpath, are all ideal for families. The linking sections are mainly on quiet residential roads but

children will need supervision, particularly at road crossings.

Hills
None.

Refreshments
Lots of choice just off the route in St Albans, Hatfield and Welwyn Garden City.
Cowper Arms PH, Cole Green (between Welwyn and Hertford). The best choice is in Hertford or Ware as the route goes right through both town centres.

Nearest railway stations
Abbey Station (St Albans), Hatfield East, Hertford North, Ware, Welwyn Garden City.

The National Cycle Network in the area
Three routes cross the area: Route 61 goes from Windsor to the Lee Valley, Route 12 from Hatfield to Stevenage, and Route 6 from Watford to Luton and Milton Keynes.

Other nearby rides (waymarked or traffic-free)
1. The Nicky Line is a railway path running north from the edge of Hemel Hempstead to Harpenden.
2. The Ayot Greenway runs east from Wheathampstead to Ayot St Peter.
3. The Grand Union Canal can be followed northwest from

London through Watford and Hemel Hempstead.
4. The Lee Navigation can be followed all the way south from Ware to London.

▲ ▼ Look out for these sculptures on the Alban Way - a reminder of Hatfield's aviation links and a blackberry arch reflecting a current image of the railway path.

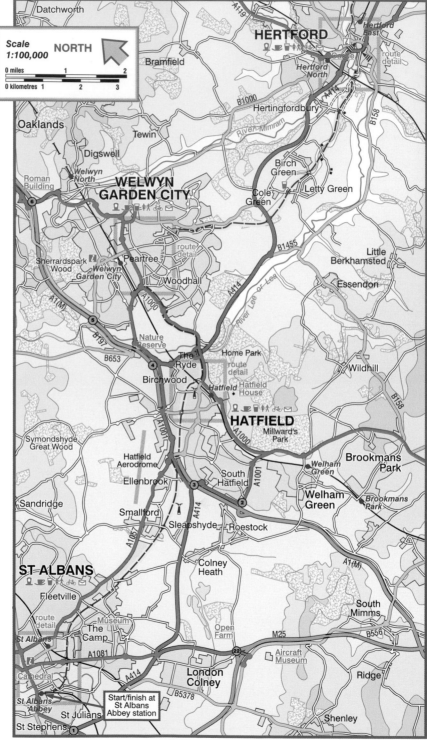

FROM ST ALBANS TO WARE VIA WELWYN GARDEN CITY AND HERTFORD

Scale
1:100,000   NORTH

0 miles   1   2
0 kilometres   1   2   3

Datchworth

HERTFORD

Hertford
East

route
detail

Bramfield

Hertford
North

Oaklands

Tewin

B1000

Hertingfordbury

River Mimram

Digswell

Roman
Building

Welwyn
North

WELWYN
GARDEN CITY

Cole
Green

Birch
Green

Letty Green

Sherrardspark
Wood

Peartree

route
detail

Welwyn
Garden City

Woodhall

B1455

Little
Berkhamsted

Essendon

A1(M)

B197

Nature
Reserve

B653

The
Ryde

Birchwood

Home Park

route
detail

Hatfield

Hatfield
House

River Lee or Lea

A414

Wildhill

B158

HATFIELD

Millward's
Park

Symondshyde
Great Wood

Hatfield
Aerodrome

Ellenbrook

South
Hatfield

A1001

Welham
Green

Brookmans
Park

Brookmans
Park

Sandridge

Smallford

Sleapshyde

Roestock

Welham
Green

ST ALBANS

Fleetville

route
detail

Museum

The
Camp

St Albans

Colney
Heath

Open
Farm

M25

A1(M)

South
Mimms

B556

Cathedral

A1081

A414

London
Colney

Aircraft
Museum

Ridge

St Albans
Abbey

St Julians

St Stephens

Start/finish at
St Albans Abbey station

B5378

Shenley

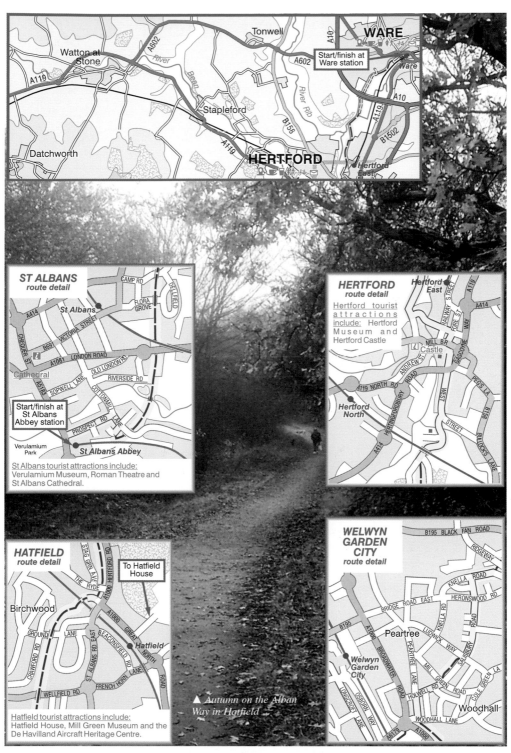

WARE

Start/finish at Ware station

Tonwell

A10

A602

Watton at Stone

River Beane

A602

A119

Stapleford

B158

River Rib

Ware

A10

A119

B1502

Datchworth

A119

HERTFORD

Hertford East

ST ALBANS
route detail

CAMP RD

DELLFIELD

FLORA GROVE

St Albans

A414

VICTORIA STREET

CHEQUER ST

B691

LONDON ROAD

A1081

OLD LONDON RD

RIVERSIDE RD

A5183

SOPWELL LANE

COTTONMILL LANE

Cathedral

Start/finish at
St Albans
Abbey station

PROSPECT RD

Verulamium
Park

St Albans Abbey

St Albans tourist attractions include:
Verulamium Museum, Roman Theatre and
St Albans Cathedral.

HERTFORD
route detail

Hertford East

A119

RAILWAY STREET

FORE ST

A414

Hertford tourist
attractions
include: Hertford
Museum and
Hertford Castle

MILL BR

GASCOYNE WAY

Castle

ANDREW ST

A119 NORTH RD

HEREFORDBURY ROAD

PEG'S LA

WEST STREET

B158

BULLOCKS LANE

**Hertford
North**

A414

HATFIELD
route detail

STAG GRN AVE

HERTFORD RD

A1000

To Hatfield
House

THE RYDE

A1000 GREAT

Birchwood

ST ALBANS RD EAST

BEACONSFIELD RD

Hatfield

GROUND RD

LANE

CRAWFORD RD

NORTH ROAD

FRENCH HORN LANE

WELLFIELD RD

Hatfield tourist attractions include:
Hatfield House, Mill Green Museum and the
De Havilland Aircraft Heritage Centre.

▲ *Autumn on the Alban
Way in Hatfield*

**WELWYN
GARDEN
CITY**
route detail

B195 BLACK FAN ROAD

RIDGEWAY

KNELLA ROAD

HERONSWOOD RD

BRIDGE ROAD EAST

KNELLA RD

LUDWICK WAY

B195

A1000

Peartree

SALISBURY

**Welwyn
Garden
City**

BROADWATER ROAD

PEARTREE LANE

MILL GREEN ROAD

COLE GREEN LA

LONGCROFT LANE

OSBORN WAY

HOLWELL RD

WOODHALL LANE

A6176

A1000

Woodhall

111

PETERBOROUGH GREEN WHEEL

The concept of Peterborough's Green Wheel is a 45-mile network of routes in and around the town including a 'rim' a 'hub' and 'spokes'. The ride described here runs west from the city centre on the 'spoke' which is signed as Route 63, following the River Nene, past the rowing lake and the Nene Valley Railway Line to Ferry Meadows Country Park, the entrance to which is marked by a wonderful centurion / frog / kingfisher / swan statue. After following traffic-free trails up to this point you join the network of quiet lanes linking the pretty villages of Marholm and Etton, both of which have pubs. Marholm's village sign represents all sectors of Marholm's community under the Fitzwilliam family coat of arms and motto - Appetitus Rationi Pareat ('may your desires be reasoned'). The second part of the ride follows the 'rim' of the Green Wheel as far as Glinton, then uses another 'spoke', Route 12, through Werrington and largely urban cycle lanes to return to the bustling pedestrianised heart of the city. Make the effort to visit Peterborough's splendid cathedral, one of England's finest Norman buildings, begun in 1118 with a magnificent west front.

Starting point
The south end of Bridge Street in the centre of Peterborough at the junction of Routes 12, 53 & 63. The route can also be easily accessed from Peterborough station, by heading north beside the railway and following signs that lead to Route 12.

Distance
21-mile circular route.

Grade
Easy.

Surface
All tarmac or fine gravel paths.

Roads, traffic, suitability for young children
The best bit for young children is from the riverside path in the centre of Peterborough as far as the old stone bridge over the River Nene at the western end of Ferry Meadows Country Park - it is traffic-free and flat.

Hills
None.

Refreshments
Lots of choice in Peterborough.
The Boathouse PH, near the rowing lake.
Two cafes at Ferry Meadows Country Park
Visitor Centre.
Fitzwilliam Arms PH, Marholm.
Golden Pheasant PH, Etton.
Bluebell PH, Glinton.

Nearest railway station
Peterborough.

The National Cycle Network in the area
Peterborough is at a crossroads of the National
Cycle Network: Route 63 goes from Wisbech
to Rutland Water, Route 12 from Huntingdon

▲ *Milton Ferry Bridge and this Millennium Milepost
form one of the gateways to the popular Ferry Meadows
Country Park.*

▼ *Peterborough Rowing Lake on Route 63 is
usually a very tranquil place, but when there is a
regatta on it is a centre of great activity, as in
this case.*

Peterborough Green Wheel

to Spalding, and Route 53 from Kettering into the centre of Peterborough. Marked in a distinct blue and white, Regional Route 21 designates the Peterborough Green Wheel and overlaps with all three National Cycle Network routes.

▼ *Relaxing at Glinton.*

Other nearby rides (waymarked or traffic-free)
There are traffic-free rides west from the centre of Peterborough on both sides of the River Nene towards Ferry Meadows and east from the centre of the city on both sides of the river to Shanks Millennium Bridge (near Whittlesey).

MARRIOTT'S WAY

Named after William Marriott, chief engineer of the Midland and Great Northern Railway, this traffic-free route out of Norwich takes you past industrial sites with tantalising glimpses of the River Wensum. Signposted 'Wensum Valley Walk' from the centre of Norwich, the route becomes the Marriott's Way near Drayton. The path takes you through the Woodlands of Mileplain Plantation, full of sweet chestnut trees making the route a special treat through the autumn. It's not all fields and woods though, since the path also follows the gently-flowing River Wensum; old metal bridges carry you back and forth across it several times. Reepham is a traditional market town with many traditional shops - butchers, bakers and cabinet makers! Established as long ago as the 13th century, the current market dates from the 18th century. There are several pubs in the village to take a welcome break before the return journey to Norwich.

▲ *The Dragon Bridge in Norwich is one of a number of bridges across the River Wensum on Marriott's Way.*

Starting points
Norwich station.
Reepham market place.

Distance
15 miles one way to Reepham.

Grade
Easy.

Surface
Tarmac at the Norwich end, stone beyond Drayton.

Roads, traffic, suitability for young children
Some on-road sections through Norwich where care is required, otherwise traffic-free and flat - great for young children just learning to ride!

Hills
None.

Refreshments
Available in Norwich, Drayton and Reepham.

Nearest railway station
Norwich.

The National Cycle Network in the area
Route 1 continues north on road to Fakenham, or south from Norwich on road to Beccles. It is part of the Hull to Harwich route and the North Sea Cycle Route.

Other nearby rides (waymarked or traffic-free):
Marriott's Way carries on for another six miles east to Aylsham, where you can join the Bure Valley Route (unsurfaced).

To find out about other cycle routes in this area visit www.sustrans.org.uk

▼ *This part of Route 1 in Norwich is one of the more urban sections of the railway path.*

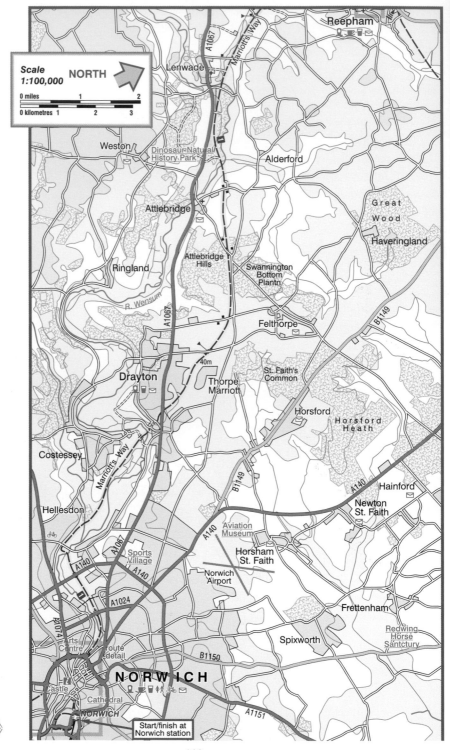

MARRIOTT'S WAY

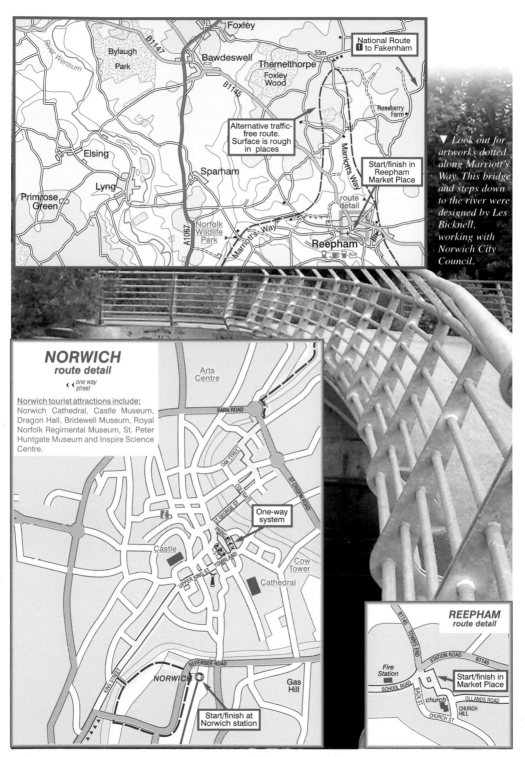

Foxley

Bylaugh Park

Bawdeswell

Themelthorpe

Foxley Wood

55m

National Route **1** to Fakenham

River Wensum

B1147

B1145

Roseberry Farm

Alternative traffic-free route. Surface is rough in places

Start/finish in Reepham Market Place

Marriott's Way

route detail

Elsing

Sparham

Lyng

Primrose Green

A1067

Norfolk Wildlife Park

Marriott's Way

Marriott's Way

Reepham

▼ *Look out for artworks dotted along Marriott's Way. This bridge and steps down to the river were designed by Les Bicknell, working with Norwich City Council.*

NORWICH
route detail

‹‹ *one way street*

Norwich tourist attractions include: Norwich Cathedral, Castle Museum, Dragon Hall, Bridewell Museum, Royal Norfolk Regimental Museum, St. Peter Huntgate Museum and Inspire Science Centre.

Arts Centre

BARN ROAD

OAK STREET

ST CRISPIN ROAD

COLEGATE

ST GEORGE ST

One-way system

Castle

ST ANDREWS ST

PRINCE ST

TOMBLAND

UPPER KING ST

Cow Tower

Cathedral

KING STREET

RIVERSIDE ROAD

NORWICH

Gas Hill

Start/finish at Norwich station

REEPHAM
route detail

B1145

TOWN'S END

STATION ROAD

B1145

Fire Station

SCHOOL ROAD

BACK ST

Start/finish in Market Place

church

OLLANDS ROAD

CHURCH HILL

CHURCH ST

119

KING'S LYNN TO SHEPHERD'S PORT

This route explores the traditional cycling country of West Norfolk. It starts at the lively port and market town of King's Lynn, at the mouth of the River Ouse, which drains much of the fertile, dark earth of the Fens.

The first part of the route is traffic-free followed by sections on quiet lanes with major roads being crossed safely. You travel through woodlands to visit the attractive village of Castle Rising with its magnificent castle and on to the royal country home at Sandringham.

If the tide is in, or if you are birdwatching, it is worth pushing on to the coast at Shepherd's Port, but be aware that when the tide is out you will be confronted by a vast expanse of mud!

Starting point
King's Lynn railway station.

Distance
15 miles one way, 30 miles return. The ride could be shortened by making the turnaround point either the attractions and refreshment stops at Castle Rising (12-mile round trip) or Sandringham Country Park (19-mile round trip).

Grade
Easy.

Surface
Tarmac.

Roads, traffic, suitability for young children
The first section, from the railway station, across the parkland and onto the dismantled railway is all traffic-free. Beyond the end of the railway path the route uses quiet lanes as much as possible. The busy main roads are all crossed via central islands.

Hills
Gently undulating.

Refreshments
Lots of choice in King's Lynn. House on the Green PH, North Wootton. Tea rooms at the Post Office, Black Horse PH, Castle Rising. Tea rooms at Sandringham

Visitor Centre.
Rose & Crown PH, Queen Victoria PH, Compasses PH, Old Bank Coffeehouse, Snittisham.

Railway stations for longer rides

It is 74 miles along Route 1 from King's Lynn to Norwich or 100 miles north to Lincoln.

The National Cycle Network in the area

The ride described is mostly part of the Hull to Harwich Cycle Route (Route 1).
1. East from Hunstanton, Route 1 turns inland through Ringstead and Burnham Market to Fakenham.
2. West from King's Lynn, Route 1 crosses the Fens to Wisbech and Boston.
3. Route 11 will run south from King's Lynn through Downham Market to Ely and Cambridge.

Other nearby rides (waymarked or traffic-free)

The Norfolk Coast Cycleway is a 100-mile linear route that runs from King's Lynn to Great Yarmouth along the North Norfolk Coast (Regional Route 30).
The Wells and Holkham Circuit uses Route 1.

The route begins at the railway station in the bustling town of King's Lynn (well worth a visit in its own right) and takes you out of the town on a traffic-free path through parkland and following a railway path. You continue on road through the woodlands of Ling Common, until you come to the attractive village of Castle Rising, with its impressive 12th century castle and 17th century almshouses. You then join a closed road which takes you onto the cycle track alongside the A149 where you follow the Route 1 signs towards the Royal Estate at Sandringham. Tea is served at the visitor centre.

The ride continues along the road to Snettisham, where this ride leaves the waymarked route and heads westwards for the coast at Shepherd's Port. This is The Wash, in which King John is reputed to have lost the crown jewels in the 13th century. The RSPB recommends visiting its Snettisham reserve there to see one of nature's great spectacles as tens of thousands of wading birds take off from their feeding grounds and flock to the islands in front of the hides when the tide covers the mudflats.

▼ *View of The Wash and Snettisham Coastal Park from near to Shepherd's Port. On a clear day you can see across to Boston Stump in Lincolnshire.*

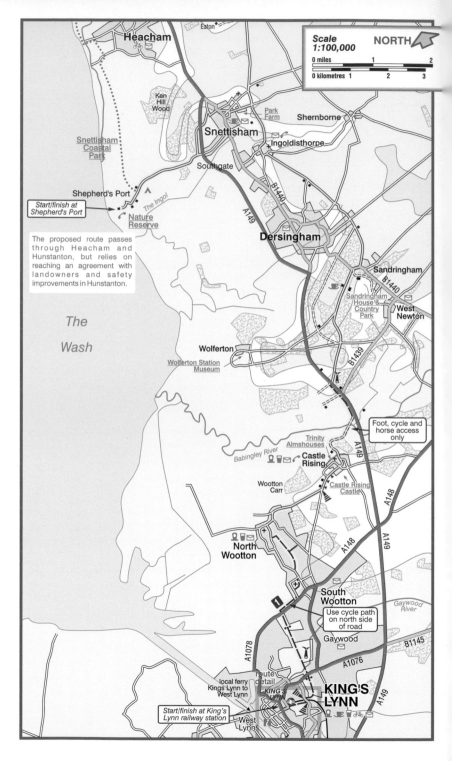

Scale 1:100,000

NORTH

0 miles · 1 · 2
0 kilometres 1 · 2 · 3

Heacham

Eaton

Ken Hill Wood

Park Farm

Shernborne

Snettisham

Ingoldisthorpe

Snettisham Coastal Park

Southgate

Shepherd's Port

Start/finish at Shepherd's Port

The Ingol

Nature Reserve

B1440

A149

Dersingham

The proposed route passes through Heacham and Hunstanton, but relies on reaching an agreement with landowners and safety improvements in Hunstanton.

Sandringham

Sandringham House & Country Park

West Newton

The

Wash

B1439

Wolferton

Wolferton Station Museum

Trinity Almshouses

Babingley River

Castle Rising

Foot, cycle and horse access only

Wootton Carr

Castle Rising Castle

A149

A148

North Wootton

A148

South Wootton

A149

Gaywood River

Use cycle path on north side of road

Gaywood

B1145

A1078

A1076

local ferry Kings Lynn to West Lynn

route detail

KING'S LYNN

KING'S LYNN

Start/finish at King's Lynn railway station

West Lynn

King's Lynn tourist attractions include:
The Old Gaol House, King's Lynn Museum, Trues Yard Heritage Centre and Guildhall of St George.

KING'S LYNN

level crossing

One-way system

ST JOHN'S WALK

Museum

Guildhall of St George (NT)

Start/finish at King's Lynn railway station

HIGH STREET

CHURCH ST

Walk through pedestrian areas

BRIDGE ST

A149

WEST LYNN

ST VALERY LA

SADDLE BOW ROAD

WISBECH ROAD

A148

KING'S LYNN
route detail

◄ one way street

pedestrian precinct

▲ *St John's Walk, King's Lynn, leads direct to the station and to the town centre.*

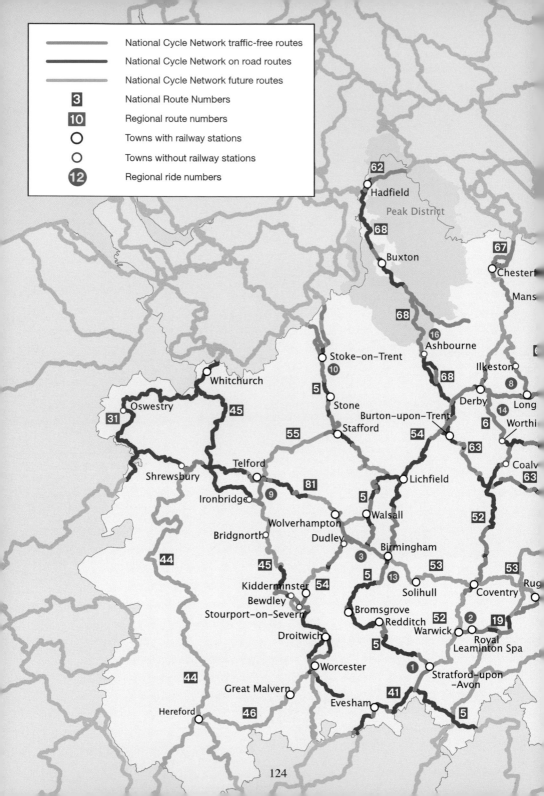

Barton
–upon–
Humber

1

Grimsby

1

12

Market Rasen

Louth

Mablethorpe

Skellingthorpe

15

12

rksop

Lincoln

64

Skegness

1

12

Newark-on-Trent

5

12

15

Boston

6

ngham

Bottesford

7

Grantham

Spalding

64

12

Melton Mowbray

rough

63

Stamford

cester

Oakham

12

63

53

64

Market
Harborough

Kettering

6

11

6

ventry

thampton

6

1. Stratford Greenway
2. Warwick to Leamington Spa
3. Birmingham to Wolverhampton
4. Leicester Riverside
5. Newark to Cotham
6. Boston to Anton's Gowt
7. Grantham to Muston
8. Nutbrook Trail
9. Silkin Way
10. Stoke Greenways
11. Brampton Valley Way
12. Rutland Water
13. Birmingham to King's Norton
14. Derby to Worthington
15. Route through Lincoln
16. Tissington and High Peak Trails

THE MIDLANDS

The Midlands offers cyclists and walkers tremendous contrasts. Though bounded to the north by the mountainous-sounding Trans Pennine Trail, most Midland riding is relatively gentle and the region boasts the highest density of traffic-free National Cycle Network routes in the country.

Here you'll find a broad patchwork of countryside dotted with old market towns and unique industrial heritage besides some of Britain's most progressive, multi-cultural cities. By utilising the extraordinary number of canal towpaths and old railways, the National Cycle Network provides an enjoyable and safe way for everyone to make daily journeys within towns and cities. It also gives city dwellers excellent rural and inter-city links, opening up possibilities for diverse and memorable longer journeys.

Major routes in the region include Route 5, running south through Stoke on Trent, Walsall, Birmingham and Stratford-upon-Avon and then onwards into the South East. Route 81 heads west from Birmingham to the World Heritage Site at Ironbridge and on to Shrewsbury, with plans in place to extend the route deep into mid-Wales. Route 6 runs down the centre of the country, linking towns and cities including Worksop, Nottingham, Derby, Loughborough, Leicester, Market Harborough, Northampton and Milton Keynes.

If the National Cycle Network in the Midlands is a dream come true for millions of people who need to get around on a daily basis, it also has its wilder side. Route 68, known as the Pennine Cycleway, is a challenging 350-mile route from the heart of the region to the Scottish border at Berwick-upon-Tweed. It incorporates the popular Tissington and High Peak Trails which reward riders with breathtaking views over the Peak District.

From visiting exciting urban regeneration sites in Birmingham and Coventry, to Lincoln's ancient towers and Boston's famous 'Stump', from learning about our amazing industrial heritage at Ironbridge to taking in the tranquillity of the Arden Forest - all these possibilities await you in the Midlands on the National Cycle Network.

▼ *The railway path between Boston and Anton's Gowt.*

126

HIGHLIGHTS

Trent Viaduct, Worthington Line
This was the first listed viaduct transferred to Sustrans, who are now responsible for nearly 3,000 bridges and structures on numerous key sections of the Network.

Humber Bridge
On this, and the similar first Severn Bridge, the cycle route is well separated from traffic, giving you the freedom to enjoy what was the longest single span in Europe.

Centenary Square, Birmingham
A real delight. Surfaced with a carpet of patterned brickwork, this has to be the country's finest city centre renewal.

Worcester Riverside Fountain
This epitomises the restoration of public spaces and the creation of attractive civic places we can all be proud of.

Southrey Station
Lies on the 30-mile long Lincoln and Boston railway, predominantly owned by Sustrans' sister charity, Railway Paths Limited, and now being gradually incorporated into Route 1.

The Leicester Space Centre
Just one of the delights of cycling along the cycle routes in Leicester which leads the way in the UK's revival of cycling.

▼ *Passing the futuristic Rocket Tower of the Leicester Space Centre.*

MIDLANDS FAMILY RIDES

**Stratford Greenway.
8.5 miles. Route 5**
This attractive, flat route offers families an easy and traffic-free ride along a canal towpath and disused railway, with our industrial and cultural heritage very much in evidence along the way. The high quality path takes riders close enough to the centre of Shakespeare's birthplace to evoke memories of famous scenes, and there are plenty of pubs and refreshment points where you can stop and soak up the atmosphere.

▼ *The canal path near Wolverhampton.*

**Warwick to Leamington Spa and Radford Semele.
4 miles. Route 41**
This short, suburban and mainly traffic-free family ride is full of highlights to enjoy. Starting at the station, you follow a route through the parks of Warwick and canalside at Leamington Spa, onto a canal path leading to the attractive village of Offchurch. There's plenty to see off the route, including the magnificent Warwick Castle, the Lord Leycester Hospital and in Leamington, the grand Royal Pump Rooms. Along the way refreshments and facilities are readily available.

**Birmingham's Gas Street basin to Wolverhampton Station.
15.5 miles. Routes 81 and 5**
This mainly canalside ride offers a great getaway from the buzz of the city. You begin near Birmingham's New Street Station at the Gas Street basin, originally a busy canal interchange. The industrial origins of the canal are still evident in the buildings on its banks. The route also passes the Galton Valley Heritage Centre where you can explore the industrial history of the area. Take time to enjoy the slower pace of life along this green oasis, and please keep your eyes open and show consideration to other users and to wildlife.

Leicester Riverside. 11 miles. Routes 6 and 48
Much of this route is traffic-free although, if you start at the Bakers Arms in Blaby, you will need to follow some roads before reaching a bridleway section. After this you take the Great Central Way as far as West Bridge and then follow the Route 6 signs to the beautiful Abbey Park. Riverside Way takes you past the Space Centre - always a favourite

with youngsters - and on to Watermead Park, a great spot to rest your legs by the boating lake. From here you could continue on to the turnaround or finish points of the White Horse in Birstall and the Hope and Anchor in Syston.

Newark to Cotham.
5 miles. Route 55

This ride takes you from the attractive market town of Newark situated on the River Trent, right out into the Nottinghamshire countryside. Starting alongside platform one at Newark North Gate station, you head south through the town to take a former railway line. Before long you are riding alongside fields to the small village of Cotham. The path's flat, smooth surface makes this an especially good day out for novice cyclists, and those with young children.

Boston to Anton's Gowt.
2.5 miles. Route 1

Boston to Anton's Gowt is a short, flat and traffic-free ride, making an ideal outing for those with young children. Following

the course of a disused railway line, the riverside route also offers striking views of the surrounding Fen countryside. The ride starts in the historic market town of Boston, in the shadow of the superb 14th century St Botolph's Church and its 271ft tower (known as the 'Stump'). To pick up the traffic-free route, you ride under the railway line on 'Sluice Bridge' - you will soon find yourself basking in the peace and quiet of a wide-open landscape.

Grantham to Muston.
7 miles. Route 15

This lovely ride combines wonderful open countryside with enjoyable canal-side views. Setting out from Grantham Station, a traffic-free path and short on road link lead you to the town's edge, where you pick up the Grantham Canal towpath and pass through the beautiful Vale of

▼ *A view from Boston Stump, looking north. The path to Anton's Gowt is on the right of the waterway.*

Belvoir. No longer a working waterway, the canal is a great place to spot local wildlife. At Woolsthorpe Wharf, try the food at the canalside Belvoir Arms (locally known as the Mucky Duck) or ride on, partly on lanes, to the Muston Gap pub where the ride ends.

Nutbrook Trail - Long Eaton to Shipley Country Park. 8 miles. Route 67

The Nutbrook Trail is a pleasant and traffic-free route along the Erewash Canal and an old railway line running through a suburban yet peaceful landscape. The ride takes you to Shipley Country Park, which consists of 600 acres of attractive parkland reclaimed from old mine workings, now full of tranquil lakes and teeming with wildlife. For children with still more energy to burn after the bike ride, there's also the American Adventure theme park to explore.

Silkin Way - Telford to Ironbridge. 7 miles. Route 45

Silkin Way is a varied, traffic-free ride which takes you to the World Heritage site at Ironbridge. Initially the route is set amidst tranquil greenery and wooded areas, disguising Telford's wider urban surroundings. As you ride along the former railway line, you'll notice reminders of the area's industrial past - the spread of the industrial revolution here mirrored the spread of Britain's influence across the globe. You follow the banks of the River Severn at Coalport, before a traffic-free path leads on to the wealth of attractions surrounding Ironbridge.

Stoke Greenway - Stoke Station to Barlaston Station. 8 miles. Route 5

This useful route provides a safe, cross-town route for cyclists and walkers, and is a fantastic resource for local people. Linking the centre of the city to the suburbs, it features plenty of greenery and some canalside views, providing a relaxing haven from the busy surroundings. This route is great for shopping trips, visiting friends, journeys to work and to school, to the nearby Staffordshire countryside, or just for a relaxing family pootle on a sunny evening! Sustrans hopes to further develop the Greenway in the future.

Brampton Valley Way - Market Harborough to Northampton. 14 miles. Route 6

This old railway ride includes two tunnels, so lights are essential. It starts at Britannia Walk off Springfield Street in Market Harborough and soon reaches open country. You climb gently to the spooky Oxenden tunnel before crossing the flat

▼ *Leamington Spa to Warwick.*

130

valley of the little River Ise. Ride on past woodlands and through the second tunnel but then prepare to take care crossing the A508 road. Near Brixworth you travel beside a heritage railway and can stop for tea at Pitsford and Brampton Station. For the mainline railway service at Northampton, stay on the path before joining a stony bridleway near Kings Heath. Follow the Route 6 signs to the town station.

Rutland Water Circuit. 14 miles (plus 6 if you ride Hambleton peninsula). Regional Route 63

This mainly traffic-free ride enjoys beautiful views over the water, picture book villages and bike-friendly refreshment stops. You can start from many points around the circuit, maybe at one of the three bike hire centres along the way. Though there are a few steep sections and the surface is rough in

▲ *Mammoth by Dan Jones, Watermead Park near Leicester.*

places, the rewards are plentiful - shady old woods, open fieldscapes, half-drowned Normanton Church and sailing boats aplenty. Stunning sunsets and amazing birdlife too - watch out for the osprey!

▼ *The Rutland Water circuit.*

BIRMINGHAM TO KING'S NORTON PARK

Despite being one of Britain's biggest and busiest cities, Birmingham has some great areas and facilities for pedestrians and cyclists. Starting right in the heart of the city, you will experience the real sense of space of Birmingham's city centre squares, surrounded by impressive buildings and with interesting sculptures to explore. After absorbing the busy and exciting Centenary Square and Birmingham streets, you can enjoy the peace of canal towpaths and riverside routes that take you through two leafy parks.

Along the route, you may be tempted by a detour to sample the delights of the chocolate factory at Cadbury World in Bournville and if there's any spare energy left at the journey's end, children will enjoy the playground in King's Norton Park. This route offers the ideal escape from the city without really leaving it at all.

Starting point
Centenary Square, Broad Street, Birmingham.

Distance
Seven miles one way, 14 miles return.

Grade
Easy.

Surface
Mixture of road, tarmac cyclepath and stone-based tracks.

Roads, traffic, suitability for young children
The ride uses some traffic-calmed streets in central Birmingham, although some streets are still busy. Once out of the centre, all the busy roads are crossed via toucan crossings. The section along the Rea Valley Route through Cannon Hill Park and along the Worcester & Birmingham Canal is traffic-free and ideal for children.

Hills
None.

Refreshments
Lots of choice in Birmingham city centre.
Cafe/tea room in Cannon Hill Park.

Nearest railway stations
Birmingham New Street in the centre of the city.
King's Norton.
Bournville.

The National Cycle Network in the area
Birmingham is at a crossroads of the National Cycle Network: Route 5 comes north from Reading through Oxford, Banbury, Stratford and Bromsgove (and is followed in this ride into the centre of Birmingham). It continues north east via Walsall, Lichfield and Burton-on-Trent to Derby. Route 53 goes east to Coventry and Rugby, and proposed north to Sutton Coldfield. Route 54 goes from Dudley to Stourbridge, with plans to continue to Hereford. Route 81 follows the Main Line Canal to Wolverhampton and Shrewsbury.

Other nearby rides (waymarked or traffic-free)
1. Although Birmingham has more miles of canal than Venice, the towpath network is not all open to cyclists. However, there is much to explore including the Worcester & Birmingham Canal towpath which is used for part of this route. For the most up-to-date information contact British Waterways on 0121 200 7400 or at www.waterscape.com
2. The proposed Route 53 will link Birmingham to Sutton

◄ *The carriage drive through Cannon Hill Park.*

► One of 1000 mileposts on the National Cycle Network.

Park, a large park just north of Birmingham where motor traffic is restricted to the outskirts.

3. The Kingswinford Railway Path runs for 10 miles from Pensnett (west of Dudley) to Wolverhampton.

4. Route 5 follows the Birmingham & Wolverhampton Canal from the centre of Birmingham to Sandwell Valley Country Park and Walsall.

You may start from the impressive Centenary Square, which is surrounded by a wealth of attractions. The square hosts the magnificent Spirit of Enterprise sculpture and the war memorial together with easy access to the ICC, Symphony Hall, National Indoor Arena and Rep Theatre. In a moment you pass the Gas Street canal basin and head off toward the Modern Mailbox complex, the Hippodrome Theatre and urban areas of the city.

Your journey from this place of vision to the traffic-free Rea Valley Route is made much easier and more enjoyable by a series of contraflow cycle lanes and toucan crossings.

A minaret at the end of Gooch Street is testimony to the high proportion of Muslims living in this multi-cultural city and stands as a contrast to the ornate façade of Edward Road Baptist Church which you will soon pass.

Cannon Hill Park is an oasis of green with bright displays of flowers and a boating lake, and marks the start of the traffic-free Rea Valley Route. You will

► Cycling through Birmingham's Centenary Square.

133

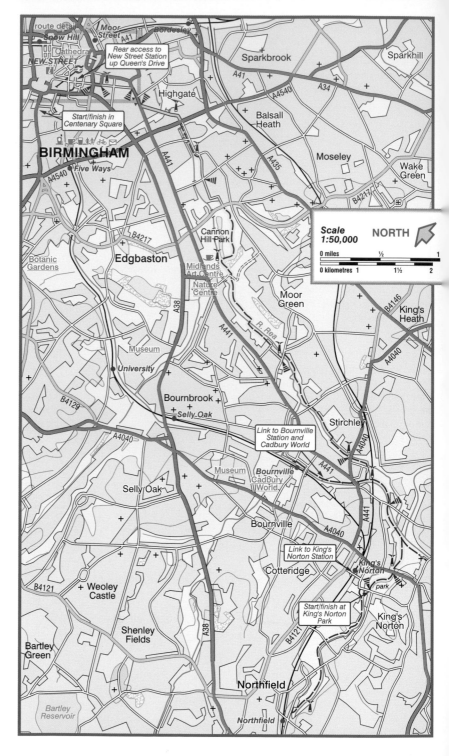

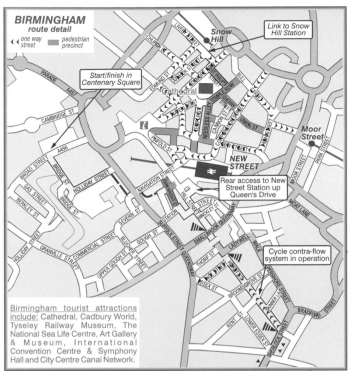

BIRMINGHAM
route detail

◄◄ one way street   pedestrian precinct

Snow Hill
Link to Snow Hill Station

Start/finish in Centenary Square

Cathedral

PARADE
A457
CAMBRIDGE ST
BROAD STREET
GAS STREET
BERKLEY ST
HOLLIDAY STREET
GRANVILLE STREET
UPPER GOUGH ST
A456
BRIDGE ST
BRIDGE ST
HOLLIDAY STREET
COMMERCIAL STREET
BLUCHER STREET
GOUGH STREET
SUFFOLK STREET QUEENSWAY
NAVIGATION STREET
STATION STREET
HILL STREET
HINCKLEY STREET
THORP ST
ESSEX ST
BROOMSGROVE ST
KENT ST
LOWER ESSEX ST
SHERLOCK STREET
CHURCH ST
EDMUND ST
PINFOLD ST
LIVERY STREET
NEEDLESS ALLEY
TEMPLE ROW
NEW STREET
CANNON ST
UNION ST
BULL STREET
SMALLBROOK QUEENSWAY
LADYWELL WALK
HURST STREET

NEW STREET

Rear access to New Street Station up Queen's Drive

Moor Street

MOOR STREET
PARK STREET
MOAT LANE
BRADFORD STREET

Cycle contra-flow system in operation

Birmingham tourist attractions include: Cathedral, Cadbury World, Tyseley Railway Museum, The National Sea Life Centre, Art Gallery & Museum, International Convention Centre & Symphony Hall and City Centre Canal Network.

follow this for four miles before joining the excellent towpath of the Worcester & Birmingham Canal for one section.

For chocoholics there's a diversion to Cadbury World at Bournville where you can find out how chocolate is made and visit the factory shop for refuelling. This route also links the ride to Bournville station. The main ride continues on to King's Norton Park where there is a playground for children.

It is possible to continue on Route 5 along the line of the river valley to Northfield, Longbridge and southwards towards Stratford-upon-Avon.

▼ *Route 5 running into Birmingham.*

DERBY TO WORTHINGTON

This is a great escape with a traffic-free path taking you right from the heart of the city deep into the countryside and the small, pretty village of Worthington. The route crosses busy roads safely and uses a mixture of specially-built cycle paths, railway paths and canal towpaths, occasionally passing through woodland.

Passing by schools and colleges and continuing into the heart of the city, this route is used for everyday trips by school children and commuters. However, it is also a wonderful resource for novices, young families or more experienced cyclists looking for a route out of the city to link with the network of country lanes.

Starting point
Derby railway station.
The Riverside Path in the centre of Derby (Bass's Recreation Ground).

Distance
13 miles one way, 26 miles return.

Grade
Easy.

Surface
Almost all on fine quality stone paths.

Roads, traffic, suitability for young children
Once onto the Riverside Path the route is excellent for young children. All the busy roads are crossed via bridges, subways or toucan crossings. There is a one-mile road section to visit Melbourne and a shorter (quieter) road section to visit Worthington.

Hills
No hills.

Refreshments
Lots of choice in Derby.
Lots of choice in Melbourne.
Malt Shovel PH in Worthington.

Nearest railway station
Derby.

The National Cycle Network in the area
Derby is at a major junction of the National Cycle Network:
Route 6 runs north from Milton Keynes through Northampton and Leicester to Derby, then on through Nottingham to join the Trans Pennine Trail in Sheffield and Barnsley.
Route 54 runs south west from Derby through Burton-on-

▼ *River Trent Viaduct in Derby.*

Trent and Lichfield to Birmingham. From Etwall, five miles along this route, you can pick up the Pennine Cycleway (Route 68) which runs all the way to Berwick-upon-Tweed. Route 54 goes northwards up to Little Eaton.

Other nearby rides (waymarked or traffic-free)

The Riverside Path alongside the River Derwent runs east to Elvaston Castle Country Park where there is a circuit of the park.

To the north of Derby city centre (Exeter Bridge) the path continues alongside the Derwent past the Industrial Museum towards Chester Green and Darley Abbey.

The Derby canal path runs between Borrowash and Breaston.

The traffic-free route starts right in the heart of the city and is well-used for everyday trips

▶ *Near Worthington.*

by schoolchildren and commuters, passing right by schools and colleges and taking people to work.

You'll take a series of specially-built cycle paths, railway paths and canal towpaths, crossing busy roads safely via toucan crossings. The route creates a green corridor linking the city centre with the countryside, passing through

▲ *Cycling on the Derby to Melbourne railway path.*

woodland and past magnificent stone sculptures.

Near Melbourne you'll cross the Grade II Listed Trent Viaduct. It was built in 1869 and repaired by Sustrans in the late 1980s.

The second half of the ride has views of the limestone bluff

137

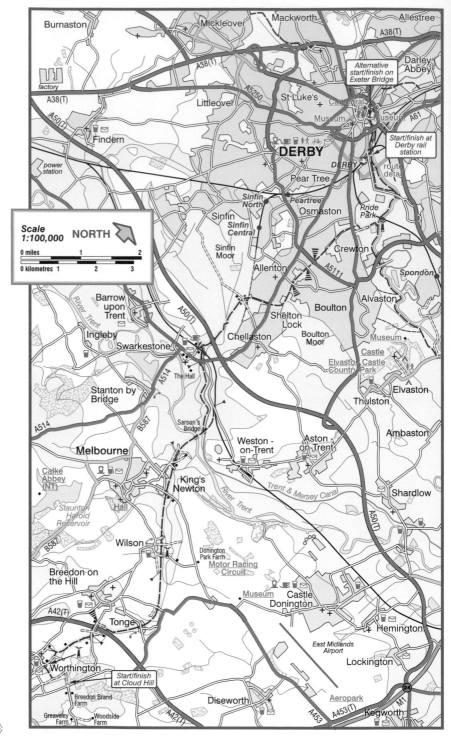

Scale
1:100,000   NORTH

0 miles   1   2
0 kilometres 1   2   3

Alternative
start/finish on
Exeter Bridge

Start/finish at
Derby rail
station

Start/finish
at Cloud Hill

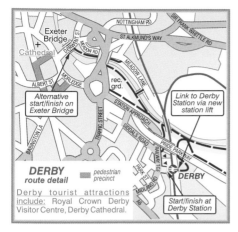

DERBY
route detail

Derby tourist attractions
include: Royal Crown Derby
Visitor Centre, Derby Cathedral.

of Breedon on the Hill, topped by a Norman church. Watch out for a left turn, just before you reach Worthington car park. Follow this around and up to the rim of Cloud Quarry which has dramatic viewpoints and a couple of enormous 'Cloud Cuckoos', vigilantly guarding their only egg.

The village of Worthington boasts an attractive church with a small wooden spire, an octagonal red-brick lock-up dating back to the 18th century, and a pub.

From Worthington it's possible to continue along quiet lanes and traffic-free sections for 10 miles to Loughborough where there is a railway station. Follow the signs for Route 6.

For maps, guides and holiday ideas visit the Sustrans on-line shop at www.sustrans.org.uk

► *Derby town centre with the River Derwent weir.*

139

ROUTES OUT OF LINCOLN TO HARBY, WASHINGBOROUGH AND FISKERTON

Traffic-free paths on either side of the historic city of Lincoln are linked via pedestrianised steets and safe crossings of busy roads to provide two wonderful rides: one into Nottinghamshire and the other out into fenland with its fields of dark earth. West from the centre of Lincoln the ride follows the watercourse known as the Fossdyke as far as the Pye Wipe Inn. It then joins a railway path to take you through Skellingthorpe to the attractive village of Harby, just inside the Nottinghamshire border, a boundary marked with a Millennium milepost. Artwork along the way has mounted photos on display boards with the subject of the photos right ahead of you, for example horses grazing or a line of trees at the far side of a field. The railway to Harby was part of a grand scheme to create a line from Warrington to a new port on the East Coast at Sutton-on-Sea, but only the section from Lincoln to Chesterfield was ever built.

Heading east from the centre of Lincoln you soon join a fine tree-lined path on the strip of land running between the River Witham to the north and a drainage channel to the south. On its way through woodland and rich agricultural land, the path verges are full of wildflowers and blossom, a veritable riot of white in late spring with hawthorn blossom, cow parsley, blackberry blossom, ox eye daisy, dog rose, clover and elderflower punctuated with the bright yellow of buttercups and the purples of vetch.

The ride to the east can be followed as far as Five Mile Bridge, where you have a choice of turning right for the tearoom at the Barn Nursery or left over the footbridge for the Carpenter's Arms pub in Fiskerton (though there are very steep steps at present so you will have to carry your bike).

▼ *View of Lincoln Cathedral.*

Starting points
The centre of Lincoln. If you wish to break the ride into two shorter traffic-free sections: Start the ride west to Harby from Foss Bank, the quiet residential road alongside Fossdyke to the south of and parallel to Carholme Road (A57).
Start the ride east to Washingborough and Fiskerton from the narrow bridge over the River Witham to the east of the town centre. The path runs along Waterside South, on the south side of the river.

Distance
Lincoln to Harby - 6 miles.
Lincoln to Washingborough or Fiskerton - 6 miles.

Grade
Easy.

▼ *View from Harby Bridge*

Surface
Smooth surfaced paths throughout.

Roads, traffic, suitability for young children
The two long stretches of railway path are ideal for children. The section on streets through the centre of Lincoln is only suitable for older children, although it isn't far to walk on pavements with younger children.

Hills
None.

Refreshments
Lots of choice in Lincoln.
Carpenter's Arms PH, stores in Fiskerton.
Barn Nursery & Tearoom at Five Mile Lane, Washingborough (on the south side of river).
Bottle & Glass PH, village shop in Harby.

Nearest railway station
Lincoln.

The National Cycle Network in the area
Route 1, the Hull to Harwich Cycle Route, passes through Lincoln on its way from Woodhall Spa to Market Rasen. Route 64 links Lincoln with Collingham and Newark and will continue on to Market Harborough.

Other nearby rides (waymarked or traffic-free)
The nearest long stretches of traffic-free trails are to the west, between Worksop and Nottingham, including rides in Clumber Park and Sherwood Forest. From South Collingham to Newark and Cotham, new traffic-free links to quiet roads are equally suitable for families.

141

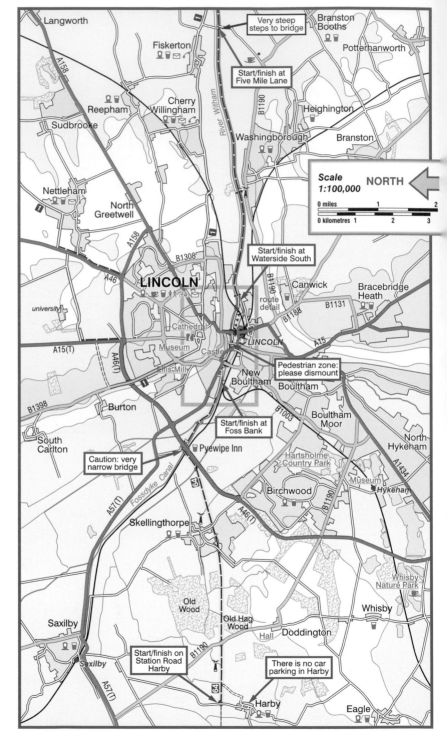

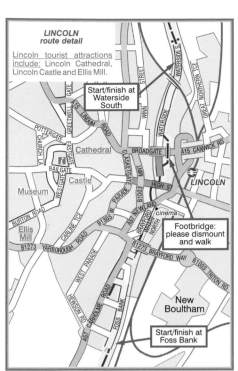

LINCOLN
route detail

Lincoln tourist attractions include: Lincoln Cathedral, Lincoln Castle and Ellis Mill.

Start/finish at Waterside South

Cathedral

Castle

Museum

Ellis Mill

LINCOLN

Footbridge: please dismount and walk

New Boultham

Start/finish at Foss Bank

▼ *Cycling in the snow in Lincoln.*   ▲ *Fossdyke Canal Path.*

TISSINGTON & HIGH PEAK TRAILS

These two traffic-free routes are the ideal way to explore the Peak District. One of the most popular traffic-free paths in the country, the Tissington Trail takes you on a steady climb up the railway path from Ashbourne right into the heart of the Peak District National Park. The trail ends in Parsley Hay where it links to the High Peak Trail which travels south east towards Cromford. On a windless day, the High Peak Trail is perfect for beginners as it was originally engineered in the 1820s to canal standards so, for the most part, it runs level through high, limestone landscape. This means that you get to have your cake and eat it - spectacular long views without the effort of climbing. There are a couple of climbs where you are advised to dismount and walk.

You may get a chance to see the old winding engine at Middleton Top operating and the nearby National Stone Centre is another attraction worth heading for.

You will find cycle hire at Ashbourne, Parsley Hay and Middleton Top.

Starting points
Station Road, Ashbourne or the other side of the tunnel near Mapleton Road. Parsley Hay. Middleton Top.

Distance
Tissington Trail 13 miles.
High Peak Trail 17.5 miles.

Grade
Easy providing you walk the few hills on the High Peak Trail.

Surface
Railway path, dust surface.

Roads, traffic, suitability for young children
Both routes are excellent for young children though you will need to take care at the occasional road crossings. In Ashbourne, the old railway tunnel has been reopened and lit so if you start from Station Road on the south side of town, your journey will have easy gradients and be traffic-free all the way.

Hills
Steady climb from Ashbourne of almost 700 ft to Parsley Hay - we recommend doing this when you are fresh, saving the easy downhill for the return trip.

Refreshments
Lots of choice in Ashbourne. Dog & Partridge pub in Thorpe. Coffees and teas at Basset Wood Farm, Tissington. Waterloo Inn in Biggin. Dawn's Refreshments at Parsley Hay Cycle Centre. Rising Sun Inn in Middleton, and cafes at Middleton Top and the National Stone Centre nearby.

Nearest railway stations
Matlock Bath, Matlock, Cromford, Buxton or Derby.

The National Cycle Network in the area

The Tissington Trail forms part of the Pennine Cycleway Route 68, a 350-mile challenge route between Derby and Berwick-upon-Tweed.

Route 54 runs from Derby south west to Burton-upon-Trent and Lichfield, and Route 6 goes from Derby to Long Eaton and Nottingham.

The High Peak Trail is on Regional Route 65.

Other nearby rides (waymarked or traffic-free)

1. Carsington Water, 8 mile cicular ride.
2. Manifold Track, Waterhouses to Hulme End.
3. Mickleover Trail, Derby to Hilton.

▶ *Ashbourne tunnel.*

▼ *Using a recumbent on the High Peak Trail.*

To find out about other cycle routes in this area visit www.sustrans.org.uk

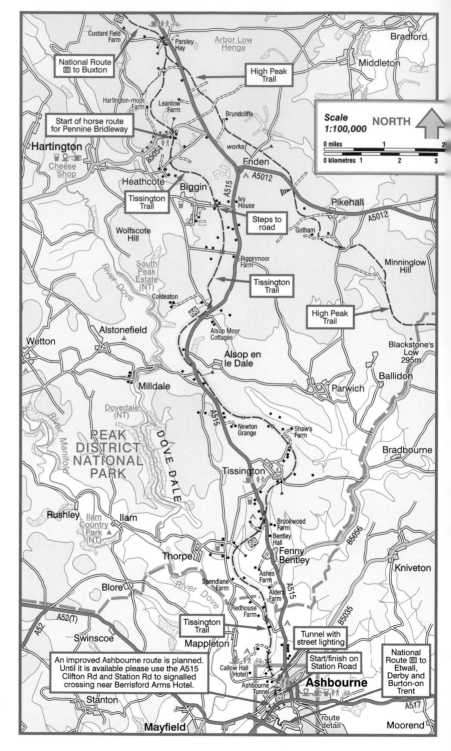

Custard Field Farm

National Route 68 to Buxton

Start of horse route for Pennine Bridleway

Hartington

Cheese Shop

Parsley Hay

Arbor Low Henge

High Peak Trail

Hartington-moor Farm

Leanlow Farm

Brundcliffe

works

Friden

A5012

Heathcote

Biggin

Tissington Trail

Wolfscote Hill

South Peak Estate (NT)

Ivy House

Steps to road

Gotham

Pikehall

A5012

Minninglow Hill

Bigginmoor Farm

Tissington Trail

River Dove

Coldeaton

High Peak Trail

Alstonefield

Wetton

Alsop Moor Cottages

Alsop en le Dale

Blackstone's Low 295m

Ballidon

Milldale

Dovedale (NT)

River Manifold

PEAK DISTRICT NATIONAL PARK

DOVE DALE

Parwich

Newton Grange

Shaw's Farm

Tissington

Bradbourne

Rushley

Ilam Country Park (NT)

Ilam

Brookwood Farm

Bentley Hall

Fenny Bentley

Kniveton

Thorpe

Ashes Farm

B5056

Blore

Spendlane Farm

Alders Farm

River Dove

A52(T)

A52

Swinscoe

Redhouse Farm

Tissington Trail

Mappleton

Tunnel with street lighting

Start/finish on Station Road

National Route 68 to Etwall, Derby and Burton-on-Trent

An improved Ashbourne route is planned. Until it is available please use the A515 Clifton Rd and Station Rd to signalled crossing near Berrisford Arms Hotel.

Callow Hall (Hotel)

Ashbourne Tunnel

Ashbourne

B5035

A515

Stanton

Mayfield

route detail

A517

Moorend

Scale 1:100,000 NORTH

0 miles — 1 — 2
0 kilometres 1 — 2 — 3

Bradford

Middleton

65

68

146

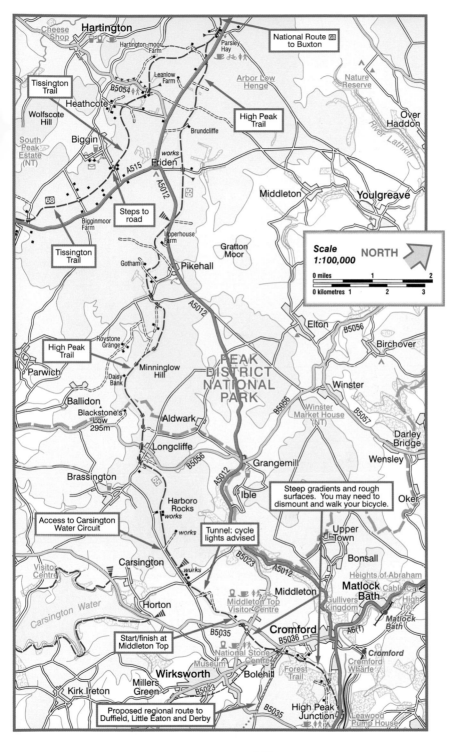

High Peak Trail

Cheese Shop
Hartington
Hartington-moor Farm
Parsley Hay
National Route 68 to Buxton

Tissington Trail
Leanlow Farm
Arbor Low Henge
High Peak Trail

Heathcote
B5054
Wolfscote Hill
Brundcliffe
Over Haddon
River Lathkill
Nature Reserve

Biggin
South Peak Estate (NT)
68
works
Friden
A515
A5012
Middleton
Youlgreave

Bigginmoor Farm
Steps to road
Upperhouse Farm
Gratton Moor

Tissington Trail
Gotham
Pikehall
Elton
B5056
Birchover

A5012
Winster
PEAK DISTRICT NATIONAL PARK

High Peak Trail
Roystone Grange
Minninglow Hill
Winster Market House (NT)
B5056
B5057
Darley Bridge

Parwich
Daisy Bank
Wensley
Oker

Ballidon
Blackstone's Low 295m
Aldwark
Grangemill

Brassington
Longcliffe
B5056
A5012
Ible
Steep gradients and rough surfaces. You may need to dismount and walk your bicycle.

Harboro Rocks
works
Upper Town
Bonsall

Access to Carsington Water Circuit
works
Tunnel: cycle lights advised
Heights of Abraham
Cable Car

Visitor Centre
Carsington
works
B5023
A5012
Middleton
Matlock Bath
High Tor

Carsington Water
Horton
Middleton Top Visitor Centre
Gullivers Kingdom
Matlock Bath
A6(T)

Start/finish at Middleton Top
B5035
Cromford
B5036
Cromford
Cromford Wharf

Wirksworth
National Stone Museum
Bolehill
Forest Trail

Kirk Ireton
Millers Green
B5023
B5035
High Peak Junction
Leawood Pump House

Proposed regional route to Duffield, Little Eaton and Derby

Scale
1:100,000
NORTH
0 miles   1   2
0 kilometres 1   2   3

ASHBOURNE
route detail

Ashbourne tourist attractions include: Oswald's Church and Elizabethan Grammar School.

Alternative start/finish

Tissington Trail

Start/finish on Station Road

Spitalhill

MAPPLETON ROAD
NORTH AVE
BUXTON ROAD
BELLE VIEW ROAD
CHURCH ST
DARK LANE
MAYFIELD ROAD
STATION RD
STATION ST
CLIFTON ROAD
NORTH LEYS
COMPTON ST
ST JOHN'S ST
PARK ROAD A515
BELPER ROAD A517
DERBY ROAD
OLD HILL
OLD DERBY ROAD
GEORGE STREET
DUNCOMBE DRIVE
PREMIER AVENUE
LODGE AVENUE
HIGHFIELD ROAD
A52
A515
A52

tunnel

An improved Ashbourne route is planned. Until it is available please use the A515 Clifton Rd and Station Rd to signalled crossing near Berrisford Arms Hotel.

Use the on-line mapping at www.sustrans.org.uk to find other National Cycle Network routes near you.

▲ *Stopping for a picnic on the Tissington Trail.*

149

Wales

1. Newport to Pontypool & Blaenavon
2. Neath to Briton Ferry
3. Merthyr Tydfil to Ponsticill Reservoir
4. Swansea Bay
5. Swiss Valley
6. Clydach to Ystalyfera
7. Brunel Trail
8. Elan Valley Trail
9. Rheidol Cycle Trail
10. Barmouth – Dolgellau
11. Dinas – Caernarfon – Y Felinheli
12. Llyn Trawsfynydd
13. Cardiff to Castell Coch
14. Quakers' Yard to Newport
15. Llanelli Millennium Coastal Park
16. Llandudno & Colwyn Bay to Prestatyn
17. Bangor to Bethesda & Llyn Ogwyn

──────	National Cycle Network traffic-free routes
──────	National Cycle Network on road routes
──────	National Cycle Network future routes
3	National Route Numbers
10	Regional route numbers
◯	Towns with railway stations
○	Towns without railway stations
12	Regional ride numbers

WALES

With some of Britain's most beautiful countryside, fascinating historical and industrial sites, and unique wildlife spotting opportunities, Wales offers cyclists many memorable experiences. The National Cycle Network provides some truly stunning longer distance routes exploring these riches, but also offers occasional and family cyclists plenty of superb, shorter and traffic-free rides.

In North Wales, two major routes set out from Holyhead on Anglesey across the Menai Bridge, one heading to Chester, the other to Cardiff. Route 5 heads east through Bangor, along the breezy coastline via popular Llandudno, Colwyn Bay and Prestatyn to Chester. Route 8, known as Lôn Las Cymru, follows an epic southerly path from Holyhead across Wales. The route passes the UNESCO World Heritage Site of Caernarfon and Harlech castles, splendid views of Snowdonia National Park, the mountains of mid-

Wales and dramatic beauty of the Brecon Beacons, before descending from Brecon along the Taff Trail to Cardiff, the Millennium Stadium and the new developments around Cardiff Bay.

Routes 4 and 47 together make up the Celtic Trail/Lôn Geltaidd, which loops through picturesque Pembrokeshire, heading east across the valleys and with an optional and remote high level route to Pontypridd, before continuing through Newport and Chepstow to the old Severn Bridge and into England. Many other routes spur from the Celtic Trail, giving varied opportunities to spot majestic red kites, explore old railway lines through remote mining valleys, visit castles and cruise gently along canal towpaths.

If you're after some inspiration to awaken or rekindle your interest in cycling, the National Cycle Network in Wales can surely help - the suggestions here barely touch the surface of what's on offer.

▼ *Caernarfon Castle.*

Pembrey Forest to Loughor Bridge
The coastal park is a huge achievement and the finest section of the whole Network. The sweep of the wide path over the newly built railway tunnels is utterly exhilarating in its achievement of reclamation with vision.

Colwyn Bay to Rhyl and Prestatyn
The Network's longest coastal section. Ride eastwards with a strong wind behind you, and you will want to cycle forever.

The mountain road from Corris to Dolgellau
We never thought this would be rebuilt but it now gives you a most stunning view of Cader Idris and the approach to Snowdonia National Park.

Cardiff Millennium Stadium
This is just the start of a whole series of highlights all the way to the Barrage.

Hengoed Viaduct
The highlight of a cross valley route from Quaker's Yard to Newport, this symbolises the vital role of the old railways in creating traffic-free routes in this crowded country.

Aberystwyth
The end of the railway and the start of many journeys.

▼ *In 'Wheel of Drams' by Andy Hazell, coal drams commemorate the haulage companies that previously used the viaduct.*

WALES FAMILY RIDES

Newport to Pontypool and Blaenavon. 16 miles. Route 46
This route follows canal towpaths and railway paths to make an attractive, convenient and traffic-free link between the towns of Newport, Cwmbran, Pontypool and Blaenavon. In places where the canal has been built over, dedicated cycle ways keep you away from traffic until the canal returns. There are some marvellous views during the journey as well as plenty of industrial heritage to explore. The ride ends at Big Pit, the National Mining Museum of Wales at Blaenavon, where you can travel 300ft underground and discover what life was really like at the coal face.

Neath Canal - Briton Ferry to Aberdulais. 5 miles. Route 47
This section of the Celtic Trail gives cyclists a green and mostly traffic-free treat, ideal for day-to-day journeys as well as for stress-free family outings. It can also form the beginning of a longer ride along the Vale of Neath to the edge of the Brecon Beacons

National Park. Starting at the old Roman ford of Briton Ferry, you drop down from Briton Ferry bridge to join the canal towpath. The canal is alive with aquatic life, a striking contrast to the nearby industrial landscape. Your ride follows the canal towpath beyond Neath to the restored canal basin at Aberdulais.

Merthyr Tydfil to Pontsticill Reservoir. 4 miles. Route 8
Beginning at the magnificent Cefn Coed viaduct near Cyfartha Castle at Merthyr Tydfil, follow the Taff Trail northwards on a disused railway through the beautiful wooded Taf Fechan valley, crossing the Pontsarn viaduct towards Ponsticill reservoir. The last section of the route leaves the traffic-free path following a country lane with a

moderate gradient to the reservoir. Refreshments are available in a converted railway carriage alongside the reservoir. Combine your ride with a trip on the narrow gauge Brecon Mountain Railway with spectacular views of the Brecon Beacons.

Swansea Bay. 5.5 miles. Route 4
An ideal ride for those with small children, this entirely traffic-free route takes in the sweep of Swansea Bay and makes a lovely family outing. Starting at Swansea Sail Bridge in the marina within Wales' resurgent second city, the route runs along just above the beach, offering wonderful views out to Mumbles Head, the gateway to the magical Gower peninsula. The ride finishes at

the Victorian seaside resort of The Mumbles, where you can enjoy an ice cream, take a stroll along the pier, visit Oystermouth Castle, or even try your hand at crazy golf.

Swiss Valley - Llanelli to Cross Hands. 12 miles. Route 47
This beautiful ride offers families a well surfaced, traffic-free path running inland from the stunning Millennium Coastal Park. The route passes through attractive woodland, past the Lleidi reservoirs to open countryside above the Gwendraith Valley and, although there is a 450ft height gain, it's a gentle and steady climb. Safely away from traffic, this route is ideal for those wanting to take children on a rewarding cycle ride, whilst giving them the opportunity to experience the exhilaration of

freewheeling back down the hill. For those with a touch more stamina, there is a link from Cross Hands (mostly on-road), to the National Botanic Gardens of Wales.

Clydach to Ystalyfera. 6 miles. Route 43
An ideal ride for those with young children this traffic-free route follows the canal towpath from Clydach to Pontardawe and then the riverside path using the dismantled railway alongside the river Tawe north to Ystalyfera. Coed Gwilwm Park north of Clydach is a good starting point with access to the route. Refreshments are available in Clydach and Ystalyfera at either end of the route, the Pontardawe Inn is directly on the route at

Pontardawe. This once heavily industrialised valley is returning to its former natural beauty, the gentle gradient of the riverside path provides a relaxing ride with views of the river, wooded hillsides and meadows.

The Brunel Trail - Haverfordwest to Neyland. 10 miles. Route 4
This enjoyable and largely traffic-free ride is full of variety, revealing a castle, industrial history and wildlife. The route is based on the vision of renowned engineer Isambard Kingdom Brunel, to create a major transatlantic transport terminus at Neyland. The ride takes you past Haverfordwest's 12th century castle through

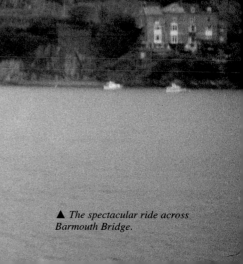

▲ *The spectacular ride across Barmouth Bridge.*

typical Pembrokeshire countryside and along the remains of the railway line Brunel completed in 1856, to an estuary-locked causeway and a nature reserve. Refreshments and facilities are available at either end of the ride.

Elan Valley Trail - Rhayader to Craig Goch Reservoir. 8 miles. Route 81

The Elan Valley Trail promises a memorable ride, full of rugged and spectacular mountain scenery, rare wildlife and impressive stone dams. The ride is essentially traffic-free along an old railway line, although there are a few short on-road sections. The railway

tunnel near the beginning of the route has been dedicated as a nature reserve to protect rare bats, and birdwatchers can also enjoy spotting red kites swooping for prey. There is a cafe and shop at the visitor centre halfway along the route, for those in need of refreshments.

Rheidol Cycle Trail - Aberystwyth to Devil's Bridge. 9 miles. Route 82

The route follows the beautiful Rheidol valley from Aberystwyth harbour to the spectacular waterfalls and three arched bridges built on top of each other at Devil's Bridge. The first two miles are traffic-free, the route then follows minor roads crossing the Vale of Rheidol narrow gauge steam railway

several times before reaching Devil's Bridge. Be aware there is a steep climb towards the end of the trail beyond Cwm Rheidol. Alternatively take the train and return by bike. From Cwm Rheidol an easier and shorter option follows the northern braid to the Rheidol Power Station, Visitor Centre and Rheidol Falls.

Lôn Mawddach - Barmouth to Dolgellau. 11 miles. Route 8

This flat route takes you through some spectacular scenery. Starting at Barmouth station, take care on the town roads, following the Route 8 signs over the Mawddach railway viaduct toll bridge. Once across the bridge, the waters of the Afon Mawddach and the peaks of Cader Idris surround you. There is a pub and an RSPB reserve at Penmaenpool, where an old signal box serves as an observation centre. The route from here to Dolgellau has been adapted with disabled users particularly in mind, continuing along the River Wnion to this fine old stone-built market town.

Dinas to Caernarfon and Y Felinheli (Lôn Eifion and Lôn Las Menai). 8 miles. Route 8

Known as Lôn Eifion to the south of Caernarfon and Lôn Las Menai to the north east of the town, this wonderful ride runs adjacent to North Wales' Menai Strait. The family-friendly, traffic-free route takes you along a former railway line offering fantastic views of mountains, coastal scenery and the amazing World Heritage site of Caernarfon Castle. You

◀ *Cwm Rheidol / Rheidol Valley reservoir near Aberystwyth.*

▲ *Swiss Valley route from Llanelli to Cross Hands.*

Llyn Trawsfynydd. 5 miles. Route 8

Starting at the Power Station Visitor Centre, follow the traffic-free path to the edge of Trawsfynydd Lake and alongside the A470 on a shared use path to the village of Trawsfynydd. Beyond the village turn right, following the quiet lane along the western edge of the lake with spectacular views of the Rhinog mountains. At present you cannot cycle all the way around the lake, so retrace your steps back to the start. To extend the ride continue on the traffic free path for two miles to the village of Gellilydan. Refreshments are available at the visitor centre or in the villages on the route.

begin the ride at the steepled church at Dinas, before following a green avenue of trees, and enjoying spectacular views of Snowdonia, passing through Caernarfon before finishing at Y Felinheli docks. You can combine your outing with a trip on the narrow gauge Welsh Highland Railway, which runs alongside you for some of the way.

▼ *Cwmbran on the way from Newport to Blaenavon.*

157

CARDIFF BAY TO CASTELL COCH

This route offers a magnificent exit from the very heart of Cardiff Bay. Starting at the waterfront this route links together some fine traffic-free trails alongside the River Taff, passing right beneath the splendid Millennium Stadium and taking you to the fairytale castle of Castell Coch.

This seven-mile ride is a taster for the full 55-mile Taff Trail which goes all the way to Brecon, itself, forming part of Lôn Las Cymru which could take you all the way to Anglesey. If you're continuing northwards from Castell Coch, descend the hill to Tongwynlais to join a traffic-free path to Taff's Well station and Pontypridd.

Starting point
Cardiff Bay.

Distance
Seven miles one way, 14 miles return.

Grade
Easy.

Surface
Mixture of tarmac and good quality gravel paths.

Roads, traffic, suitability for young children
The route is almost entirely traffic-free from Cardiff to Tongwynlais. There is a short section on road through Tongwynlais.

▼ *The Taff Trail takes you right past the Millennium Stadium.*

Hills
The route is flat as far as Tongwynlais then there is a short steep climb up to Castell Coch.

Refreshments
Lots of choice in Cardiff centre. Pubs in Tongwynlais. Cafe in Castell Coch (you will need to pay to enter the castle).

Nearest railway stations
Cardiff Bay.

The National Cycle Network in the area
The Taff Trail forms part of Route 8 which links with a number of city centre routes and extends to Holyhead in North Wales. Just north of Castell Coch the Taff Trail joins the Celtic Trail/Lôn Geltaidd (Route 4) which runs from Fishguard to Chepstow.

Other nearby rides (waymarked or traffic-free)
1. The Taff Trail continues north from Castell Coch (starting with an exceedingly steep climb!) along dismantled railways through Nantgarw and Rhydyfelin to Pontypridd. The low level alternative drops back down to Tonwynlias and heads north from the Lewis Arms to join a traffic-free path north of Taff's Well Station. South from Cardiff centre the trail runs to Cardiff Bay and the Barrage.
2. There are good quality towpaths along the canals leading from Newport north west to Crosskeys (Route 47) and north to Cwmbran and Pontypool (Route 46).

Between Llandaff and Tongwynlais you pass the Mellingriffith Water Pump -

a water-powered beam engine erected in 1807 to lift water 11 feet up from the river to the Glamorganshire Canal. The pump worked for 140 years until 1948 when the canal was closed and filled in.

After a short road section through Tongwynlais and a very steep climb up the drive you reach the fairytale Castell Coch, a Grade 1 listed building built on medieval remains and lavishly decorated and furnished in the Victorian Gothic style. With its conical turrets rising above the surrounding beech woodland, it is an outstanding landmark. This route forms part of the 55-mile Taff Trail which continues on to Merthyr Tydfil and Brecon and which itself is part of the long-distance route, Lôn Las Cymru all the way up through Wales to Anglesey.

▲ *Taff Trail Marker by Angharad Jones.*

▼ *Castell Coch lies at the top of an exceedingly steep hill.*

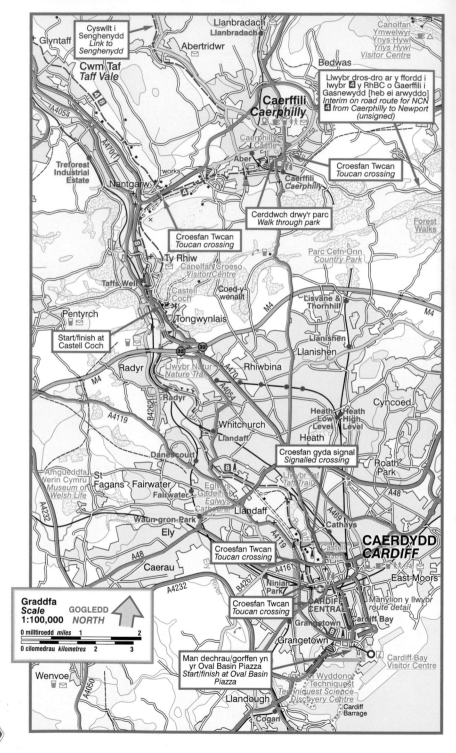

Cyswllt i
Senghenydd
Link to
Senghenydd

Llwybr dros-dro ar y ffordd i
lwybr 4 y RhBC o Gaerffili i
Gasnewydd [heb ei arwyddo]
Interim on road route for NCN
4 from Caerphilly to Newport
(unsigned)

Croesfan Twcan
Toucan crossing

Cerddwch drwy'r parc
Walk through park

Croesfan Twcan
Toucan crossing

Start/finish at
Castell Coch

Croesfan gyda signal
Signalled crossing

Croesfan Twcan
Toucan crossing

Croesfan Twcan
Toucan crossing

Man dechrau/gorffen yn
yr Oval Basin Piazza
Start/finish at Oval Basin
Piazza

Graddfa
Scale
1:100,000

GOGLEDD
NORTH

0 milltiroedd miles   1   2
0 cilomedrau kilometres   2   3

160

▼ *The Millennium Stadium.*

Manylion llwybr CAERDYDD
CARDIFF route detail

Ymhlith yr atyniadau i ymwelwyr yng Nghaerdydd mae: Bae Caerdydd, Amgueddfa Bywyd Cymreig, Techniquest, Stadiwm y Mileniwm.

Cardiff tourist attractions include: Millennium Waterfront, Museum of Welsh Life, Techniquest, Millennium Stadium.

NEWPORT TO TRELEWIS
AND QUAKER'S YARD

The route from Newport to Crosskeys is one of the best canal towpaths in Wales - a wide gravel track runs alongside what was once a major artery carrying coal down to the docks at Newport. There are views of wooded hills rising to over 1,000 feet to either side of the canal as you approach Crosskeys. From there you join a high quality railway path through the Sirhowy Valley County Park. Set in 1,000 acres of mixed woodland, the park boasts great walking and cycling paths, both along the Sirhowy River and through the Flatwoods Meadows Local Nature Reserve. For those who like a challenge, the climbs to Graig Goch Wood or Twyn yr Oerfel will oblige, but also reward you with spectacular views.

At Hengoed, the spectacular viaduct dominates. Completed in 1858, it spans over 850 feet with 16 arches, nearly 130 feet above the Rhymney valley floor. The path remains traffic-free all the way to Quaker's Yard where you can pick up a return journey by train or carry on along the Network to many other parts of Wales.

Starting points
Quaker's Yard Station.
Newport Station.

Distance
19 miles.

▼ *Newport to Crosskeys*
Monmouthshire and Brecon canal,
Crumlin Arms.

For a shorter ride, you might go from either start point as far as Sirhowy Valley Country Park, about 9 miles.

Grade
Easy.

Surface
Gravel towpath for first 8 miles

(Newport to Crosskeys), then tarmac cycle path.

Roads, traffic, suitability for young children
A short on-road section from Newport station, then traffic-free to Crosskeys where there are a couple of short on-road sections before Sirhowy Park.

Then traffic-free all the way to Quaker's Yard. A couple of crossings where care is needed near Hengoed.

Hills
Flat from Newport to Sirhowy Park, gentle hills to Quaker's Yard.

Refreshments
Choice in Newport, Risca and Crosskeys.

▼ *Dragonfly sculpture Fourteen Locks Canal near Newport.*

Nearest railway stations
Quaker's Yard, Hengoed, Ystrad Mynach, Newport.

The National Cycle Network in the area
The whole route is on Route 47, part of Celtic Trail (Lôn Geltaidd) which runs from Fishguard to the old Severn Bridge near Chepstow. At Quaker's Yard, you can pick up Route 8 (Lôn Las Cymru) which would take you south to Cardiff or north all the way to Holyhead.

Other nearby rides (waymarked or traffic-free)
1. Newport to Cwmbran and Pontypool along the canal towpath, Route 46.
2. Newport to Caerphilly, mostly on-road and many more hills! Route 4.
3. Lots of waymarked walking routes in Sirhowy Valley Country Park.

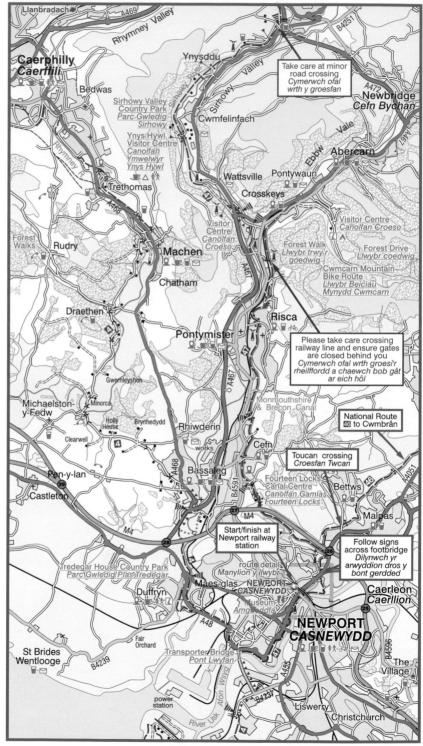

Llanbradach
Rhymney Valley
A469
B4251

Caerphilly
Caerffili
Bedwas
Ynysddu
Take care at minor
road crossing
*Cymerwch ofal
wrth y groesfan*
A472
Newbridge
Cefn Bychan

Sirhowy Valley
Country Park
*Parc Gwledig
Sirhowy*
Cwmfelinfach
Sirhowy Valley
A467

Ynys Hywl
Visitor Centre
*Canolfan
Ymwelwyr
Ynys Hywl*
Ebbw Vale
Abercarn

Trethomas
Wattsville
Pontywaun
Crosskeys
Visitor Centre
Canolfan Croeso

Forest
Walks
Rudry
Visitor
Centre
*Canolfan
Croeso*
Forest Walk
*Llwybr trwy'r
goedwig*
Forest Drive
Llwybr coedwig

Machen
Chatham
Cwmcarn Mountain
Bike Route
*Llwybr Beiciau
Mynydd Cwmcarn*

Draethen
Pontymister
Risca
Please take care crossing
railway line and ensure gates
are closed behind you
*Cymerwch ofal wrth groesi'r
rheilffordd a chaewch bob gât
ar eich hôl*

Gwernleyshen
Monmouthshire
& Brecon Canal
National Route
47 to Cwmbrân

Michaelston-
y-Fedw
Minorca
Brynhedydd
Rhiwderin
works

Holly
House
Clearwell
A468
Cefn
Toucan crossing
Croesfan Twcan

Pen-y-lan
29
Castleton
Bassaleg
B4591
Fourteen Locks
Canal Centre
*Canolfan Gamlas
Fourteen Locks*
Bettws
Malpas

M4
27
M4
Start/finish at
Newport railway
station
26
Follow signs
across footbridge
*Dilynwch yr
arwyddion dros y
bont gerdded*

28
Tredegar House Country Park
Parc Gwledig Plas Tredegar
route detail
Manylion y llwybr
Caerleon
Caerllion
25

Duffryn
Maes-glas
NEWPORT
CASNEWYDD
Museum
Amgueddfa

Fair
Orchard
A48
NEWPORT
CASNEWYDD
B4596
The
Village

St Brides
Wentlooge
B4239
Transporter Bridge
Pont Lwyfan
A455

power
station
River Usk
B4237
Liswerry
Christchurch

164

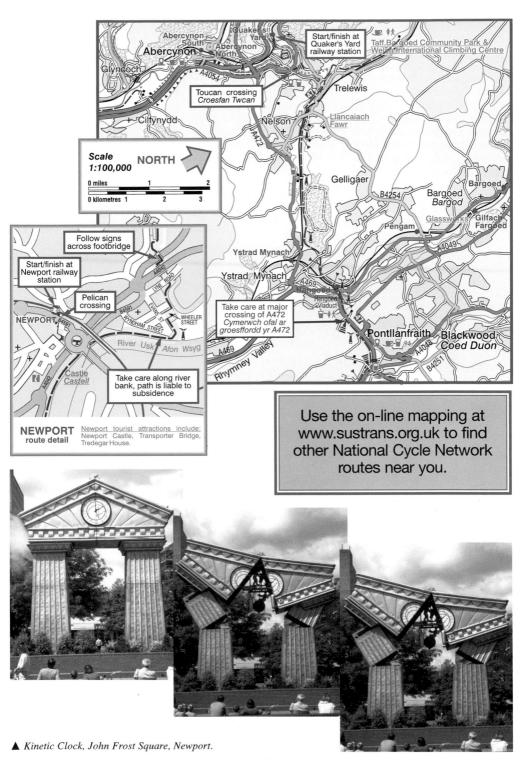

Scale 1:100,000

NORTH

| 0 miles | | 1 | | 2 |
| 0 kilometres | 1 | 2 | 3 |

Abercynon South
Abercynon North
Abercynon
Glyncoch
Cilfynydd

Quaker's Yard
Start/finish at Quaker's Yard railway station

Taff Bargoed Community Park & Welsh International Climbing Centre

Trelewis

Toucan crossing
Croesfan Twcan

Nelson

Llancaiach Fawr

Gelligaer

Bargoed
Bargod

Bargoed

Glassworks
Pengam
Gilfach Fargoed

Ystrad Mynach
Ystrad Mynach

Hengoed
Hengoed Viaduct

Take care at major crossing of A472
Cymerwch ofal ar groesffordd yr A472

Pontllanfraith
Blackwood
Coed Duon

Rhymney Valley

Newport route detail

Follow signs across footbridge

Start/finish at Newport railway station

Pelican crossing

NEWPORT

LYNE ROAD
EVANS ST
WYNDHAM STREET
WHEELER STREET

River Usk *Afon Wsyg*

Castle
Castell

Take care along river bank, path is liable to subsidence

NEWPORT route detail Newport tourist attractions include: Newport Castle, Transporter Bridge, Tredegar House.

Use the on-line mapping at www.sustrans.org.uk to find other National Cycle Network routes near you.

▲ *Kinetic Clock, John Frost Square, Newport.*

KIDWELLY TO LLANELLI

This is an easy mainly traffic-free route with magnificent views across the Loughor Estuary towards the Gower Peninsula.

Starting in Kidwelly with its dramatic castle, you soon follow a traffic-free path that takes you through the sandy woodland of Pembrey Forest. Pembrey Country Park has plenty on offer with an eight-mile beach, refreshments, an adventure playground and dry ski slope.

The section between Pembrey Forest and Llanelli is on purpose-built traffic-free paths through the magnificent Millennium Coastal Park: a linear park landscaped from millions of tons of earth that was once derelict land. Providing there isn't a strong wind, this makes an excellent place for new cyclists and children to practice their skills.

Halfway along is Burry Port with its harbour and facilities. Llanelli North Dock now boasts a new cafe and visitor centre and, if you continue eastwards, you will arrive at the Wildfowl and Wetlands Centre at Penclacwydd.

▼ *Looking towards the Gower Peninsula.*

Starting points
The centre of Kidwelly.
The Wildfowl & Wetlands
Centre, Penclacwydd, southeast
of Llanelli.
North Dock, Llanelli.

Distance
18 miles one way, 36 miles
return.
Shorter options include:
Burry Port to Pembrey Country
Park 3½ miles.
Kidwelly to Pembrey Country
Park 6 miles.
Penclacwydd to Llanelli 4½ miles.
Penclacwydd to Burry Port 7
miles.

Grade
Easy.

Surface
Mixture of tarmac and gravel
paths.

Roads, traffic, suitability for
young children
There is a short road section at
the start in Kidwelly where care
should be taken. This is an
excellent route for young
children (as long as you take
account of the wind!).

Hills
None.

Refreshments
Lots of choice in Kidwelly,
Burry Port and Llanelli.
Cafe at North Dock, Llanelli.
Cafe at Pembrey Country Park
(just off the route).
Cafe at the Wildfowl &
Wetlands Centre at the end of
the ride at Penclacwydd.

Nearest railway stations
Kidwelly, Burry Port, Llanelli.

The National Cycle Network
in the area
The ride described here is part
of Route 4, the Celtic Trail (Lôn
Geltaidd), which runs from

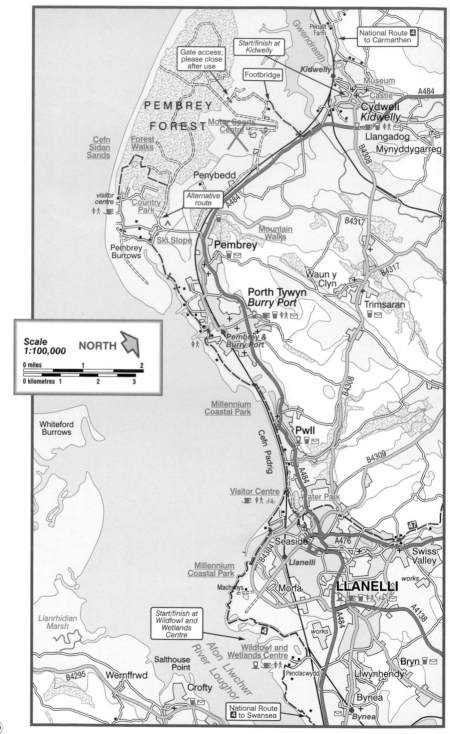

Scale
1:100,000

NORTH

Fishguard to the old Severn Bridge near Chepstow. Route 47 runs north from Llanelli via Swiss Valley to Cross Hands with 13 miles of spectacular traffic-free route. Route 43 will link Swansea to Builth Wells where it joins Lôn Las Cymru from Cardiff to Anglesey (Route 8).

Other nearby rides (waymarked or traffic-free)
1. There are many more tracks to explore in Pembrey Forest, around the Country Park.
2. You can cycle traffic-free from the Wildfowl & Wetlands Centre to Bynea around the Loughor estuary.

Starting from Kidwelly, with its dramatic castle, you soon join a traffic-free path that continues more or less unbroken to the Wildfowl and Wetlands Centre east of Llanelli.

Throughout the ride there are many views of estuaries that flood in exceptionally high tides. The first, Gwendraeth, has a backdrop of rounded green hills rising up over 600 ft from the shoreline.

You soon enter the sandy woodlands of Pembrey Forest, a 1000-hectare sand dune forest and Site of Scientific Special Interest. There are many tracks based around the visitor centre which you could use as a detour to explore the country park. The country park also offers a wide range of attractions including a dry ski slope, the longest toboggan run in Wales, a nine hole pitch & putt course, a miniature railway, a large adventure playground and an eight-mile long beach. You can also hire bikes from the centre.

Beyond Pembrey Forest there are long sections of cycle paths with wonderful views out over the estuary that separates the Gower Peninsula from the mainland.

Between Burry Port and Llanelli you cross the railway line twice via huge land bridges covered with earth and grass, a wonderful piece of landscaping. In fact, along the whole length of the route, millions of tons of earth have been moved to regenerate what was once a derelict wasteland.

At the end of the ride you could visit The Wildfowl & Wetlands Centre, with its Millennium Wetland complex, home to wildlife as diverse as dragonfly and Little Egret.

From here, you have the option of pressing on to Swansea and catching the train back, or cycling all or part of the way back as far as the stations at Llanelli or Burry Port.

▲ *The Millennium Coastal Park has turned derelict land into a magnificent linear park.*

LLANDUDNO TO PRESTATYN

Enjoy this wonderful open, breezy ride along the wide sea promenade. After following quiet roads and new cycle paths from the edge of Llandudno, it stretches traffic-free almost unbroken for 16 miles from Rhôs-on-Sea to Prestatyn, with the sea and sandy beaches on one side and a background of wooded hills rising to over 600ft behind Abergele on the other. Along the way you'll see the tiny chapel of St Trillo in Rhôs-on-Sea which is reputed to be the starting point for Madoc ap Owain Gwynedd's epic voyage to America in 1170, and the atmospheric Gwrych Castle up in the wooded hills between Llanddulas and Abergele. Rhyl's ice cream stalls will give you the boost you need to complete the last few miles to the journey's end at Prestatyn.

NB This is an open coastal ride where you should be very aware of the wind (normally from the west). If you are going to cycle there and back it is best to cycle into the wind at the start, while you are fresh, and have the wind help you on the return journey. Alternatively, contemplate catching the train then doing a one way trip, blown back to the start!

▼ *Coastal sea defences, like modern sculptures, at Llanddulas near Colwyn Bay.*

Starting point
Llandudno Junction station. Eastern end of the promenade in Llandudno Bay.

Distance
19 miles from Llandudno Bay promenade, 38 miles return. 22 miles from Llandudno Junction, 44 miles return.

Grade
Easy but take good note of the wind direction! Catch the train into the wind and cycle with the wind behind you.

Surface
Tarmac or good stone-based track.

Roads, traffic, suitability for young children
After taking quiet roads from Llandudno Junction station to the seafront at Rhôs-on-Sea, the route is almost entirely traffic-free. If starting at Llandudno promenade, the route is almost completely traffic-free. There are short road sections from Prestatyn railway station to the seafront and at the western end of Rhyl over the Blue Bridge. There are no difficult road crossings along the seafront and this section is ideal for children.

Hills
Between Llandudno promenade and Penrhyn Bay there is a climb up and over Penrhyn Hill. There are a couple of short steep climbs around the jetties at Llandulas.

Refreshments
Lots of choice in Llandudno, Colwyn Bay, Rhyl and Prestatyn.

Nearest railway stations
Llandudno, Llandudno Junction, Colwyn Bay, Abergele & Pensarn, Rhyl and Prestatyn.

▲ *Take in the funfair in Rhyl.*

The National Cycle Network in the area
The ride is part of Route 5, which runs east-west from Chester to Holyhead. At its eastern end Route 5 connects with the Southport to Hull Trans Pennine Trail; at its western end it links with Lôn Las Cymru, (Route 8) from Holyhead to Cardiff.

Other nearby rides (waymarked or traffic-free)
1. There are two railway paths starting from Caernarfon, one heads south to Bryncir, the other runs north east towards Bangor.
2. A railway path runs south from Porth Penrhyn (near Bangor) to Bethesda and Llyn Ogwen.
3. There are waymarked forestry routes in the woodlands around Betws-y-Coed.
4. Chester to Connah's Quay Railway Path (see page 186).

To find out about other cycle routes in this area visit www.sustrans.org.uk

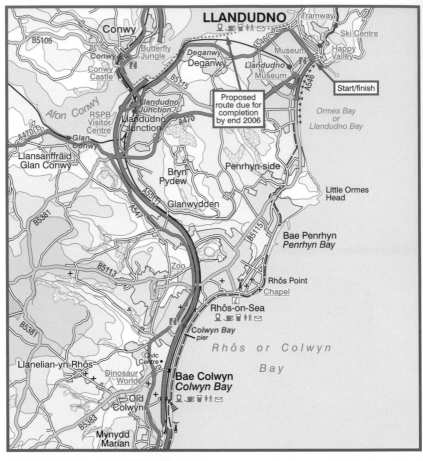

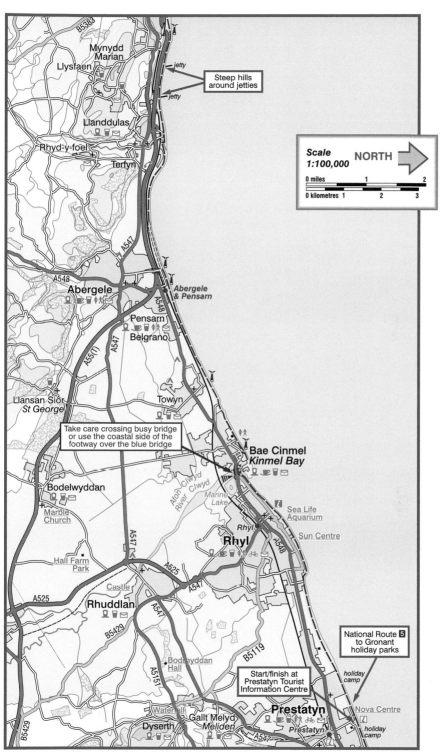

Steep hills around jetties

Take care crossing busy bridge or use the coastal side of the footway over the blue bridge

National Route 5 to Gronant holiday parks

Start/finish at Prestatyn Tourist Information Centre

Scale
1:100,000
NORTH

0 miles   1   2
0 kilometres   1   2   3

Mynydd Marian
Llysfaen
jetty
Llanddulas
jetty
Rhyd-y-foel
Terfyn
B5383

A548
Abergele
Abergele & Pensarn
Pensarn
Belgrano
A547
A5(1?)
Llansan Siôr
St George
Towyn
Bodelwyddan
Marble Church
Afon Clwyd
River Clwyd
Marine Lake
Bae Cinmel
Kinmel Bay
Sea Life Aquarium
Sun Centre
Rhyl
A548
Hall Farm Park
A525
Castle
Rhuddlan
B5429
Bodrhyddan Hall
A5151
B5119
Waterfall
Gallt Melyd
Meliden
Dyserth
Prestatyn
Nova Centre
holiday camp
holiday camp
A547
B5429

173

BANGOR TO BETHESDA AND LLYN OGWEN

Known as Lôn Las Ogwen, this superb ride offers excellent mountain views as you climb south from the coast at Bangor via a railway path through mature woodland alongside streams to the village of Tregarth. After a short section on-road, the ride continues on up through the spoils of the slate quarry on a well-designed path with ever better views of the mountains of Snowdonia ahead. The path joins a minor road that runs parallel with the busy A5 and therefore carries very little traffic. A final climb takes you to Llyn Ogwen where there is a cafe and normally several groups of outdoor enthusiasts either walking, climbing or cycling. In future the route will continue eastwards to Capel Curig and Betws-y-Coed. The narrow gauge railway on which the first part of the path is built was constructed by the Penrhyn Estate to transport slate from the quarries at Bethesda for export at Porth Penrhyn. With the fortune they made from the slate trade they had the mock-Gothic Penrhyn Castle built which now houses a doll museum, a collection of industrial locomotives and a variety of stuffed animals.

NB There is a climb of almost 1000ft from Bangor to Llyn Ogwen so it will be considerably slower on the way up than on the way back down. For a more gentle ride, go only as far as Tregarth, which involves a climb of less than 300ft.

Starting points

Porth Penrhyn / Abercegin, on the northeastern edge of Bangor, just off the A5122 at the brow of the hill (signposted 'Porth Penrhyn').
Ogwen Cottage, Llyn Ogwen, on the A5 towards Capel Curig and Betws-y-Coed.

Distance

11 miles.

Grade

Moderate to Tregarth, then some strenuous sections south from Tregarth to Llyn Ogwen.

Surface

Tarmac or good quality stone-based path.

Roads, traffic, suitability for young children

The gentle climb on the traffic-free section from Port Penrhyn to Tregarth is the best part for families. Beyond the end of the railway path there is a 1½ mile section on the B4409 through Tregarth. South from Tregarth there is a further 2½ mile traffic-free stretch, then a very quiet lane to reach Llyn Ogwen but there are several short steep climbs on the second half of the ride.

Hills

Gentle climb from Porth Penrhyn to Tregarth then several short steep climbs on the path through the quarry. Final climb on the minor road up to Llyn Ogwen.

Refreshments

Lots of choice in Bangor. Pant Yr Ardd PH, stores, Tregarth. Cafe at Llyn Ogwen.

▼ *Lôn Las Ogwen passes the old slate tips as it traverses Penrhyn Quarry, reputedly the largest slate quarry in the world.*

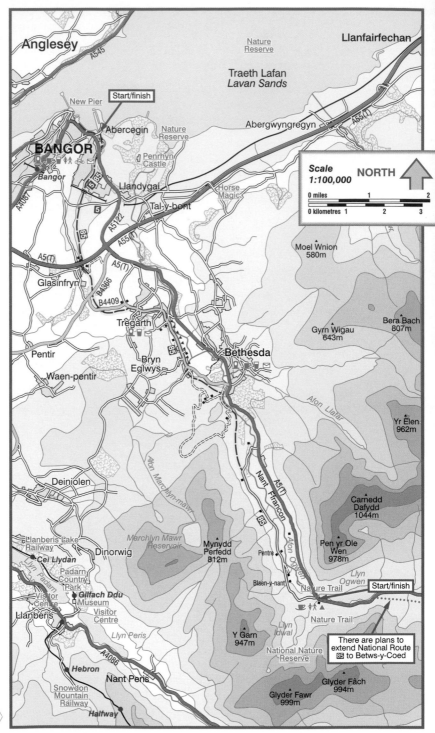

Nearest railway station
Bangor.

The National Cycle Network in the area
Route 5 passes through Bangor on its way from Anglesey to Chester.

Route 8 (Lôn Las Cymru) passes to to the west of Bangor, crossing Menai Bridge then heading southwest to Caernarfon.

Other nearby rides (waymarked or traffic-free)
There are two traffic-free trails starting in Caernarfon: Lôn Las Menai runs northeast along the coast to Y Felinheli, and Lôn Eifion heads south to Bryncir.

▼ *Spectacular views of Tryfan in Snowdonia.*

1. Longdendale Trail east of Manchester
2. Middlewood Way
3. Calder Valley Cycleway
4. Fallowfield Loop
5. Dunford Bridge to Penistone
6. Harland Way
7. Blackburn & Accrington
8. Aire Valley Towpath
9. Six Bridges: Stockton to Middlesbrough
10. Whitby to Scarborough
11. Haltwhistle to Lambley Viaduct
12. Keswick to Threlkeld
13. Chester to Connah's Quay
14. Spen Valley Greenway
15. Camerton – Cleater Moor
16. Selby – Beningbrough
17. Consett to Sunderland
18. Morecambe to Crook of Lune

Hornsea

verley

65

Kingston
–upon–
Hull

————	National Cycle Network traffic-free routes
————	National Cycle Network on road routes
————	National Cycle Network future routes
3	National Route Numbers
10	Regional route numbers
O	Towns with railway stations
O	Towns without railway stations
12	Regional ride numbers

THE NORTH

The North of England encompasses a huge diversity of landscapes, and the National Cycle Network provides practical routes through densely populated and industrialised areas as well as stirring rides through remote countryside. Here, on the Network you will see the scars left by the old heavy industries of coal, steel, shipbuilding and textiles, but also England's most rugged scenery, mystical spots, and best-loved National Parks.

The National Cycle Network gives cyclists and walkers access to many spectacular and well-known places, but vitally, it also provides practical access to everyday destinations. Many cities in the region, such as Liverpool, Manchester, Hull, Doncaster and York, feature prime urban routes for commuting to work and school, going shopping, visiting friends and so on. In numerous cases these routes also provide fantastic green corridors, creating a pleasant escape whilst still within urban surroundings. Network routes such as the Spen Valley Greenway enhance this feeling of escape, by incorporating the display of many memorable works of art.

Justifiably one of the Network's best known and loved long distance rides is the Sea to Sea Route (C2C) from Whitehaven or Workington in Cumbria to Tynemouth or Sunderland on the North Sea coast. The Trans Pennine Trail marks the southern extent of the region, following sections of Routes 62 and 65 to link Southport and Liverpool on the west coast to Hull on the east coast. Route 6 runs roughly north-south down the western side of the region, connecting the Lake District with Morecambe, Lancaster and Preston and continuing down to the Midlands. Hadrian's Cycleway follows Route 72 through the UNESCO World Heritage Site, tracing the remains of the famous Roman wall.

To the east of the region, Route 1 continues its inexorable path up the North Sea coast from Kent to the tip of Scotland. The section from Newcastle to Edinburgh is known as the Coast and Castles route, taking in the magic of Lindisfarne (Holy Island) and providing an unforgettable journey. Other longer routes include the White Rose Cycle Route north from Hull, through the Vale of York and along the fringes of the North York Moors to Middlesbrough. From here, riders can continue northwards to Newcastle along the Three Rivers route.

The following pages are full of ideas for exploring the North of England. Whether you want to get to work or the local shops in Liverpool, coast around a seaside resort in Yorkshire or spot rare red squirrels in the quiet woodlands of Northumberland, your bike will get you there on the National Cycle Network.

▼ *Burnley-Colne canal path.*

John Grimshaw's
HIGHLIGHTS

Terris Novalis sculpture by Tony Cragg
This marks the site of a once great enterprise – the Consett steelworks, in its heyday the largest in Europe and which provided some of the steel for the Sydney Harbour Bridge. At the junction of four railway paths, the sculpture takes the form of a theodilite and a level - the two surveying instruments which marked out the industrial revolution and our urban lives today.

The Lancaster Lune Bridge
Truly unites the city with its neighbours north of the river. This striking bridge is a brilliant example of the bold action needed to turn around cycling.

The Mersey Ferry
Remains the best way of seeing Liverpool and Birkenhead and grasping the scale of the seaway around which this great port was built.

The Lindisfarne tidal causeway
The longest tidal crossing on the Network - there is no closer way of touching the sea. This is the centrepiece of the altogether memorable coastal part of the Coast & Castles Route, from Berwick to Whitley Bay.

The York Millennium Bridge
Another example of tipping the balance of travel in favour of cycling. This links together 20 years of route construction in York by Sustrans.

Summit
In this case the summit of the Rochdale Canal. Summits are always highlights and this one is called Summit! It reveals an unexpected cleft through the Pennines avoiding the need for a tunnel.

Keswick boardwalk
Fifty tonnes of English Oak around a beech-clad promontory were needed to bridge the gap in the Keswick and Threlkeld railway route, previously severed by the construction of the A66 viaduct above.

▼ *The Terris Novalis sculpture on the C2C route.*

North of England Family Rides

**The Longendale Trail.
6.5 miles. Route 62**
This short, traffic-free route along a valley from Hadfield station offers fine views of the Longendale Valley, making a great family ride. The trail runs to the south of a series of reservoirs (Bottoms, Rhodeswood, Torside and Woodhead), which formed the world's largest artificial expanse of water when created in 1877. Look out for the mysterious, eerie flickering lights, which have been seen for centuries and have come to be known as 'The Devil's Bonfire'. Facilities are available at the beginning of the ride.

**Middlewood Way -
Macclesfield to Marple.
10 miles. Route 55**
The Middlewood Way is a traffic-free ride taking in Macclesfield's rich industrial heritage, as well as lovely views of the Peak District. Starting in Macclesfield, famed for its silk industry, you pick up the route at the main station, following the Route 55 signs to the start of the railway path. You follow the route through the village of Bollington, set among attractive hills in the Cheshire countryside. During the ride you overlook the Macclesfield Canal, one of the last narrow canals to be built in Britain, as you proceed on towards Middlewood and finally, the village of Marple.

**Calder Valley Cycleway -
Sowerby Bridge Station to
Warland. 13 miles. Route 66**
Enjoy the splendid West Yorkshire scenery on this ride, which takes in the restored Rochdale Canal path and quiet roads. The cycleway takes you from Sowerby's picturesque canal boat lined wharf to Mytholmroyd, birthplace of the poet Ted Hughes. From here you pedal on through the vibrant town of Hebden Bridge. Look out for aliens at Todmorden, which has been the site of countless reported UFO sightings! From here, cyclists follow the route to its restful conclusion at the pub at Warland.

**Fallowfield Loop Line -
Chorlton cum Hardy to
Debdale. 6.5 miles. Regional
routes 55, 6 and 66**
This ride is the perfect tonic to Manchester's busy urban surroundings, providing ideal family cycling - and access to relaxing green

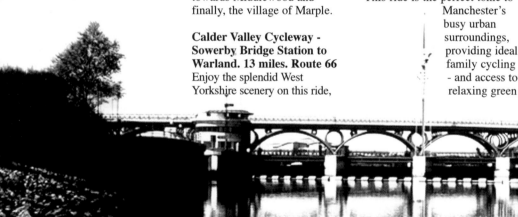

spaces. The Fallowfield Loop Line is a high quality and popular traffic-free route which winds its way through southern Manchester, creating an important wildlife habitat as well as a perfect place for youngsters to learn and practise their bike skills. For commuters, shoppers and families alike, this is a brilliant way to get about the city to local centres, schools, shops, workplaces, parks and other amenities.

Dunford Bridge to Penistone. 6 miles. Route 62

Following the River Don, this traffic-free path along a disused railway is an easy way to experience the Pennines. Starting at the village of Dunford Bridge, the ride cuts through some wild and remote open moorland, yet involves fairly easy cycling to access such breathtaking countryside. The ride ends at Penistone, a Pennine market town with 13th century church and 18th century remnants of the cotton industry, plus a smattering of cafes, pubs and restaurants. If

you're feeling game, you can opt to carry on to Wharncliffe wood and follow the forest trails towards Sheffield.

Harland Way - Wetherby to Spofforth. 3 miles. Route 66

This short, traffic-free and child-friendly ride explores the attractive open farmland and wooded railway cutting which make up the Harland Way. Wetherby's attractive medieval centre creates an interesting and historic setting in which to start the excursion, while at Spofforth there's a castle to visit not far off the route, home of the Percy family since Norman times. Refreshments are readily available at each end of the ride, and there's also a short optional extension to the route southeast of Wetherby, which is planned to link to Tadcaster and York.

Blackburn to Accrington. 7 miles. Route 6

This route provides a refreshing, fun and traffic-free option for cyclists and walkers travelling between these two Lancashire towns. Starting at

Blackburn station, you pick up the revitalised Leeds and Liverpool canal (Britain's longest canal) and quickly find yourself in a different world. This tranquil waterway was once used to transport raw cotton to the area's mills and factories. Soon you ride into open countryside and are treated to great views of the surrounding Pennine hills, before entering Accrington, the somewhat unlikely birthplace of Butch Cassidy!

Aire Valley towpath - Leeds to Saltaire. 14 miles. Route 66

This traffic-free ride along the canal towpath forms a great, green route out of Leeds (please always show consideration to other towpath users). Starting at the canal basin, you soon pass the evocative ruins of the 12th century Kirkstall Abbey, (its museum features a reconstruction of the streets of 1880s Leeds). Continue through beautiful countryside to the World Heritage Site at

▼ *Tees Barrage.*

Saltaire, a village built by Victorian philanthropist Sir Titus Salt to create model housing for his mill workers. Saltaire also houses the Salts Mill art gallery (a 'must' for David Hockney fans), shops and restaurants.

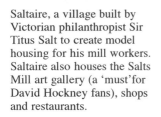

▼ Berwick-upon-Tweed.

Six Bridges Route - Stockton to Middlesbrough.
8 miles. Routes 1 and 14

What a great way to get around between Stockton and Middlesbrough! This circular and mostly traffic-free route is brilliant for regular journeys, and if you've time on your hands, is a fascinating way to appreciate the regeneration of the area. The Tees Barrage has become a catalyst for the transformation of derelict land along the river, and as you'll see on your ride along this green retreat, the scheme has generated attractive waterside developments along new canals, a stream, a lake and the riverside.

Whitby to Scarborough.
18 miles. Route 1

This is a spectacular ride, suitable for families ready for a bit of a challenge - the path's a little rough in places (mountain bikes recommended). From Whitby, the railway path takes you over some wondrous open moorland and coast, along Robin Hood's Bay and on to the famous resort of Scarborough. Explore the cobbled streets of Robin Hood's Bay (also a great place for rock pools and fossil hunting), before continuing to the delights of Scarborough's Victorian seafront - and a well-earned cup of tea!

Haltwhistle to Lambley Viaduct. 4.5 miles. Route 72

Starting from Haltwhistle station, this delightful ride takes you along an old railway line through woodland, quiet villages and upland meadows. Look out for red squirrels, rare now in England but still present in this beautiful corner of Northumberland. This mainly traffic-free route includes some gentle gradients,

but refreshments are available at Rowfoot's Wallace Arms pub. At Coanwood, you can opt to follow the signs to the South Tynedale narrow gauge railway at Alston, or continue on the railway path to traverse the amazing Lambley Viaduct, which stands 110 feet above the River South Tyne.

▲ Crossing Lambley Viaduct on the South Tyne Trail.

▼ Mother and child sculpture in Blackburn.

Keswick to Threlkeld. 3 miles. Route 71

This is an easy, traffic-free family ride through the beautiful, tree-clad Greta Gorge. The ride begins by Keswick's swimming pool and follows the old Cockermouth, Keswick and Penrith railway. A series of eight bridges engineered by Thomas Bouch, designer of the ill-fated Tay Bridge, take the route across the River Greta. Keswick is a thriving holiday and outdoor activities venue surrounded by stunning fells and lakes, whilst Threlkeld offers distractions such as a quarry and mining museum. The more adventurous can continue on a round trip back to Keswick via Castlerigg Stone Circle.

CHESTER TO HAWARDEN BRIDGE AND CONNAH'S QUAY

Chester is a town ringed by medieval walls with fragments dating back to Saxon and even Roman times. Opposite the centre is the site of the Roman amphitheatre; and Roman archaeological finds, as well as displays on local history, can be seen at the Grosvenor Museum. There is a cyclepath along the towpath of the Shopshire Union Canal that links the centre of town to the railway path, an attractive open ride taking you from the north side of Chester out into the Wirral's rich farmlands, planted with potatoes, maize and grain. The Mickle Trafford to Dee Marsh railway line once carried steel to and from the steelworks on the banks of the Dee at Hawarden Bridge. Wide open railway paths like these are great for side-by-side conversations with no traffic to worry about, and good visibility enables you to be aware of other path users whether on bike or on foot. Away in the distance are the Clwyd Hills. The ride crosses the tidal River Dee via Hawarden Bridge and ends on the south bank of the river opposite the Corus Steelworks. In the near future Route 5 will be completed along the north coast of Wales and will run west all the way from Chester to Anglesey.

Starting points
The railway path starts to the northeast of Chester city centre. Turn off the A56 Hoole Road about one mile after Chester railway station onto Fairfield Road. This crosses the old railway line after about 400 yards. The wharf at Connah's Quay, about one mile west of Hawarden Bridge and the railway stations at Hawarden Bridge and Shotton.

Distance
8 miles.

Grade
Easy.

Surface
Tarmac.

▼ *Wide open railway paths are great for side-by-side conversations.*

Roads, traffic, suitability for young children
All traffic-free and flat. You will need to negotiate roads to go in search of refreshments in Connah's Quay.

Hills
None.

Refreshments
Nothing on the route itself. Lots of choice just off the route on the waymarked link to the city centre, for example Telford's Warehouse PH at the end of the canal towpath.

Nearest railway stations
Chester, Hawarden Bridge, Shotton.

The National Cycle Network in the area
Route 5 uses this ride on its way along the north coast of Wales from Anglesey to Stoke on Trent.

Other nearby rides (waymarked or traffic-free)
1. There are waymarked woodland rides in Delamere Forest Park to the east of Chester.
2. The Whitegate Way is a railway path just a little further east from Delamere.

▶ *Along the canalside in Chester.*

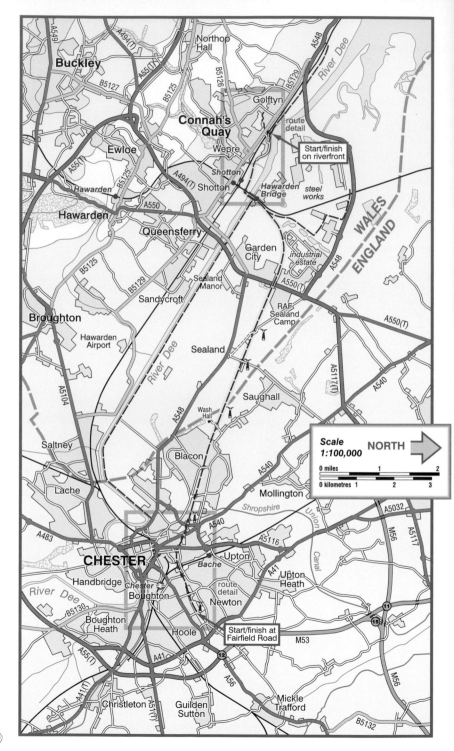

► *One of the painted mileposts along the route, this one is three miles from Connah's Quay.*

CONNAH'S QUAY
route detail

Golftyn

Start/finish on riverfront

Wepre

Shotton

Shotton

Hawarden Bridge

RIVER DEE

CHESTER
route detail

Chester tourist attractions include: Chester Abbey, City Walls, Roman Ampitheatre and Chester Castle Museum

Hoole

Newton

Start/finish at Fairfield Road

Bache

Boughton

Chester

City Walls

Abbey

189

SPEN VALLEY GREENWAY BETWEEN BRADFORD AND DEWSBURY

A quick look at an Ordnance Survey map of the area would give you no indication of this wonderful hidden green corridor running along the course of an old railway line. It is one of those self-contained rides, floating above the urban areas and heavy industry that lies to either side. There is also a fine sense of humour evident along the course of the route with signs shaped like bicycle pedals, a chair made of old digger parts, 'road'signs warning of 'blossom opening', and a flock of sheep formed from recycled industrial machine parts. There is a

signposted cycle route from the city hall and railway station in Bradford city centre through Bowling Park and along Bierley Lane to join the start of the Spen Valley Greenway in Oakenshaw. The ride travels gently downhill through a golf course past verges of willowherb, elderflower, clover and campion, seemingly over the top of Cleckheaton, Liversedge and Heckmondwike and finishes by following a riverside path along the River Calder to Dewsbury town centre.

Starting points
Bradford City Hall.
Green Lane, Oakenshaw.
Dewsbury Health Centre, Mill Street West, Dewsbury Town Centre.

Distance
12 miles.

Grade
Easy to moderate.

Surface
Tarmac or good stone path.

Roads, traffic, suitability for young children
There are several roads to negotiate between Bradford centre and the start of the Spen Valley Greenway in Oakenshaw. The best bit for families is the 7-mile section

from Oakenshaw south to the Calder & Hebble Navigation. There is one busy road crossing at the southern end to arrive in the centre of Dewsbury.

Hills
There are a few moderate climbs from Bradford to

the start of the Spen Valley Greenway, then a gentle descent from Oakenshaw to Dewsbury.

Refreshments
Although the Spen Valley Greenway passes very close to or even through built-up

◀ *A ram looks on in Sally Matthews 'We all walk the same path'.*

areas, almost all the refreshment opportunities lie off the path as it crosses streets via railway bridges or beneath road bridges.
Lots of choice in Bradford, Cleckheaton, Heckmondwicke and Dewsbury.

Nearest railway stations
Bradford, Dewsbury, Ravensthorpe.

The National Cycle Network in the area
Route 66 runs its zig zag course from York to Leeds, northwest to Shipley then south through Bradford to Dewsbury before turning west again along the Calder Valley.

▼ *Jason Lane created seats, marker posts and entrance gateways from local scrap material.*

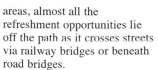

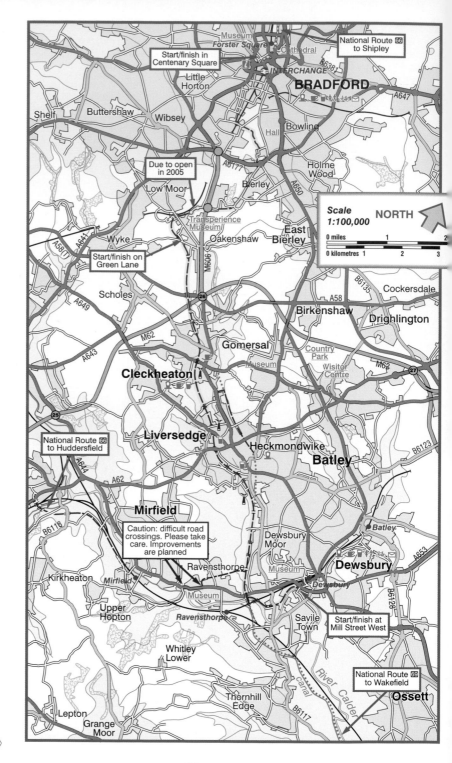

SPEN VALLEY GREENWAY
BETWEEN BRADFORD AND DEWSBURY

Museum
Forster Square
National Route 66 to Shipley
Cathedral
INTERCHANGE
Start/finish in Centenary Square
BRADFORD
A6381
A647
Little Horton
Shelf
Buttershaw
Wibsey
Bowling
Holme Wood
Hall
A6177
A650
Due to open in 2005
Low Moor
Bierley
Transperience Museum
East Bierley
Wyke
Oakenshaw
Start/finish on Green Lane
M606
Scale 1:100,000

NORTH

0 miles 1 2
0 kilometres 1 2 3

Scholes
B6135
Cockersdale
A58
Birkenshaw
Drighlington
M62
Gomersal
Country Park
Museum
Visitor Centre
M62
Cleckheaton
Liversedge
National Route 66 to Huddersfield
Heckmondwike
Batley
B6123
Batley
Mirfield
Caution: difficult road crossings. Please take care. Improvements are planned
Dewsbury Moor
Ravensthorpe
Museum
Dewsbury
A653
Kirkheaton
Mirfield
Museum
Dewsbury
B6128
Upper Hopton
Ravensthorpe
Savile Town
Start/finish at Mill Street West
Whitley Lower
River Calder
National Route 69 to Wakefield
Ossett
Lepton
Thornhill Edge
Grange Moor
B6117

192

Other nearby rides (waymarked or traffic-free)
There are two long traffic-free trails either side of Leeds:
1. The Leeds & Liverpool Canal northwest to Shipley.
2. The Aire & Calder Navigation southeast to Woodlesford.
3. Further south there are many traffic-free sections of the Trans Pennine Trail close to Barnsley.

> **Use the on-line mapping at www.sustrans.org.uk to find other National Cycle Network routes near you.**

▲ *Mothers with their young children at Heckmondwike.*

▼ *Cycling through 'Rotate' by Trudi Entwistle.*

ROUTES OUT OF LANCASTER: MORECAMBE AND THE CROOK O'LUNE

Reflecting the city's maritime heritage, the Millennium Bridge in the heart of Lancaster is the centrepiece of the city's cycle network and stands on the location of the first bridge over the River Lune. You have a choice of rides from this point: to the west, a railway path popular with commuters and children walking to school runs through a largely urban area to the railway station in Morecambe, from where it is just a short ride on quiet streets to the seafront. To the north of Lancaster's Millennium Bridge, Route 6 follows the Lancaster Canal towards Kendal. To the northeast, the ride described here follows the lovely majestic River Lune through mixed woodland and a riot of wildflowers beneath the mighty stone aqueduct carrying the canal, beneath the M6 motorway bridge, then twice crosses the river at the Crook o'Lune, where the river describes a U-shaped bend between Halton and Caton. Along the way are interpretation boards with details of birds you may see along the river, and historical facts - for example William Turner painted here.

Starting points
Morecambe railway station.
The Millennium Bridge in Lancaster.
Crook o'Lune picnic site.

▼ *Signposts for Route 6 in Lancaster.*

Distance
Morecambe to Lancaster - 3 miles.
Lancaster to Crook o'Lune - 5 miles.

Grade
Easy.

Surface
Tarmac or fine gravel path.

Roads, traffic, suitability for young children
Ideal for children, with no dangerous road crossings.

Hills
None,

Refreshments
Lots of choice in Morecambe and Lancaster,
Pubs just off the route in Halton and Caton,

Nearest railway stations
Morecambe or Lancaster,

The National Cycle Network in the area
Route 6 passes through Lancaster on its way from Preston to Kendal with links to the centre of Lancaster to Morecambe and Caton

(described here). Route 62 runs close to the coast southwest to Fleetwood and Blackpool; Route 72 explores South Lakeland on its way to Barrow; further east, the Pennine Cycleway links Settle to Appleby-in-Westmorland.

Other nearby rides (waymarked or traffic-free)
1. There is another traffic-free trail that links Lancaster to Glasson following the River Lune out to Morecambe Bay.
2. The towpath of the Lancaster Canal can be followed through Lancaster and north to Carnforth (Route 6).

3. The Lancashire Cycleway uses Regional Routes 90 and 91 to link Carnforth, Lancaster and Blackpool, and circle the Forest of Bowland on a 260-mile ride.

> **To find out about other cycle routes in this area visit www.sustrans.org.uk**

▼ *River Lune Bridge in Morecambe, The Millennium Bridge is the centrepiece of the Lune Millennium Park, an environmental upgrade project.*

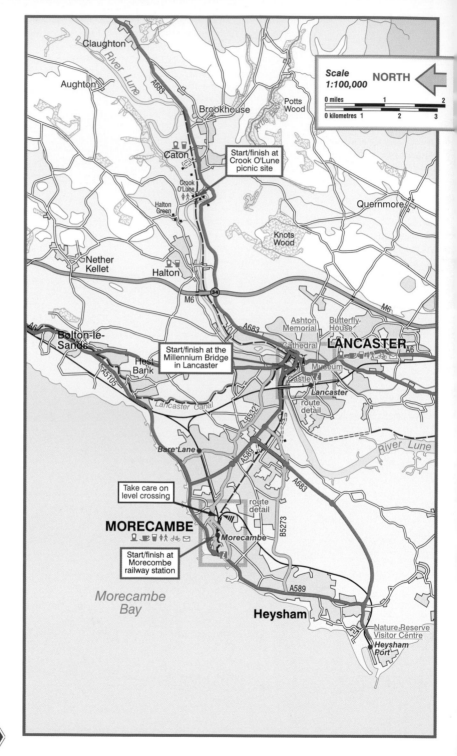

▼ *An attractive path beside Morecambe Road approaching the Lune Millennium Bridge in Lancaster.*

MORECAMBE
route detail

Morecambe tourist attractions include: Morecambe Prom. and Morecambe Winter Gardens

Start/finish at Morecombe railway station

OUT MOSS LANE
EUSTON ROAD
CENTRAL DRIVE
B5274
A589 MARINE ROAD CENTRAL
WOODHILL LANE
Morecambe
ACRE MOSS LANE
WEST END ROAD
BALMORAL ROAD
ELLESMERE ROAD
MARINE RD CENTRAL

LANCASTER
route detail

A683 A6 CATON RD
A6
A683
A6 THURNHAM ST
A6 OWEN ROAD
A589 MORECAMBE ROAD
GREYHOUND BRIDGE RD
CABLE ST
Start/finish at the Millennium Bridge in Lancaster
RIVER LUNE
ST GEO'S Q.
Castle
Lancaster
MEETING HSE LA.
DALLAS ROAD

Lancaster tourist attractions include: Lancaster Castle, Lancaster City Museum and Lancaster Maritime Museum.

Camerton to Workington, Whitehaven and Cleator Moor in West Cumbria

The C2C (Sea to Sea), the most famous of all the long distance cycle routes on the National Cycle Network, has two starting points on the west coast of Cumbria: Workington and Whitehaven. This ride links these two towns and explores the first few miles of both options: from Workington northeast to the end of the traffic-free path at Camerton, and from Whitehaven southeast towards the edge of the fells at Cleator Moor. With easy access from the train, Whitehaven harbour is an attractive start / finish point for both rides offering a choice of trips: gently uphill towards Cleator Moor along the railway path, which starts on the outskirts of the town, to the very edge of the Lake District National Park with ever better views of the mountains ahead; OR north along the coast on a newly created cyclepath parallel with the existing railway, which soon joins an old mineral railway line running almost unbroken to Workington. After crossing the bridge over the River Derwent on the northern edge of town, another railway path is followed uphill through ever more lush countryside to Camerton, where there is a chance of stopping for refreshments then turning around, or of continuing along the C2C route to the handsome town of Cockermouth.

Starting points
Camerton, northeast of Workington. The railway path starts from beneath the road towards Flimby.
Workington, by the footbridge over the River Derwent, just off the A596 North Side Road (near Brow Top car park).
The harbour in Whitehaven.

Distance
5 miles from Camerton to Workington.
9 miles from Workington to Whitehaven.
4 miles from Whitehaven to Cleator Moor.

Grade
Moderate.

Surface
Tarmac.

Roads, traffic, suitability for young children
From Camerton to Whitehaven is almost all railway path or specially built cyclepath. The best section for families is from Mirehouse Road on the

southern edge of Whitehaven to Cleator Moor (and beyond).

Hills
There is a gentle descent from Camerton to Workington. There are a few gentle ups and downs between Workington and Whitehaven, then a steady climb up to Cleator Moor from Whitehaven.

Refreshments
Black Tom Inn, Camerton. Lots of choice in Workington. Lots of choice in Whitehaven. Cafe and pubs just off the route in Cleator Moor.

Nearest railway stations
Workington or Whitehaven.

The National Cycle Network in the area
The C2C has two options at its start:
1. Workington to Cockermouth and Bassenthwaite Lake.
2. Whitehaven to Rowrah, Lorton Vale and Whinlatter Forest.
The routes join to the west of Keswick.

Other nearby rides (waymarked or traffic-free)
1. Traffic-free trails along the shores of Ennerdale Water.
2. Waymarked woodland routes in Whinlatter Forest.
3. The Keswick Railway Path to Threlkeld.

▲ *An underpass avoids a busy road crossing.*

▼ *Bridge Parapet by Alan Dawson.*

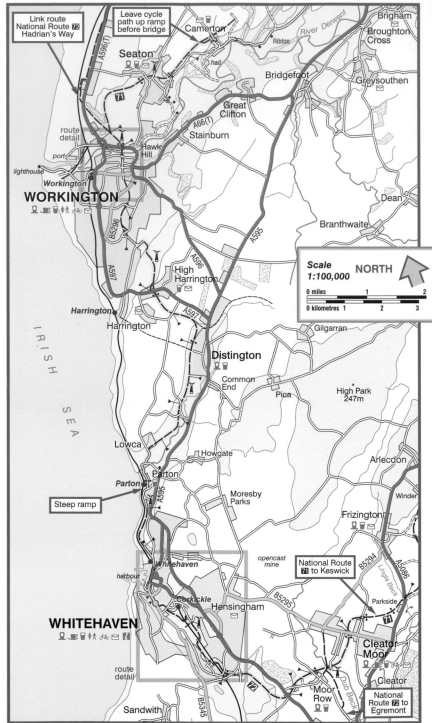

CAMERTON TO WORKINGTON, WHITEHAVEN AND CLEATOR MOOR IN WEST CUMBRIA

200

▼ *Steel Route Images by Richard Farrington showing different types of transport.*

WHITEHAVEN
route detail
Whitehaven tourist attractions include: The Beacon Centre.

Whitehaven

harbour

Corkickle

1 NEW TOWN
2 PRESTON STREET
3 JAMES STREET
4 MARKET PLACE
5 SWINGPUMP LANE
6 STRAND STREET
7 EAST STRAND
8 ALBION STREET

1 CROASDALE AVENUE
2 NEWLANDS AVENUE

WORKINGTON
route detail
Workington tourist attractions include:
Helena Thompson Museum.

Workington

SELBY TO BENINGBROUGH

A peaceful route on railway paths, alongside rivers and on quiet lanes which takes in the beautiful walled city of York on its way to Beningbrough.

From the market town of Selby, with its ancient abbey church, the route follows the River Ouse, then joins quiet roads to Barlby and Ricall. At Ricall, the route joins the popular railway path all the way to York's famous Knavesmire race course.

You then go through historic York to Beningbrough, crossing the grazed Rawcliffe Meadows. You will pass several curious sculptures - seats that look like horse-drawn carriages and farm implements, a weather vane with a bicycle and dog, and a metalwork globe with depictions of York Cathedral and the city's wall.

Beningbrough Hall - a National Trust property - offers a view of life in an English country house from Georgian to Victorian times.

Starting points
Selby Station.
York Station (if chosing a shorter section of the ride).
Beningbrough Hall.

Distance
24 miles one way; 15 miles from Selby to York and another 9 miles from York to Beningbrough

Grade
Easy.

Surface
Tarmac cycle paths and quiet lanes.

Roads, traffic, suitability for young children
Mainly traffic-free and flat; short sections on quiet lanes in Ricall and Barlby. The last five miles, from Overton to Beningbrough, follow quiet country lanes. Cycle facilities throughout York are excellent and children could easily manage a ride in either direction from there.

Hills
None.

Refreshments
Lots of choice in Selby and York; also try Riccall and Bishopthorpe.
The Sidings Hotel & Restaurant, Shipton (open for coffee, lunch, tea).
The cafe at Beningbrough Hall is open from Easter to October.
Downay Arms pub, Blacksmith Arms pub, Newton-on-Ouse (just beyond Beningbrough).

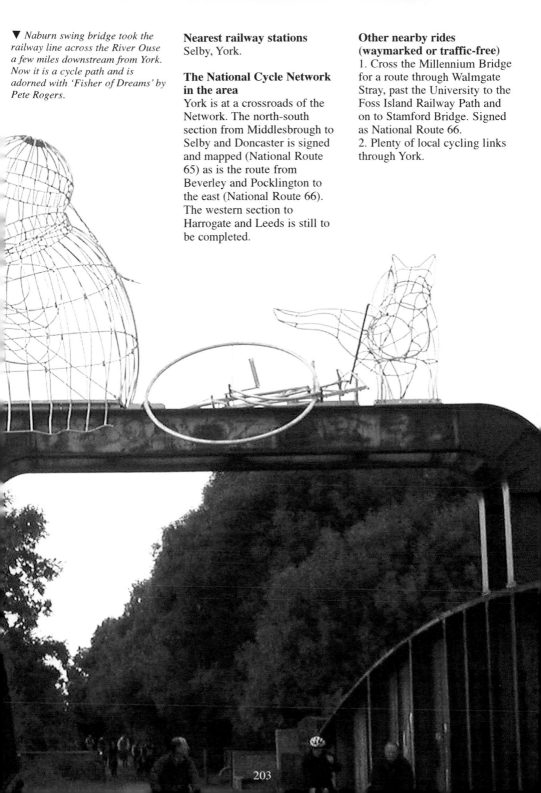

▼ *Naburn swing bridge took the railway line across the River Ouse a few miles downstream from York. Now it is a cycle path and is adorned with 'Fisher of Dreams' by Pete Rogers.*

Nearest railway stations
Selby, York.

The National Cycle Network in the area
York is at a crossroads of the Network. The north-south section from Middlesbrough to Selby and Doncaster is signed and mapped (National Route 65) as is the route from Beverley and Pocklington to the east (National Route 66). The western section to Harrogate and Leeds is still to be completed.

Other nearby rides (waymarked or traffic-free)
1. Cross the Millennium Bridge for a route through Walmgate Stray, past the University to the Foss Island Railway Path and on to Stamford Bridge. Signed as National Route 66.
2. Plenty of local cycling links through York.

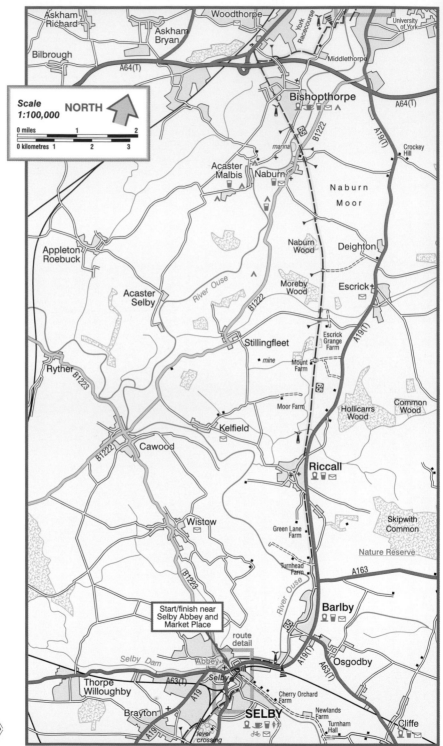

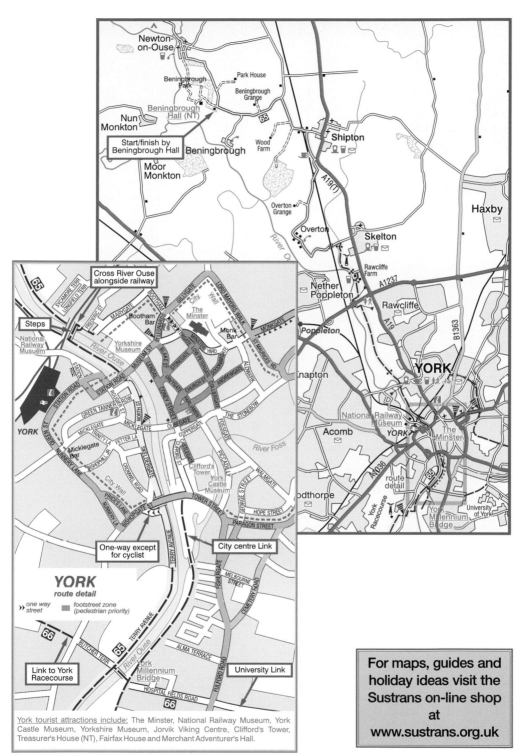

Newton-on-Ouse

Park House

Beningbrough Park

Beningbrough Grange

Nun Monkton

Beningbrough Hall (NT)

Start/finish by Beningbrough Hall

Beningbrough

Wood Farm

Moor Monkton

Shipton

Overton Grange

Overton

Skelton

Haxby

Rawcliffe Farm

Nether Poppleton

Rawcliffe

A1237

A19

B1363

Poppleton

Knapton

YORK

Acomb

National Railway Museum

YORK

The Minster

route detail

A1036

...dthorpe

York Racecourse

York Millennium Bridge

York Castle Museum

University of York

Cross River Ouse alongside railway

SYCAMORE TERR
LONGFIELD TERR

MARYGATE

Steps

FREDERIC ST

Bootham Bar

National Railway Museum

River Ouse

Yorkshire Museum

STATION ROAD

STATION RD

QUEEN ST

YORK

GREEN

TANNER ROW

MICKLEGATE

Micklegate Bar

TRINITY LA

FETTER LA

BISHOPHILL JR

CROMWELL ROAD

City Wall

PRICE'S LANE

NUNNERY LA

BISHOPGATE ST

TERRY AVENUE

BOOTHAM

GILLYGATE

LORD MAYORS WALK

The Minster

City Wall

Monk Bar

MONKGATE

ST MAURICE'S RD

ST LEONARD'S

MUSEUM ST

BLAKE ST

CONEY STREET

DEANGATE

MINSTER YARD

GOODRAMGATE

ALDWARK

SKELDERGATE

OUSEGATE

COPPERGATE

PICCADILLY

CLIFFORD ST

FOSSGATE

WALMGATE

River Foss

Clifford's Tower

York Castle Museum

GEORGE STREET

HOPE STREET

PARAGON STREET

CEMETERY ROAD

MELBOURNE STREET

One-way except for cyclist

City centre Link

TOWER STREET

YORK
route detail

⟩⟩ one way street

■ footstreet zone (pedestrian priority)

FISHERGATE

Link to York Racecourse

BUTCHER TERR

River Ouse

York Millennium Bridge

ALMA TERRACE

FULFORD ROAD

HOSPITAL FIELDS ROAD

University Link

York tourist attractions include: The Minster, National Railway Museum, York Castle Museum, Yorkshire Museum, Jorvik Viking Centre, Clifford's Tower, Treasurer's House (NT), Fairfax House and Merchant Adventurer's Hall.

Consett to Sunderland

In its entirety it would be a very long, although immensely satisfying, day to ride from Consett to Sunderland and back again (52 miles). It is a ride that is best split into shorter sections, for example Consett to the Beamish Open Air Museum, or from the museum to the Washington Wildfowl & Wetlands Centre, or from the wetlands centre to the finish at the North Sea Coast. The ride is one of the two finishing options for the Sea to Sea (C2C) cycle route, the most popular long distance challenge on the whole of the National Cycle Network. For those of you just wishing to try out a short stretch of the famous ride it is worth bearing in mind that cycling downhill towards Sunderland with the prevailing westerly wind behind you is considerably easier than cycling uphill into the wind, so plan accordingly. The ride is a mixture of railway path, specially built cyclepath, a few short sections of quiet roads and a splendid finish along the Stadium of Light riverside route on the banks of the River Wear, past the National Glass Centre to the new marina and the coast. There are sculptures all along the way, from the mighty shining Terris Novalis surveying instruments with animal feet at Consett to the metal transformers with faces, the scrap metal cows and then a whole series of artworks along the riverside path down to the marina in Sunderland.

Starting points

Lydgetts Junction to the south of Consett (just off the A692 Castleside road).
Sunderland Marina.

Distance

26 miles.

Grade

Easy on the eastbound downhill ride to Sunderland. Moderate on the westbound uphill ride to Consett.

Surface

Tarmac or good quality gravel path.

Roads, traffic, suitability for young children

Although the ride is almost entirely traffic-free, there are several roads to cross between Consett and Stanley. The longest unbroken railway path section is between Annfield Plain and the James Steel Park in Washington. Between Washington and the Stadium of Light in Sunderland the route is a mixture of paths, roads and shared-use pavements. From the Stadium of Light to the coast is a wide, open, traffic-free promenade alongside the river past a series of sculptures.

Hills

There are some short but steep hills climbing out of the Wear Valley, and from Chester-le-Street to Annfield Plain the railway climbs at a steady 1:50. Together with a prevailing westerly wind, it would be advisable to calculate taking (at least) twice as long cycling westbound as eastbound.

▼ *The busy Sunderland Marina. The ride through the marina is stunning.*

Refreshments
Lots of choice in Sunderland.
Snow Goose Cafe by the
Sunderland marina.
Cafe in the National Glass
Centre on the riverside
promenade.
Shipwrights PH on the route to
the southeast of Washington.
Cafe in the Washington
Wetlands Centre (no need to
pay an entry fee if you just
want to use the cafe).
Mary Inn, Beamish (just off
the route).
Jolly Drovers PH, Leadgate
roundabout.
Lots of choice just off the
route in Chester-le-Street,
Stanley, Annfield Plain and
Consett.

Nearest railway stations
Sunderland, Chester-le-Street,
about one mile south of the
route.

▶ *King Cole by David Kemp.*

The National Cycle Network in the area
Lydgetts Junction, Consett is an
important crossroads of the
National Cycle Network with
traffic-free paths extending in
all directions. To the north lies
Route 14, the Derwent Valley
Trail, leading towards
Newcastle and one of the
options for finishing the C2C
route; to the east lies the
Consett and Sunderland
railway path, described in this
ride; to the southeast the
Lanchester Valley Walk (Route
14) links to Durham; to the
southwest the Waskerley Way
(Route 7) climbs high into the
Pennines as the C2C route
heads towards Cumbria. At the
eastern end of the ride,
Sunderland also lies on
Route 1 as it travels up the
coast from Middlesbrough to
Newcastle and then up the
Northumbrian coast to
Berwick, the Scottish Borders
and Edinburgh.

To find out about other
cycle routes in this
area visit
www.sustrans.org.uk

207

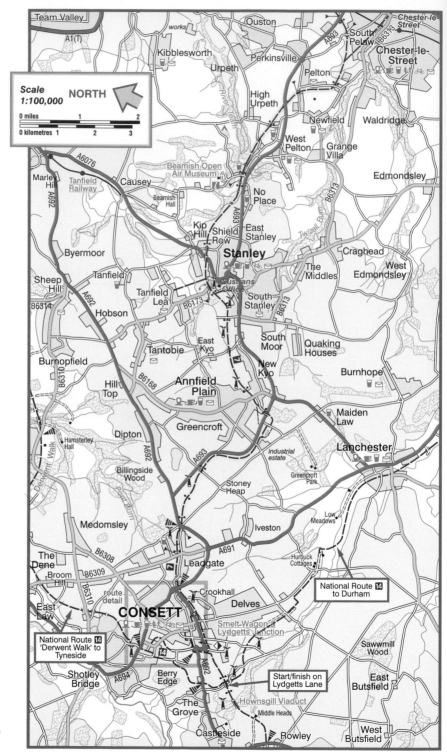

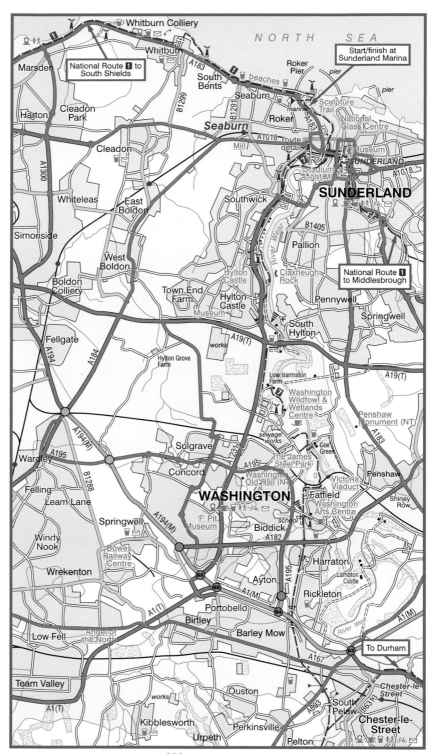

SHETLANDS ISLANDS

1. Dalkieth to Penicuik
2. Paisley & Clyde Railway Path
3. Clydebank to Loch Lomond
4. Water of Leith & Union Canal
5. Millennium Link
6. Clyde Corridor Cycle Route
7. Ayrshire Coast Cycleway
8. Aberfoyle to Callander
9. Tentsmuir Forest
10. Perth to Almond Bank
11. Cunninghame Cycleway
12. Aviemore to Boat of Garten
13. Haymarket, Edinburgh – Forth Road Bridge
14. Airdrie to Bathgate
15. Paisley to Kilbirnie
16. Tayport to Broughty Ferry, Dundee
17. Callander – Killin

————	National Cycle Network traffic-free routes
————	National Cycle Network on road routes
————	National Cycle Network future routes
3	National Route Numbers
10	Regional route numbers
O	Towns with railway stations
O	Towns without railway stations
12	Regional ride numbers

SCOTLAND

Scotland is the most mountainous and spectacular region in the United Kingdom, with mile upon mile of breathtaking scenery, and many remote and unspoilt places. If it's amazing scenery you're after, the National Cycle Network will take you there on a mixture of forest tracks, riverside and lochside paths, dismantled railways and quiet roads. In Scotland, the Network will also take you through famous towns and cities, past castles, alongside legendary lochs and world famous golf courses, and by everything from rare wildlife to the remains of Scotland's shipbuilding and industrial heritage.

Because Scotland's population is concentrated in the Glasgow-Edinburgh corridor, much of the rest of the country is sparsely inhabited - ideal territory for exploring by bike. Many roads here are much quieter than their English counterparts, enabling safe rides on B-roads and in some cases even A-roads, except in the peak holiday period. As you would expect, Scotland's two principal cities are both well served by the Network. National Route 1 (the North Sea Cycle Route) links Edinburgh south to the English border at Berwick-upon-Tweed, and north to John o'Groats (and the Orkney and Shetland Islands by ferry)

via Dundee, Aberdeen and Inverness. National Route 7, the Lochs and Glens Cycle Route, links Glasgow south to the English border at Gretna, and north to Inverness via Callander, Pitlochry, and Aviemore. Glasgow and Edinburgh are connected by the east-west oriented National Route 75, the Clyde to Forth Cycle Route.

Scotland is the perfect setting in which to experience cycling as it should be enjoyed - safely, and with that closeness to the outdoors which fills you with a sense of freedom and wellbeing. From the vibrant atmosphere of Glasgow to the architectural magnificence of Edinburgh; from the legacy of the Clyde shipbuilding industry to the majesty of the mountain scenery further north, the National Cycle Network provides the perfect vantage point.

▼ *Taking a break at Loch Garten.*

HIGHLIGHTS

John Grimshaw's

Glen Ogle

The whole of Route 7 from Callander to Killin is a tribute to the perseverance of Sustrans' Scottish team over years of negotiation. The result is a spectacular approach to the Highlands, avoiding the A85 main road throughout.

Forth Bridge and Tay Bridge

Two monumental highlights in any cycling journey.

The Big Water of Fleet Viaduct

Is just that – big. Route 7 passes under this abandoned structure, standing isolated miles and miles from anywhere.

Edinburgh

The cycling city of Scotland. It is a delight and a privilege just to be able to cycle here, let alone on such wonderful routes. The Meadows Path was an early achievement by the Spokes Cycling Campaign.

Loch Venachar

The site of one of Sustrans' most heroic summer workcamps, where, despite the rain and the midges, a beautiful waterside route was carved out by hand

to link Callander to Aberfoyle through the Queen Elizabeth Forest Park.

Bardrainney

If high points are summits, then the rock behind Bardrainney, above Port Glasgow, signals the start of the long downhill glide to Kilmacolm, Bridge of Weir, Paisley and Glasgow. In the other direction the railway route plummets down to the Clyde.

Orkney Ferry

Leaving the mainland for Orkney simply has to feature as a highlight. Reaching Scrabster at all is quite an achievement and going further, across the sea to Orkney, is even more memorable.

▼ *Enjoying the view from the old railway viaduct in Glen Ogle.*

SCOTLAND
FAMILY RIDES

Dalkeith to Penicuik.
8 miles. Regional Route 1
This attractive and mainly traffic-free ride can be reached from a number of towns, and also links to the Esk Valley route to Musselburgh. It takes you through some lovely Lothian countryside and shady wooded sections, and offers great views of the Pentland Hills. There are plenty of sites of historical interest just off the route, including the remains of Old Woodhouselee Castle, Roslin Chapel (supposed resting place of the Holy Grail), Wallace's Cave and the site of the bloody battle of Rosslyn Glen in 1302.

Paisley and Clyde Railway Path (Johnston to Greenock).
13.5 miles. Route 75
This is a varied and rewarding family route - almost entirely traffic-free with no difficult road crossings - with lots to see and plenty of amenities along the way. Open countryside beckons from the fringes of Glasgow, taking you to the Firth of Clyde to admire the sweeping views. At Port Glasgow you'll find hidden gems such as Newark Castle, and experience the atmosphere of the working shipyard. There is a steep descent into

great ride is mainly traffic-free, and passes Glasgow's proud shipbuilding heritage, as well as interesting new projects like The Saltings Ecology Park. Utilising railway paths and the towpath of the Forth and Clyde Canal, the route takes you through Bowling and on minor roads into Dumbarton. From here, you follow a riverside path to Balloch and the southern shore of the majestic Loch Lomond. Those with children should note the occasional light-controlled road crossings that dissect the route.

Greenock. If the return journey seems too much, riders can opt to take the train back.

Clyde and Loch Lomond Cycleway. 20 miles. Route 7
Starting in Glasgow from the north side of Bell's Bridge, this

Water of Leith and Union Canal - Balerno to Edinburgh. 7 miles. Route 75
A mostly traffic-free and downhill ride. It e begins at Balerno High School (which can be reached via quiet roads from the stations at Curriehill or Kirknewton) where you

join the traffic-free railway path beside the Water of Leith. Keep your eyes peeled and you may glimpse a kingfisher or even an otter, as you scoot downhill with the city of Edinburgh spread out before you. At Colinton you follow the old railway line through a tunnel, and at Slateford aqueduct the route joins the Union Canal into Edinburgh.

The Millennium Link - Linlithgow to Falkirk. 10 miles. Route 76

Linlithgow to Falkirk on the Millennium Link is a wonderfully rural, traffic-free route along the Union Canal. In Linlithgow, you can visit the Linlithgow Canal Centre. Then, find your way to the northern side of the Union Canal and simply follow it westwards to Falkirk. It's a remarkable waterway, featuring stunning canal architecture including the 'smilin' and greetin' bridge', Scotland's longest waterway tunnel, and the magnificent Avon Aqueduct. Your journey ends in Falkirk at the spectacular Falkirk Wheel, the world's only rotating boat lift. You can reach this ride via the stations at Linlithgow, Polmont and Falkirk.

Clyde Corridor Cycle Route. 12 miles. Route 75

This high quality, traffic-free route follows the banks of the River Clyde from the heart of Glasgow's city centre out into the Lanarkshire countryside. You join the route at Bell's Bridge next to the Scottish Exhibition and Conference Centre, or at any point along the northern bank of the Clyde through the city centre. This route is great for easy, car-free access to the Science Centre, the People's Palace at Glasgow Green and many other central Glasgow tourist attractions. You can shorten the ride by picking-up the regular rail service from Carmyle, Cambuslang, Newton and Uddingston stations.

Ayrshire Coast Cycleway - Irvine and Troon to Prestwick and Ayr. 13 miles. Route 7

This popular route provides a great opportunity to explore Ayrshire's coastline. This is a largely flat and open section which offers wonderful views across the sea to the Isle of Arran. Starting at the Irvine Beach Park or the station, a smooth, traffic-free path takes you through two nature reserves, until a brief on-road section leads you to the coastline skirting Troon, and then along the edge of the world famous golf course. With the airport on your left, the route continues to Prestwick, running along the promenade to the centre of town and Ayr.

Aberfoyle to Callander. 13 miles. Route 7

This ride along forest tracks and minor roads between Aberfoyle and Callander takes you through a beautiful mountain forest and along the shore of Loch Venachar. Your rewards for the initial

◄ *Sculpture in Irvine.*

climb include the exhilarating descent, and you can also follow optional cycle paths within the forest to Loch Katrine and the village of Brig o' Turk.

The seasonal 'Trossachs Trundler' bus may be able to help transport you and your bike between Stirling and the ride's start and finish points. We recommend getting up-to-date information on this service before you travel - Tel: 01786 442707. Bikes can be hired from Aberfoyle and Callander.

Tentsmuir Forest. 5.5 miles plus links. Route 1

A fun, family friendly and traffic-free route through this dense, 'spooky' pine forest. From Leuchars Church you follow signs pointing north for Route 1, proceeding into the forest where, in medieval times, locals believed devils lurked! You ride close to the wildlife reserve at Tentsmuir Point, a gathering place for huge numbers of birds. Follow the route signs to the north west edge of the wood (ignoring the on-road signed route). Turn left, following the path until you emerge again at the lane, before retracing your steps on link routes to Leuchars or continuing to Tayport for the new path to the Tay Bridge and Dundee.

Perth to Almondbank. 5.5 miles. Route 77

This leisurely pedal to Almondbank weir is mainly traffic-free, and is punctuated by some impressive views. You begin the ride alongside the

◄ *This beautiful, single span bridge on General Wade's Military Road was constructed in the early 1830s, following the destruction of the previous bridge in a great flood in 1829.*

River Tay, Scotland's longest river, and follow it for nearly 2½ miles before turning alongside the River Almond. Your ride finishes at Almondbank, where the riverbank becomes more wooded, and salmon fishing is a popular pastime.

Cunninghame Cycleway. 9 miles. Route 73

This mainly traffic-free route offers a great way to get some exercise between Irvine and Kilmarnock. Picking up the path at Irvine's Tourist Information Centre or the station, the route follows the River Irvine until the start of the railway path at Dreghorn, where you emerge into open countryside. At the edge of Kilmarnock, a light-controlled crossing takes you over the road, and you then follow a short, signed road route to the town centre. Many families enjoy exploring Kilmarnock's Dean Castle Country Park,

whilst adults may fancy a visit to the whisky distillery for a 'wee dram'!

Aviemore to Boat of Garten. 5 miles. Route 7

Nature lovers will go really 'wild' on this stunning 5-mile route! The ride is almost entirely traffic-free, and offers unique wildlife spotting opportunities as you cross heather covered moorland, before reaching what's become known as the 'Osprey Village' at Boat of Garten. On this breathtaking route you'll be surrounded by spectacular mountain ranges and dense forests - and since you start and finish at either end of the Strathspey Railway, you can choose to return by steam train if anyone's legs are too tired. Refreshments are available at each end of the ride.

◀ *Union Canal, Edinburgh. Originally designed and built to transport coal into Edinburgh.*

EDINBURGH TO FORTH BRIDGE

Riding across the Forth Road Bridge must be one of the most extraordinary cycling experiences in Scotland. Hundreds of feet above the Firth of Forth, with views to the east of the magnificent Forth Rail Bridge (the one where, as the saying goes, they start painting at one end the moment they have finished at the other!) you can cross from South Queensferry to North Queensferry in complete traffic-free safety.

The crossing makes an exciting ride for children, though the route uses road sections in Haymarket, Dalmeny and North Queensferry.

Starting point
Haymarket Station, Edinburgh. Northern end of the Forth Road Bridge.

Distance
11 miles one way, 22 miles return.

Grade
Easy to moderate.

Surface
Tarmac.

Roads, traffic, suitability for young children
Quiet residential streets from Haymarket station car park are used until the start of the railway path. Care should be taken on the roads and crossings in Dalmeny. If you decide to visit North Queensferry, there is a road section from the cycle path on the bridge down to the village. The most exciting section for children is the crossing of the Forth Road Bridge itself, which has traffic-free cycle lanes on both sides.

Hills
Rolling.

Refreshments
Albert Hotel, Ferrybridge Hotel, Post Office Café, North Queensferry.
Cramond Brig Pub, Cramond. The tearoom in Dalmeny House is open on Sunday, Monday and Tuesday afternoons in July and August. The Forth Bridges Hotel, South Queensferry.
Various choices in South Queensferry village.

▶ *On the Forth Road Bridge during the Sustrans Route 76 Trailblazing Ride in 2003.*

Nearest railway stations
Edinburgh Haymarket,
Dalmeny and North
Queensferry.

**The National Cycle Network
in the area**
1. Route 75, the Clyde to Forth
Cycle Route runs across
Scotland from Gourock to
Leith.
2. Route 1 northbound connects
Edinburgh with St Andrews and
Dundee and continues along the
coast to Aberdeen and
Inverness.
3. Route 1 southbound is the
Coast and Castles Route which
runs from Edinburgh to
Dalkeith then south through the
Scottish Borders to Berwick-
upon-Tweed to follow the
coast to Newcastle upon Tyne.
4. Still under development,
Route 76 runs from Edinburgh
to Stirling around both sides
of the Forth Estuary.

**Other nearby rides
(waymarked or traffic-free)**
There are many traffic-free
trails in or near Edinburgh,
such as the Innocent
Railway Path, the Water of
Leith, the Union Canal,
plus several sections of
railway path in North
Edinburgh.

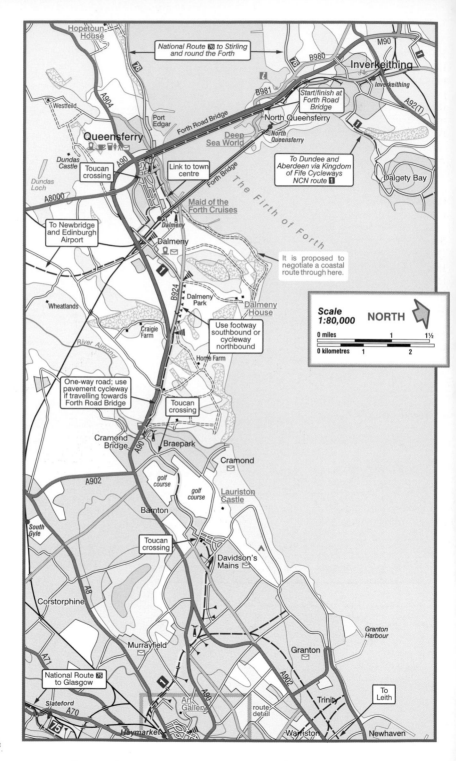

EDINBURGH TO FORTH BRIDGE

National Route **76** to Stirling and round the Forth

Inverkeithing

M90

B980

B981

Inverkeithing

A92(T)

Start/finish at Forth Road Bridge

Hopetoun House

Westfeild

A904

Port Edgar

Forth Road Bridge

Deep Sea World

North Queensferry

North Queensferry

Queensferry

To Dundee and Aberdeen via Kingdom of Fife Cycleways NCN route **1**

Dalgety Bay

Dundas Castle

A90

Toucan crossing

Link to town centre

Forth Bridge

Dundas Loch

A8000

Maid of the Forth Cruises

The Firth of Forth

To Newbridge and Edinburgh Airport

Dalmeny

Dalmeny

It is proposed to negotiate a coastal route through here.

B924

Dalmeny Park

Dalmeny House

Scale 1:80,000

NORTH

0 miles   1   1½

0 kilometres   1   2

Wheatlands

Craigie Farm

River Almond

Home Farm

Use footway southbound or cycleway northbound

One-way road; use pavement cycleway if travelling towards Forth Road Bridge

Toucan crossing

Cramond Bridge

A90

Braepark

Cramond

A902

golf course

golf course

Lauriston Castle

Barnton

South Gyle

Toucan crossing

Davidson's Mains

A8

Corstorphine

A90

Granton Harbour

Murrayfield

A902

Granton

A71

National Route **75** to Glasgow

A8

Slateford

A70

75

Art Gallery

route detail

A99

Trinity

To Leith

Haymarket

Warriston

Newhaven

220

Starting from Haymarket Station car park, the ride out from central Edinburgh uses a mixture of cycle paths, railway paths and quiet roads through Barnton, Davidson's Mains and over the lovely old Cramond Brig to cross the River Almond.

You use quiet streets and cycle paths through Queensferry, named after Queen Margaret who used the ferry to cross the Forth in the 11th century.

You cross the bridge from South Queensferry to North Queensferry in complete traffic-free safety along the cycle lanes that run either side of the bridge.

After crossing the bridge you have the choice of returning or going into North Queensferry using a road section from the cycle path down to the village for refreshments, a visit to Deep Sea World and train trip back to Edinburgh across the Forth Rail Bridge.

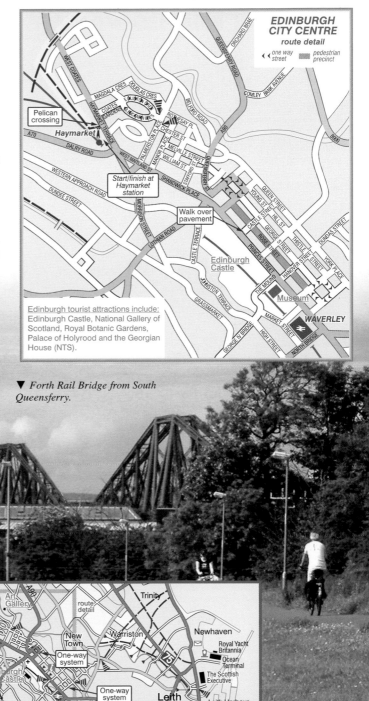

EDINBURGH CITY CENTRE
route detail

◄◄ one way street   ▬ pedestrian precinct

Pelican crossing

Haymarket

Start/finish at Haymarket station

Walk over pavement

Edinburgh Castle

Museum

WAVERLEY

Edinburgh tourist attractions include: Edinburgh Castle, National Gallery of Scotland, Royal Botanic Gardens, Palace of Holyrood and the Georgian House (NTS).

▼ *Forth Rail Bridge from South Queensferry.*

Slateford

Art Gallery

Trinity

route detail

New Town

Watriston

Newhaven

Royal Yacht Britannia

Merchiston

Union Canal

Ocean Terminal

The Scottish Executive

National Route 75 to Gourock Clyde to Forth Cycle Route

Start/finish at Haymarket station

Edinburgh Castle

One-way system

One-way system

Leith

Leith Harbour and Docks

Bruntsfield Links

WAVERLEY

Morningside

EDINBURGH

HILLEND LOCH RAILWAY PATH

This high plateau ride in Scotland's Central Belt features some of the most famous sculptures on the whole of the National Cycle Network: the huge stone Bedrock Bicycle, the tall metal keyhole and the magically suspended bucket pouring molten metal, not to mention others such as 'Calormen Fishing', 'Steam', 'Tower' and 'Fruit Barra'. There is a real sense of space enhanced by wide open vistas on the middle part of the ride, with wonderful views across Hillend Reservoir. The old Airdrie to Bathgate Junction Railway carried coal, ironstone and limestone to and from the numerous works in the area and much of this land was scarred by two centuries of heavy industry: it is a tribute to the local authorities that so much is now greened over. Riding east from Drumgelloch Station, Airdrie, the urban landscape is soon left behind as you climb into the green countryside. The highpoint is reached at the east end of the reservoir and after passing the series of sculptures there is a noticeable descent into Bathgate.

▼ *Bedrock Bike by Dave Holladay and team. The granite millstones are from former mills at Caldercruix.*

Starting points
Drumgelloch railway station, Airdrie (off the A89 Armadale Road, about ½ mile east of the A89 / A73 roundabout). About ½ mile southwest of Bathgate railway station, just off the B7002 near the Leisure Centre.

Distance
14 miles.

Grade
Easy.

Surface
Tarmac.

Roads, traffic, suitability for young children
With the exception of a ¼-mile section on a quiet road in Caldercruix, the ride is all traffic-free from Drumgelloch railway station to the edge of Bathgate.

Hills
There is a gentle climb of 50m (165ft) over about 5 miles from Airdrie to the highpoint just east of Hillend Reservoir. There is a more noticeable climb from Bathgate up to the 'plateau section' that runs west to the reservoir.

Refreshments
Lots of choice in Airdrie. Cafe at the Airdrie and District Angling Club, Hillend Reservoir. Lots of choice in Bathgate.

Nearest railway stations
Drumgelloch, Airdrie and Bathgate.

The National Cycle Network in the area
The ride forms part of Route 75, the Clyde to Forth Cycle Route running from Gourock on the Firth of Clyde (west of Glasgow) to the main Scottish Executive building by the shore in Leith, Edinburgh.

Other nearby rides (waymarked or traffic-free)
1. The towpaths of the Forth & Clyde Canal and the Union Canal have in the past few years been brought up to a high standard all the way from Glasgow to Edinburgh.
2. East of Bathgate, there is a largely traffic-free section of Route 75 through Livingston to East Calder and then again from Balerno along the Water of Leith Walkway into the heart of Edinburgh.
3. About 10 miles west of Airdrie, the Clyde Walkway runs from Cambuslang through Rutherglen into the heart of Glasgow.

▲ *Path construction between Airdrie and Bathgate.*

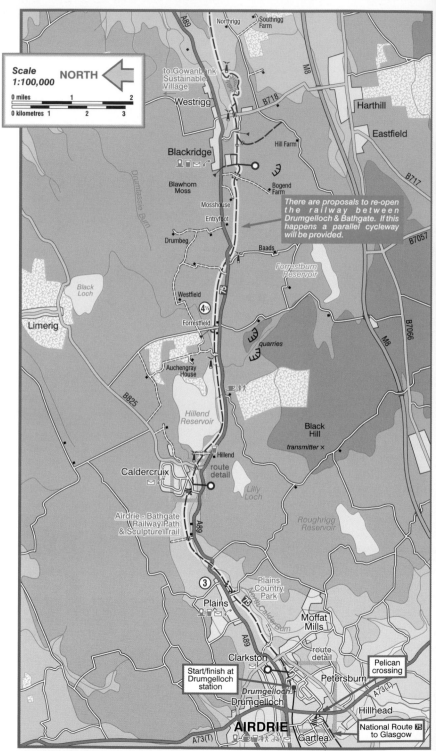

Scale
1:100,000

NORTH

0 miles   1   2
0 kilometres   1   2   3

to Gowanbank Sustainable Village

Northrigg

Southrigg Farm

Westrigg

Harthill

Eastfield

Blackridge

Hill Farm

Blawhorn Moss

Bogend Farm

Mosshouse

Entryfoot

There are proposals to re-open the railway between Drumgelloch & Bathgate. If this happens a parallel cycleway will be provided.

Drumbeg

Baads

Forrestburn Reservoir

Black Loch

Westfield

Limerig

4½

Forrestfield

quarries

Auchengray House

Black Hill

Hillend Reservoir

transmitter ×

Hillend

route detail

Caldercruix

Lilly Loch

Airdrie - Bathgate Railway Path & Sculpture Trail

Roughrigg Reservoir

3

Plains Country Park

Plains

Moffat Mills

route detail

Clarkston

Pelican crossing

Start/finish at Drumgelloch station

Petersburn

Drumgelloch

Hillhead

AIRDRIE

Gartlea

National Route 75 to Glasgow

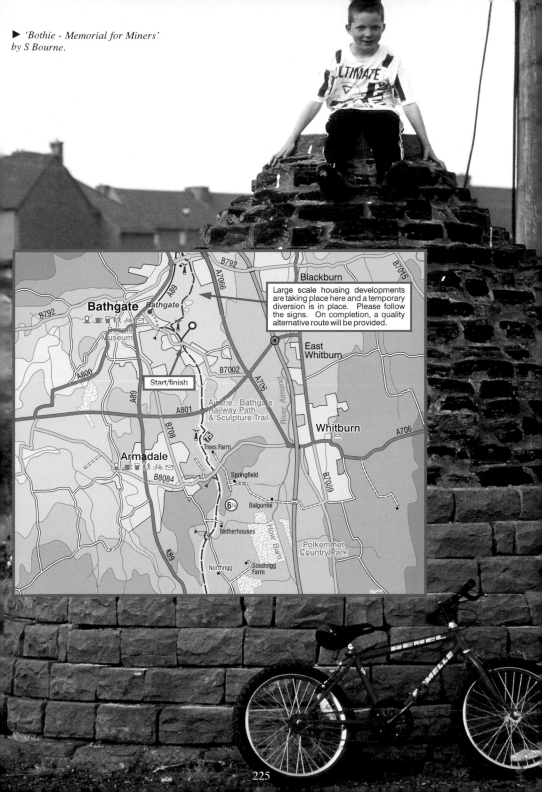

▶ *'Bothie - Memorial for Miners'*
by S Bourne.

Blackburn

Bathgate

Large scale housing developments are taking place here and a temporary diversion is in place. Please follow the signs. On completion, a quality alternative route will be provided.

East Whitburn

Start/finish

Airdrie - Bathgate Railway Path & Sculpture Trail

Whitburn

Armadale

Trees Farm

Springfield

6½ Balgornie

Netherhouses

Polkemmet Country Park

Northrigg

Southrigg Farm

LOCHWINNOCH LOOP LINE

Glasgow is the hub of several traffic-free paths that radiate out to the west, southwest and east of the city. It is the meeting point of the Lochs & Glens Cycle Route (Route 7) which travels the length of Scotland from south to north and the Clyde to Forth Cycle Route (Route 75) which crosses the country from west to east. This ride, forming part of Route 7, leaves the southwest edge of the Glasgow conurbation on a green corridor following the course of an old railway. After a safe, traffic-free section running west from Paisley Canal Station, there is a short stretch through Elderslie where great care should be taken on the

B789. You soon rejoin the course of the old railway, passing the dramatic Borealis sculpture at the junction of Routes 7 and 75. A series of interpretation boards tell you the history of some of the attractions along the way such as Lochwinnoch Temple, Barr Castle and Castle Semple Collegiate Church. The railway path continues past the glittering expanse of Castle Semple Loch and Barr Loch, passing the villages of Lochwinnoch and Kilbirnie, and ends on the edge of Glengarnock.. The best, most easily accessed, refreshments are either in the village of Lochwinnoch or in Castle Semple Country Park Visitor Centre.

Starting points
Paisley Canal railway station, southwest of Glasgow.
End of the railway path in Glengarnock.

Distance
14 miles.

Grade
Easy

Surface
Tarmac.

Roads, traffic, suitability for young children
There is one short section through Elderslie where care should be taken on the busy B789 (it is not far and you may prefer to walk along the pavement). A second, less busy road is used close to

▼ *Lochwinnoch Loop Line. The beginnings of Lochwinnoch go back to the stone age about 3000BC. Well preserved bronze age artefacts have been found and an iron age fort can still be seen on Knockmade Hill. Hollowed out tree trunks used as canoes in the shallow lochs have also been found. The remains of Barr Castle, and early 16th-century square tower can be found near Lochwinnoch.*

Lochwinoch. You will need to use short stretches of road if you choose to visit Lochwinnoch or Kilbirnie for refreshments. Lochwinnoch is recommended for better choice and quieter approach roads.

Hills
There is a gentle climb south from Lochwinnoch to a highpoint about halfway towards Kilbirnie.

Refreshments
Garthland Arms PH, Brown Bull PH, Junction Cafe, shops in Lochwinnoch.
Basic cafe, fish and chip shop, the Bowery PH in Kilbirnie (accessed via busy road).

Nearest railway stations
Paisley Canal (southwest of Glasgow) is at the start and Glengarnock lies just beyond the end of the railway path.

The National Cycle Network in the area
1. Route 7 (the Lochs & Glens Cycle Route) continues southwest beyond Kilbirnie to the Ayrshire Coast. To the north, beyond Paisley, Route 7 continues into the centre of Glasgow, crosses Bell's Bridge then follows the Firth of Clyde and the River Leven to Loch Lomond on its way towards the Highlands.
2. Route 75 (the Clyde to Forth Cycle Route) goes west from Paisley to Johnstone then continues up to the Firth of Clyde and to Greenock and Gourock. To the east it passes through the centre of Glasgow and links with the Hillend Loch Railway Path (see page 222).

Other nearby rides (waymarked or traffic-free)
These are part of the National Cycle Network:
1. The Forth & Clyde Canal towpath.
2. The Clyde and Loch Lomond Cycleway through Dumbarton to Loch Lomond.
3. Paisley and Clyde Railway Path.
4. The Clyde Corridor Cycle Route east of Glasgow Green
5. Strathblane to Kirkintilloch, north of Glasgow.

▼ *A peaceful ride along the Lochwinnoch Loop Line, highly recommended.*

227

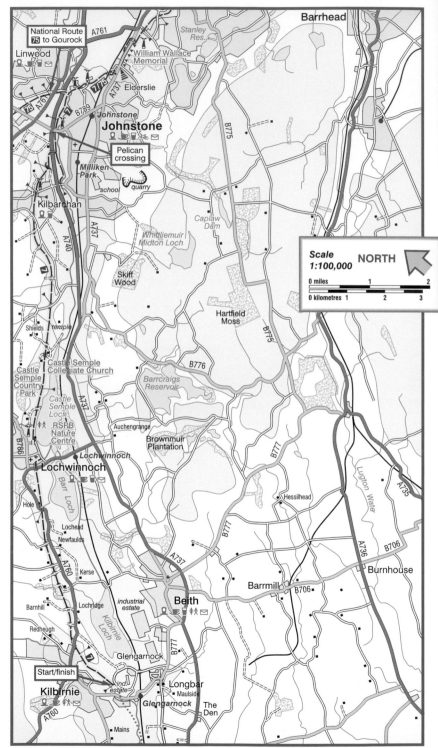

National Route 75 to Gourock
Linwood
Barrhead
William Wallace Memorial
Stanley Res.
A761
Elderslie
B789
Johnstone
Johnstone
Pelican crossing
Milliken Park
school
quarry
Kilbarchan
A737
A740
Caplaw Dam
Whitliemuir Midton Loch
Skiff Wood
Hartfield Moss
B775

Scale
1:100,000
NORTH
0 miles   1   2
0 kilometres 1   2   3

Shields
temple
Castle Semple Collegiate Church
B776
Castle Semple Country Park
Castle Semple Loch
Barrcraigs Reservoir
RSPB Nature Centre
B786
A737
Auchengrange
Brownmuir Plantation
Lochwinnoch
Lochwinnoch
Barr Loch
Hole
B777
Lugton Water
A735
Hessilhead
Lochead
Newfauld
A760
Kerse
A737
B777
Barrmill
B706
Burnhouse
Barnhill
Lochridge
industrial estate
Beith
B777
A736
B706
Redheugh
Kilbirnie Loch
Glengarnock
ind estate
Longbar
Maulside
Start/finish
Kilbirnie
A760
Glengarnock
The Den
Mains

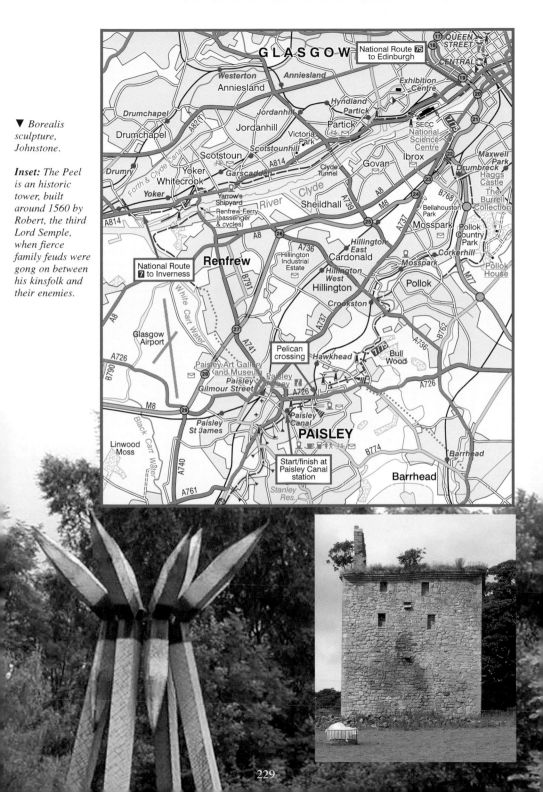

▼ *Borealis sculpture, Johnstone.*

Inset: *The Peel is an historic tower, built around 1560 by Robert, the third Lord Semple, when fierce family feuds were gong on between his kinsfolk and their enemies.*

ROUTES OUT OF DUNDEE: TO TAYPORT AND BROUGHTY FERRY

There are many unusual and memorable features on these rides either side of the estuary of the Firth of Tay, not least the lift that takes you and your bike up through the centre of the Tay Road Bridge to set you right in the middle on a safe and segregated cycle lane, slightly above the traffic running either side of you, with fantastic views out along the estuary in both directions. For once you can truly feel King of the Road! At the southern end of the bridge, the route soon links with a railway path taking you to the edge of Tayport with fine views of the lighthouse and across the estuary to Broughty Castle. There is a

tea room and pub in Tayport and, if you are feeling fit, you can continue on Route 1 into Tentsmuir Forest and explore the waymarked woodland tracks that form part of the Kingdom of Fife Millennium Cycle Routes. Back on the north side of the Tay Road Bridge, long and painstaking negotiations have created a segregated cycle lane all the way through the security zone of Dundee docks (a permit is issued at the control point on production of photo ID). Following close to the shoreline, Broughty Castle comes into sight: entry is free and there are refreshments nearby in Broughty Ferry.

Starting points
The cycle lane access point at the northern end of the Tay Road Bridge, Dundee.
Broughty Castle, Broughty Ferry, four miles east of Dundee.
The harbour in Tayport.

Distance
9 miles.

Grade
Easy.

Surface
Tarmac.

Roads, traffic, suitability for young children
A newly-built segregated cyclepath through Dundee docks links via a quiet road to a stretch of traffic-free shoreline promenade ending at the western edge of Broughty Ferry. The crossing of the Tay Bridge is via an excellent

traffic-free path running along the middle of the bridge; at its southern end you soon join a shared-use pavement and railway path that take you to the edge of Tayport. There are no busy roads but care should be taken with young children at the crossings and various points where the route is shared with (minimal) traffic.

Hills
There is a noticeable climb from Tayport up to the southern end of the Tay Bridge. At the northern end of the bridge a lift takes you from street level up to the central cycle lane.

Refreshments
Ship Inn, Broughty Ferry. Lots of choice in Dundee. Cafe/kiosk in the car park at the southern end of the bridge. Jane's Harbour Tearoom, Bell Rock Tavern in Tayport.

Nearest railway stations
Dundee, Broughty Ferry and Leuchars.

The National Cycle Network in the area
The ride forms part of Route 1 which crosses Fife from Edinburgh, then passes through Dundee on its way up the east coast. Route 77 heads west from Dundee to Perth and north to Pitlochry and Aberdeen.

Other nearby rides (waymarked or traffic-free)
There are easy, waymarked traffic-free trails in Tentsmuir Forest, to the southeast of Tayport, which can be accessed by following Route 1 beyond the end of this ride towards Leuchars and St Andrews. There are three other forests in Fife with waymarked trails: Pitmedden, Devilla and Blairadam - see www.fife-cycleways.co.uk for more details.

▲ Sailing boat on the Tay Estuary.

▼ Tay Road Bridge has a special cycle lane offering fantastic views.

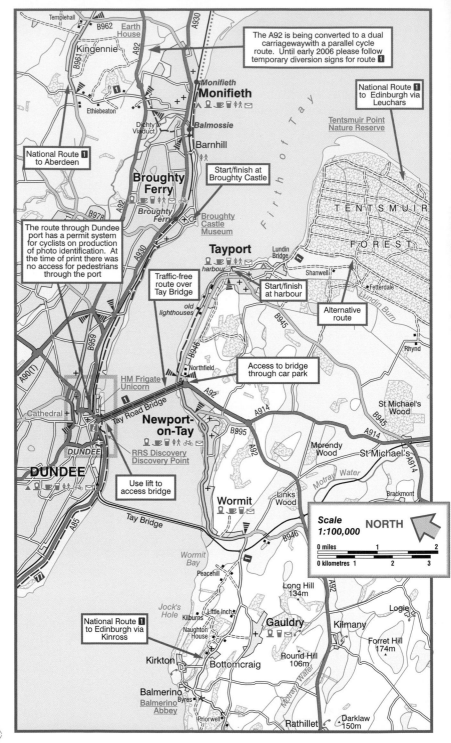

The A92 is being converted to a dual carriageway with a parallel cycle route. Until early 2006 please follow temporary diversion signs for route **1**

National Route **1** to Edinburgh via Leuchars

National Route **1** to Aberdeen

Tentsmuir Point Nature Reserve

Start/finish at Broughty Castle

The route through Dundee port has a permit system for cyclists on production of photo identification. At the time of print there was no access for pedestrians through the port

Traffic-free route over Tay Bridge

Start/finish at harbour

Alternative route

Access to bridge through car park

HM Frigate Unicorn

Cathedral

Use lift to access bridge

RRS Discovery Discovery Point

National Route **1** to Edinburgh via Kinross

Scale 1:100,000 NORTH

National Route **1** to Edinburgh via Kinross

232

▼ *RRS Discovery, Dundee. Explore Scott's famous polar exploration ship Discovery and visit the Antarctic Museum.*

DUNDEE
route detail

Dundee tourist attractions include: Verdant Works, Discovery Point & RRS Discovery, the Frigate Unicorn, Art Gallery & Museums, Dundee Contemporary Arts Centre, Dundee Observatory, Green Circular Cycle Route, Shaw's Sweet Factory.

Firth of Tay

Port of Dundee

MARKET ST

A92

ALBERT STREET

ARTHURSTONE TERRACE STREET

LYON STREET

VICTORIA STREET

PRINCES STREET

DENS ROAD

PEEP O'DAY LANE

ARBROATH ROAD

BROUGHTY FERRY ROAD

KING STREET

EAST MARKETGAIT

MARY ANN LANE

bus station

COW GATE

SEAGATE

TRADES LANE

CANDLE LANE

SOUTH MARKETGAIT

HM Frigate Unicorn

Use lift to access bridge

Tay Road Bridge

city centre

MURRAYGATE

STREET

VICTORIA ROAD

HILLTOWN

NORTH MARKETGAIT

MEADOWSIDE

MEADOWSIDE

COMMERCIAL

HIGH STREET

NETHERGATE

RRS Discovery Discovery Point

SOUTH MARKETGAIT

DUNDEE

RIVERSIDE DRIVE

A85

Pelican crossing

233

CALLANDER TO KILLIN VIA BALQUHIDDER OR TO LOCH VENACHAR

A most spectacular setting of lochs and mountains provides the backdrop for these two rides north and south from the holiday centre of Callander.

On one ride, you make your way to the entrance to the Highlands, visit Rob Roy's grave and travel through the spectacular Glen Ogle. You'll cycle alongside rushing rivers, over viaducts, along railway paths and an ancient military road. There are several climbs, a couple of which are steep, but your reward is some great views.

The other option is a shorter ride that will take you along the quiet shores of Loch Venachar where you can see dinghies and windsurfers out on the water. Past Blackwater Marshes, a site of Special Scientific Interest, you cycle on forest tracks towards Brig o'Turk. This ride has more rolling hills with the occasional steep climb.

Starting points
The centre of Callander, Callander Meadows.
Brig o'Turk village hall.

Distance
a) Callander to Balquhidder 13 miles.
b) Balquhidder to Killin 12 miles.
c) Callander to Brig o'Turk eight miles.

Grade
Moderate to difficult.

Surface
Mixture of tarmac and stone-based tracks. There are rougher sections at the north end of Loch Lubnaig and going into Killin.

Roads, traffic, suitability for young children
a) Callander to Balquhidder.

A traffic-free path starts from the Meadows car park in Callander. There may be a little traffic along the road serving the holiday chalets at the southern end of Loch Lubnaig. A very quiet road is used between Strathyre and Balquhidder. There is considerable holiday traffic between Balquhidder and Kinghouse. Take extreme care crossing the trunk road at Glenoglehead.

▼ *Kinghouse to the Glen Ogle summit.*

b) Callander to Loch Venachar. There is a short section (½ mile) on the A81 south from the centre of Callander where care should be taken. You then join the minor road to Invertrossachs, which carries very little traffic. There is a three-mile cycle path/forestry track between Invertrossachs and Brig o'Turk.

Hills

a) Callander to Strathyre. There is a steady 200ft climb from Callander past the Falls of Leny up to Loch Lubnaig. There are several other short climbs, including a steep one up a series of zig zags at the north end of Loch Lubnaig (fantastic views!).

b) Balquhidder to Killin. There is a very steep climb from Lochearnhead to Glenogle, and a steep descent from

▼ The Kendrum viaduct near Lochearnhead, now completely restored.

Glenoglehead.

c) Callander to Brig o'Turk. Generally rolling with the occasional short steep climb.

Refreshments

a) Lots of choice in Callander.
b) Cafe and pubs in Strathyre.
c) Teashop at the museum in Stronvar just south of Balquhidder.
d) The Byre Inn at Brig o'Turk.
e) Lots of choice in Lochearnhead.
f) Lots of choice in Killin.

Nearest railway stations

Dunblane and Bridge of Allan.

The National Cycle Network in the area

1. From Killin, Route 7 continues to Loch Tay, Pitlochry, Aviemore, and Inverness.
2. To the south of Loch Venachar, Route 7 crosses the Dukes Pass via forestry tracks, then passes through Aberfoyle

▲ Construction on the Kendrum viaduct.

and Drymen on its way to Loch Lomond and Glasgow.

Other nearby rides (waymarked or traffic-free)

1. There are plenty of forest routes in Queen Elizabeth Forest Park (maps from the Tourist Information Centres or the Queen Elizabeth Forest Park Visitor Centre north of Aberfoyle).

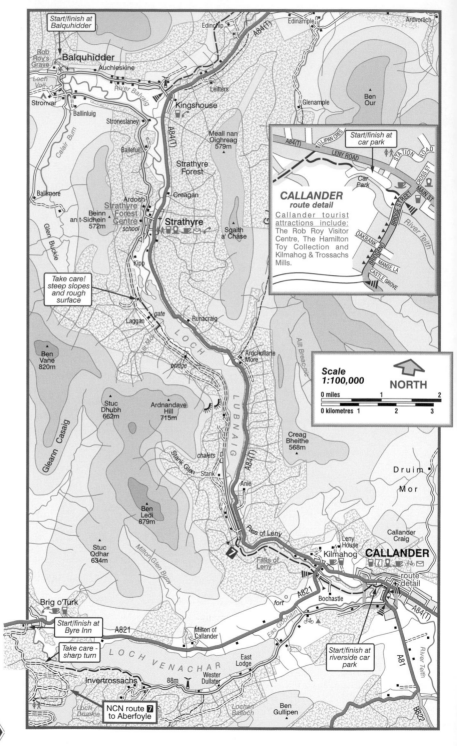

Start/finish at Balquhidder

Rob Roy's Grave

Balquhidder

Auchleskine

Edinchip

A84(T)

Edinample

Ardvorlich

Loch Voil

River Balvaig

Leitters

Ben Our

Stronvar

Ballinluig

Kingshouse

Glenample

Stroneslaney

Baileful

Meall nan Oighreag 579m

Calair Burn

Strathyre Forest

Ballimore

Ardoch Strathyre Forest Centre

Beinn an t-Sidhein 572m

Creagan

school

Strathyre

Sgaith a' Chase

Glen Buckie

Start/finish at car park

A84(T)

KILPAN CRS

LENY ROAD

STATION

ROAD

Car Park

MAIN ST

CROSS ST

BRIDGE STREET

CALLANDER
route detail

Callander tourist attractions include: The Rob Roy Visitor Centre, The Hamilton Toy Collection and Kilmahog & Trossachs Mills.

OAKBANK

BRIDGEND

MANSE LA

CASTLE GROVE

River Teith

Kipp

Take care! steep slopes and rough surface

Laggan

gate

Runacraig

LOCH

Ardchullarie More

Allt Breac na

Ben Vane 820m

bridge

Mill Mor

Scale
1:100,000

NORTH

0 miles   1   2

0 kilometres   1   2   3

Stuc Dhubh 662m

Ardnandave Hill 715m

LUBNAIG

chalets

Creag Bheithe 568m

Gleann Casaig

Stank Glen

Stank

Druim

Mor

Ben Ledi 879m

Anie

A84(T)

Stuc Odhar 634m

Milton Glen Burn

Pass of Leny

Leny House

Callander Craig

Kilmahog

CALLANDER

route detail

Brig o'Turk

Falls of Leny

Start/finish at Byre Inn

A821

fort

A821

Bochastle

Eas Gobhain

A84(T)

Take care - sharp turn

LOCH VENACHAR

Milton of Callander

Start/finish at riverside car park

A81

River Teith

Invertrossachs

88m

East Lodge

Wester Dullater

Loch Drunkie

NCN route 7 to Aberfoyle

Lochan Balloch

Ben Gullipen

B822

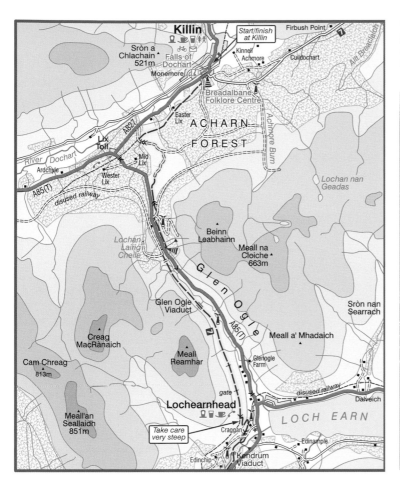

▼ Loch Vennachar, between Aberfoyle and Callander, such amazing views.

2. There is also a delightful ride on a traffic-free Scottish Water road along the northern side of Loch Katrine, which can be continued on minor roads as far as Loch Lomond or Aberfoyle.

The first ride travels north to Balquhidder along the course of the old Caledonian railway line which until 1965 used to run from Callander to Oban. Passing through woodland, alongside the swift waters and spectacular falls of the River Leny, you are cycling a parallel course to the Pass of Leny, known as the entrance to the Highlands. There are fine views of Ben Ledi where it is said that 2000 years ago the

Druids lit fires at the top to celebrate the changing of the seasons.

At the end of Loch Lubnaig the route takes a quiet road to Balquhidder where you can visit Rob Roy's grave. From here you can continue through the spectacular Glen Ogle, with excellent views of Loch Earn in places, using the old military road, two railway paths and two listed viaducts to make your way to Killin and Loch Tay.

Your other option is a shorter ride to the south and west of Callander. This route follows the shores of Loch Venachar, passing splendid isolated houses set above the water's edge and

offering views across to Ben Ledi.

The loch ends at Blackwater Marshes, a Site of Special Scientific Interest where there are reeds, willow, birch trees and patches of bog myrtle. This special combination of plants and water provides home and food for Greylag geese, goosanders, teal and wigeons. The open territory is also excellent for birds of prey.

You then follow a short section on forest roads to reach the refreshment stop / turnaround point at Brig o'Turk.

Malin Head

Carndonagh

Greencastle　Castlerock

P

Buncrana

Creeslough

Limavady

Magilligar Point

15

Burtonport

Derry

Claudy

92

93

Letterkenny

Raphoe

13

Strabane

Sperrins

Por

Newtownstewart

Donegal

95

Gortin

95

Pettigoe

Omagh

6

Cookstown

Ballyshannon

Bundoran

8

91

92

Fintona

4

Dungannon

9

Belleek

Lower Lough Erne

95

Portac

Enniskillen

5

Upper Lough Erne

Armagh

Manorhamilton

Sligo

91

91

Tynan

91

Collooney

Dowra

91

Clones

91

Carrick-on-Shannon

Du

To Du

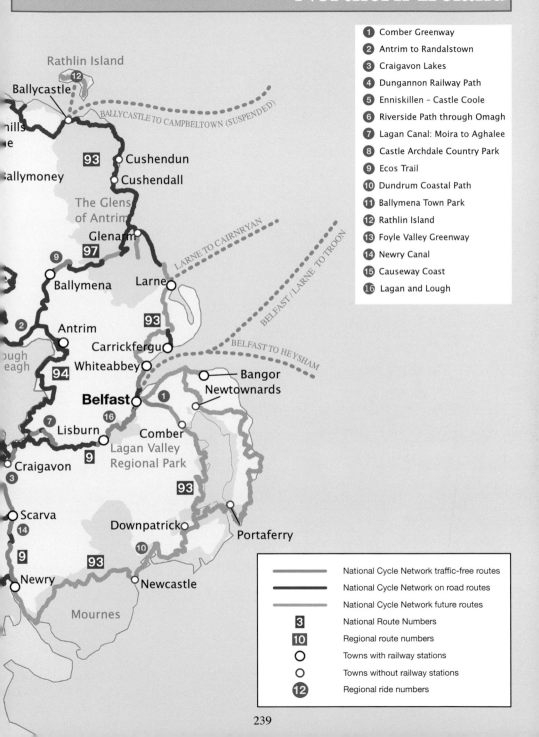

Northern Ireland

1. Comber Greenway
2. Antrim to Randalstown
3. Craigavon Lakes
4. Dungannon Railway Path
5. Enniskillen – Castle Coole
6. Riverside Path through Omagh
7. Lagan Canal: Moira to Aghalee
8. Castle Archdale Country Park
9. Ecos Trail
10. Dundrum Coastal Path
11. Ballymena Town Park
12. Rathlin Island
13. Foyle Valley Greenway
14. Newry Canal
15. Causeway Coast
16. Lagan and Lough

Rathlin Island

Ballycastle

BALLYCASTLE TO CAMPBELTOWN (SUSPENDED)

Ballymoney

93 Cushendun

Cushendall

The Glens of Antrim

Glenarm

97

9

Ballymena

Larne

LARNE TO CAIRNRYAN

BELFAST / LARNE TO TROON

2

Antrim

93

Carrickfergus

Whiteabbey

94

BELFAST TO HEYSHAM

Bangor
Newtownards

Belfast

1

16

7

Lisburn

Comber

Lagan Valley
Regional Park

9

93

Craigavon

3

Scarva

14

Downpatrick

Portaferry

9

93

10

Newry

Newcastle

Mournes

National Cycle Network traffic-free routes
National Cycle Network on road routes
National Cycle Network future routes

3 National Route Numbers
10 Regional route numbers
○ Towns with railway stations
○ Towns without railway stations
12 Regional ride numbers

239

NORTHERN IRELAND

The rural road network of Northern Ireland provides a range of cycling opportunities for everyone from the novice family group to the long-distance tourer. On your journey you'll see rich farmland and dramatic coastline, fine parks and country houses. You'll also find plenty of evidence of history through the ages, from prehistoric burial sites and iron age forts, to castles and cathedrals. Northern Ireland's countryside is full of pleasant, relaxed towns and villages, and of course, you'll encounter the legendary Irish welcome from the locals.

Water is perhaps the dominant theme in describing the National Cycle Network here. The Ballyshannon to Ballycastle Cycle Route takes you from the Atlantic to the Irish Sea along the beautiful north coast, passing the unforgettable Giant's Causeway, a UNESCO World Heritage Site and designated Area of Outstanding Natural Beauty. Route 94 is known as The Loughshore Trail, and makes a complete circuit of Lough Neagh, the largest inland lake in the UK and Ireland.

Route 9 runs east-west between Belfast and Ballyshannon, and includes extended traffic-free riding in Belfast alongside the River Lagan. Likewise, the National Cycle Network in Derry enjoys traffic-free passage beside the River Foyle. Further south, the Kingfisher Trail explores a long distance loop including Upper and Lower Lough Erne, while the Newry to Portadown canal towpath offers lovely, easy traffic-free riding with the option to make the return leg by train.

Northern Ireland is a great area for family rides, as the following pages illustrate. You'll experience incredible coastal scenery and tranquil towpaths; and have opportunities for wildlife watching in remote spots, such as at the RSPB bird watching viewpoint on Rathlin Island. The National Cycle Network is a brilliant way for cyclists to explore and enjoy the area, as well as to make routine journeys through the busier towns and cities.

▼ *Using the Cott ferry to cross Upper Lough Erne at Crom Castle is a pleasant alternative to a very busy road.*

John Grimshaw's
HIGHLIGHTS

Rivers, Towpaths and Greenways.
From one end of the country to another, towpaths, riverside paths and former railway tracks provide flat traffic-free routes to and from all the cities of Northern Ireland through idyllic countryside teeming with wildlife

The Sperrins.
Cycling between Cookstown and Omagh on quiet rural lanes and roads is challenging but rewarding. Following the trail of prehistoric settlers, travellers get a sense of remoteness in the rolling landscape.

Craigavon.
A centre of cycling excellence! Miles of flat traffic-free paths around the lakes with a trip to Oxford Island thrown in for good measure, to admire the grandeur of Lough Neagh and enjoy some great home cooking.

The North Coast.
From the geological wonder of The Giant's Causeway to Castlerock via some of the best beaches on Northern Ireland with views of distant Donegal - not to be missed. Ice cream and rock!

Belfast.
Becoming more and more cycle friendly with the attractive Laganside area from Stranmillis to Belfast Lough simply awash with cityscapes, art pieces and numerous places to stop off for a snack or quick pint!

Derry/Londonderry - Gateway to the northwest.
The city with its superb, award-winning, riverside path along the Foyle and increasing network of link routes makes it easier to cycle to work and school whilst also providing a pleasant day ride to picnic by the waters-edge.

▼ *Prominent cycle parking at Bishopsgate National Trust property in Downhill.*

NORTHERN IRELAND FAMILY RIDES

Comber Greenway.
2.5 miles. Route 93
Families, this one's for you - a short, traffic-free and level ride along a disused railway line through East Belfast! Great efforts have been made to enhance the route, including the planting of trees, shrubs and wildflowers, and a safe crossing is in place at the Holywood Arches (where the railway line used to cross the junction on a series of arches). A traffic-free path also links to Victoria Park alongside the Connswater River. This ride represents the first phase of a planned cycle and walking route all the way from Belfast Lough to Comber.

Antrim to Randalstown.
4 miles. Route 94
This short ride along the Loughshore Trail provides plenty of points of interest and lovely, level cycling between these two County Antrim towns. Starting at Lough Neagh, you ride out along a recently improved path towards Randalstown. Clothworthy Arts Centre, set in magnificent woodlands, is worth a visit and the viaduct in Randalstown gives a fantastic view over the town. There are plans for an

additional three-mile cycle route inland along the magnificent Six Mile Water, due for completion in 2007.

Craigavon Lakes.
3 miles. Routes 9 and 94

Family cycling heaven is found along the shores of Craigavon Lakes! The main route is just three miles long, and there are plenty of additional tracks for you to explore the 250 acres of parkland that surround the lakes. The paths along the lake shore and through the woods are entirely traffic-free and have well maintained tarmac surfaces, so are particularly ideal for family cycling. For a break from the pedalling, you can enjoy the delights of the Tannaghmore Animal Farm and the Barn Museum. Bikes are available for hire from the highly rated Craigavon Watersports Centre.

Dungannon Lake Park.
2 miles. Route 95

This traffic-free route is great for a family ride with young children. Dungannon Park, on the edge of Dungannon, is a beautifully kept area with a trout-fishing lake and lots of activities, and is wonderful for exploring by bike. The path also features a signposted traffic-free link to the Linen Green, which is situated in a refurbished linen weaving mill and contains an interesting exhibition on the rich heritage of the area. Retail facilities and refreshments are also available.

Enniskillen to Castle Coole. 2 miles.

This is a perfect route for a quiet potter on a bike, finishing at Castle Coole, one of the finest neo-classical houses in Ireland. Following a refreshing bike ride by wandering its landscaped grounds and sumptuous interior makes for a great day out. From Enniskillen Castle on the banks of the River Erne, you follow a cycle path around the Lakeland Forum, over a bridge and briefly onto a minor road, until the path brings you past Ardhowen Theatre and into the grounds of Castle Coole. There are plenty of refreshments and toilets at either end of the ride.

▼ *Cycling past Enniskillen Castle on the Kingfisher Trail.*

Riverside Path, Omagh.
6 miles. Route 92

This generally flat and mostly traffic-free route takes you from Omagh, a bustling market town in the foothills of the Sperrins, to Gortnagarn. The route along the banks of the Camowen River begins from the car park at Cranny Fields off the Hospital Road. You cross a small wooden bridge, joining a private road which crosses the A505 and enters the leisure centre grounds. The signed path runs alongside Grange Park, to the stunning Wishbone sculpture, created by Niall Laird. The path continues, taking you all the way out to Gortnagarn. Toilets and refreshments are available along the route.

▼ *Dundrum Coastal Path will form part of Route 93 in County Down.*

Lagan Canal - Moira to
Aghalee. 3.5 miles. Route 9

SSShhhhhhh! This flat, peaceful and predominantly traffic-free bike ride is lovely, running alongside an expanse of water known in parts as the Broadwater and the Lagan Navigation Canal. In this quiet rural setting the only sounds you're likely to hear are the gentle lowing of cattle in the fields, birdsong escaping from the hedgerows, or the splashing of waterfowl on the canal. Many swans glide by on the waterway in summertime, not to mention mallards, grebes and tufted ducks. Take care on the last half mile or so of the ride, which uses the public road into Aghalee.

Castle Archdale. 3 miles.
Route 91

This rural route offers lovely country park and waterside scenery, and is largely traffic-free. The area features views of Lower Lough Erne and a wide variety of leisure attractions, with opportunities to combine cycling with other activities. The path runs through the grounds of Castle Archdale Country Park, and is part of the Kingfisher Trail. Remains of the Archdale manor house, which was built in 1773, now house a youth hostel, tearooms, a countryside centre and museum. Other activities and facilities in the park include boat hire, fishing, pony trekking, a campsite, nature trail, wildlife pond and rare breeds enclosure.

ecos Trail. 1.5 miles. Route 97

The riverside paths along the River Braid offer families a short and pleasant traffic-free route, which extends to Ballykeel Housing Estate crossing the old wooden

bridge. ecos Centre is the Environmental Centre for Northern Ireland, and gives visitors a chance to explore environmental issues. It's set in 150 acres of woodland, so you really can cycle and walk on the wild side! To extend this route you can travel to the village of Brougshane along the on-road cycle lanes - Broughshane has a worldwide reputation for its amazing floral displays.

Dundrum Coastal Path.
1.5 miles. Route 93

This short, entirely traffic-free coastal route is simply breathtaking! You follow the path of the former GNR railway line, hugging the shoreline and getting close to the many wading birds which frequent Dundrum Bay. This path is due for resurfacing in 2007. Isambard Kingdom Brunel's ship the Great Britain famously grounded here in 1846 during a transatlantic voyage. In early summer the path is a riot of colour when the yellow whin blossom is at its finest, whilst the Mourne Mountains provide a spectacular backdrop as they sweep majestically down to the sea at nearby Newcastle.

Ballymoney Town Park.
Route 96

Ballymoney is a fairly level, compact town and so worth developing for cycling. The Council is building a marvellous Riverside Park and has upgraded paths for shared use. To access the route start at the Railway Station. These traffic-free paths are useful for families and there is a play park en route with cycle parking. The plan is to link the path as far as the bypass and create a circular route for cyclists. Route 96 will use the park as a section of the Lower Bann Cycle Way.

Rathlin Island.
4.5 miles. Route 93

Biking on Rathlin Island is a terrific way to explore this magical, wild spot. Thirty minutes by ferry from Ballycastle, the ride starts at the harbour (bikes are available for hire), and you can head off towards either the South or the West lighthouses. At Mill Bay, seals bask on the rocks near the Boathouse Visitors' Centre, whilst the RSPB viewpoint at West Light is a tremendous, cliff hugging location from which to see puffins and other sea birds including guillemots, razorbills, kittiwakes and fulmars. Only 100 people live on the island, so you shouldn't see much traffic. A little hilly and the surface will be improved in the future.

THE FOYLE VALLEY CYCLE ROUTE: LONDONDERRY / DERRY TO STRABANE

Crossing and recrossing the border with the Republic of Ireland, this ride along the valley of the River Foyle links the historic walled city of Londonderry / Derry with Strabane (pronounced 'Stra-bann' with the emphasis on 'bann'), just back over the border in Northern Ireland, near the confluence of the River Mourne with the River Foyle. The ride starts with a flat 4 ½-mile traffic-free section right alongside the River Foyle, with views across to the green hills of Corrody,

▼ *Overlooking the river at Queen's Quay on the Foyle Valley Cycle Route.*

Slievekirk and Gortmonly. This first section forms an excellent there-and-back ride for families and novices. The nearest refreshments beyond the end of the riverside section are at the Carrig Inn in Carrigans, although this will involve almost a mile on the R236, which can be busy. The ride passes through an area predominantly given over to pasture, with the occasional field of grain or potatoes. Many of the houses are new, an indication of the tremendous rise in the economic fortunes of the Republic in the last 15 years. A final climb leaves you with a long descent to Lifford and across the bridge over the River Foyle back into Northern Ireland, and the magnificent stainless steel and bronze figure sculptures known as Let the Dance Begin. Standing 18ft high, the figures represent a shared cultural vision for the area, a merging of two cultures rich in music and dance.

Starting points
The Tourist Information Centre in Londonderry / Derry.
The Tourist Information Centre in Strabane.

Distance
21 miles from Londonderry / Derry to Strabane. The traffic-free section at the start is about 4½ miles long.

Grade
The traffic-free section is easy. The rest is moderate.

Surface
Tarmac.

Roads, traffic, suitability for young children
The first 4½ miles are ideal for children on a flat, well-surfaced traffic-free path. The second section down to Strabane occasionally uses or crosses fairly busy roads.

Hills
There are several climbs in the second half of the ride, most notably just before Lifford.

Refreshments
Lots of choice in Londonderry / Derry.
Carrig Inn, stores in Carrigans.
Pub, stores in St Johnstown.
Lots of choice in Lifford.
Lots of choice in Strabane.

Nearest railway stations
Londonderry / Derry is served by regular trains from Belfast via Coleraine.
The cross country buses can normally fit one or two bikes in the luggage storage areas.

The National Cycle Network in the area
The ride described here (Route 92) forms part of the Ballyshannon to Ballycastle Cycle Route which goes east from Ballyshannon on the Atlantic coast to Ballycastle (just beyond the Giant's Causeway) on the Irish Sea.

Other nearby rides (waymarked or traffic-free)
There is another traffic-free ride on the other side of the River Foyle, running for 3 miles from the double-decker Craigavon Bridge to New Buildings. This is the start of Route 93.

▲ *The Foyle Valley Cycle Route is perfect for families to enjoy traffic-free cycling.*

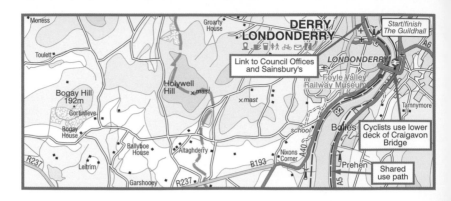

▲ *Cycling and walking on the Foyle Valley Cycle Route.*

Starting points
The Tourist Information Centre in Newry Town Hall.
The Bann Bridge in Portadown.

Distance
20 miles.

Grade
Easy.

Surface
Mainly tarmac with sections of very good quality gravel path.

Roads, traffic, suitability for young children
The ride is ideal for young children in that it is flat and largely traffic-free. There are some stretches where the ride runs along minor roads parallel with the canal, but these carry very little traffic. Care should be taken at the road crossings. There is a good cafe at Scarva Visitor Centre which would make an ideal turnaround point for a shorter there-and-back ride from Portadown or Newry.

Hills
None.

Refreshments
Lots of choice in Newry.
Rice Hotel, Railway Bar, stores in Poyntzpass.
Excellent cafe at the Scarva Visitor Centre.
Park Hotel, stores in Scarva.
Lots of choice in Portadown.

Nearest railway stations
Newry and Portadown. This is an excellent ride to use the train one way and cycle back. Taking the train to Newry is recommended as Newry station is at the top of a hill and the prevailing southwesterly wind is more likely to be of help as you ride from Newry north to Portadown. Although there are stations at Scarva and

▲ *Overlooking the Newry-Portadown canal at Moneypenny's Lock.*

Poyntzpass there are very few trains a day (in the very early morning and early evening) and none on Sunday, so these are not very useful.

The National Cycle Network in the area
The northern part of the ride is on Route 9, part of the Belfast to Ballyshannon cycle route which goes east from Portadown to Lisburn and Belfast. To the west of the canal towpath, Route 91 goes

to Armagh, then in a circuitous route via Dungannon, Cookstown and Omagh to Enniskillen and Ballyshannon. Route 94 is the Lough Neagh Circuit.

Other nearby rides (waymarked or traffic-free)
There are short traffic-free trails on the east side of Craigavon Lake and, a little further east, between Moira and Aghalee.

NEWRY TO PORTADOWN ALONG THE CANAL

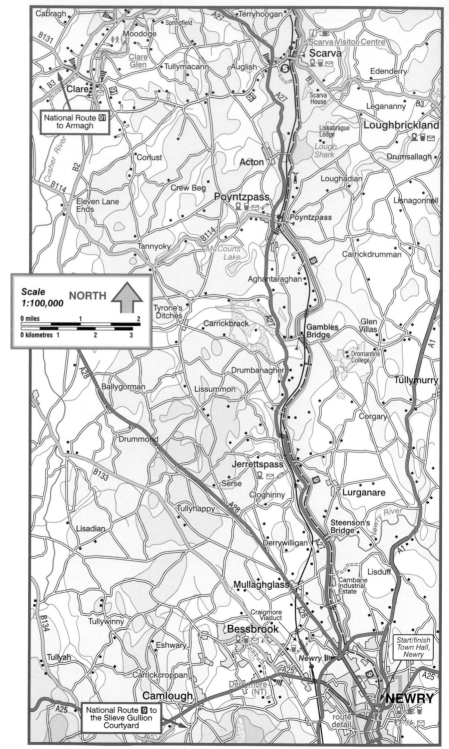

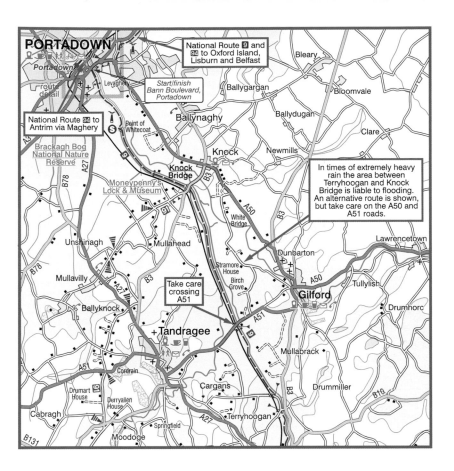

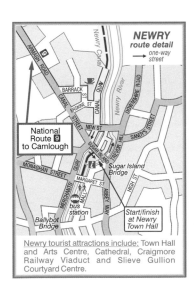

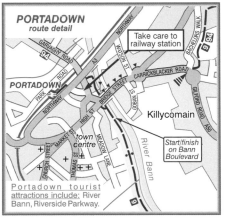

CASTLEROCK TO GIANT'S CAUSEWAY

The Giant's Causeway, a World Heritage Site, is a splendid destination for this scenic ride along the beautiful north coast of Ireland. Created from a volcanic eruption 60 million years ago, this is a designated Area of Outstanding Natural Beauty and has attracted visitors for centuries.

From Coleraine the ride uses cycle lanes and segregated cycle tracks to Portstewart and Portrush with fine sea views across to the Mull of Kintyre.

From Portrush to Bushmills, home of the famous Irish whiskey, the route follows quiet lanes parallel to the busy coast road with a climb up to 300ft with wonderful views.

From Bushmills, a delightful section of railway path takes you almost to the door of the Giant's Causeway Visitor Centre. **NB** For safety reasons (a steep hill with a blind bend and lots of pedestrians) you are NOT allowed to cycle the mile down to the Giant's Causeway from the Visitor Centre. Please do not abuse this sensible safety precaution.

You may well choose to break this ride up into several shorter sections, with Coleraine or Portrush as good starting points, both served by railway stations.

Starting points
Castlerock Station.
The new Millennium Bridge over the River Bann in Coleraine.
West Strand, Portrush.

Distance
Castlerock to Coleraine: seven miles one way, 14 miles return.
Coleraine to Portrush: seven miles one way, 14 miles return.
Portrush to Giant's Causeway: nine miles one way, 18 miles return.

Grade
Moderate.

Surface
All tarmac, with the exception of the railway path into Giant's Causeway which is a high-grade stone path.

Roads, traffic, suitability for young children
Most of the ride is on quiet roads, cycle lanes and segregated cycleways where the route runs (safely) alongside busier roads. The section between Portstewart and Portrush has fine views out to sea. The final traffic-free section from Bushmills to Giant's Causeway is along the course of a disued railway.

Hills
There are several short hills and two longer climbs of almost 300ft: one to the north west of Coleraine on the way to Castlerock, the other between Portrush and Bushmills, both on very quiet stretches of road.

Refreshments
Pubs, cafe in Castlerock.
Lots of choice in Coleraine.
Lots of choice in Portstewart.
Lots of choice in Portrush.
Cafe at the Giant's Causeway.

Nearest railway stations
Castlerock, Coleraine, Portrush.

The National Cycle Network in the area
1. West of Castlerock, Route 93 climbs steeply on Bishop's Road to over 1,000ft with magnificent views to the Inishowen Peninsula and, on a fine day, to the Scottish Isles of Islay and Jura. It then drops down to Limavady via Binevenagh Forest.
2. East of Giant's Causeway Route 93 continues inland towards Ballycastle and the ferries to Scotland and Rathlin.

Other nearby rides (waymarked or traffic-free)
1. A ferry link from Magilligan Point to Greencastle on the Inishowen Peninsula, will link to the route.
2. Rathlin Island, a ferry ride from Ballycastle, offers challenging cycling and walking to famous birdnesting sites and dramatic cliffs.

▼ *The North Coast beaches are ideal for a picnic by the sea.*

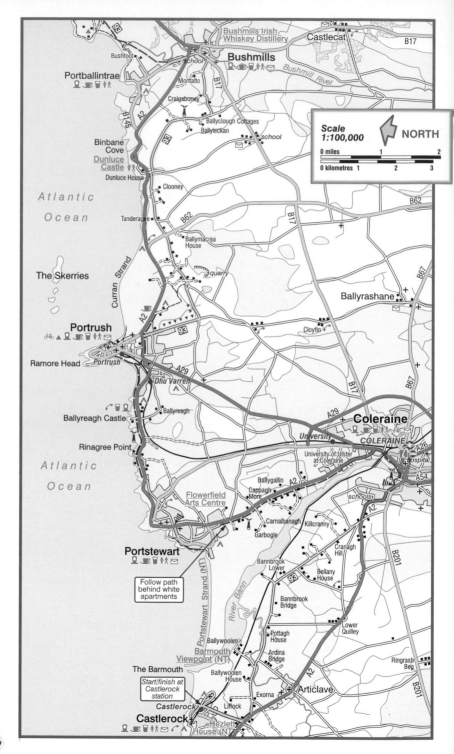

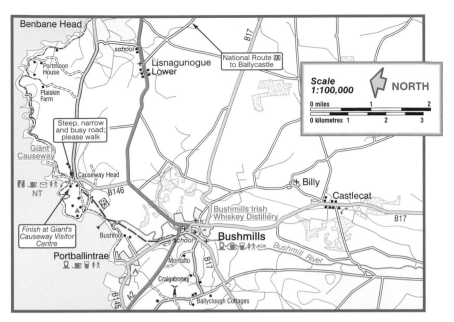

▼ *The Giant's Causeway, at the end of the spectacular ride along the North Antrim Coast.*

LAGAN AND LOUGH CYCLE ROUTE

Water is the linking theme of this ride as it makes its way along the River Lagan and Lagan Navigation Canal from Lisburn into the regenerated heart of Belfast, then out along the shores of Belfast Lough towards the Loughshore Park at Jordanstown via the North Foreshore Path.

From Lisburn a long wooded river and canalside section leads past former linen mills and right into the centre of Belfast via safe crossings at the Ormeau and Albert Bridges. Along the way you'll spot some great artworks including some weights (where you can check out your eyesight!),a flying angel and one of only two huge

ceramic UK maps showing the National Cycle Network routes throughout the country.

The Belfast Hills, particularly the dramatic outline of the Cave Hill, form a fine backdrop to the second part of the ride. After the ferry terminals and the dockland area you'll cross onto the North Foreshore Path, which will take you all the way to Hazelbank Park and Whiteabbey with the vast shimmering expanse of Belfast Lough off to your right.

The fence along the first part of this section was erected to protect the numerous wading birds from being disturbed by dogs and walkers.

Starting Points
Lisburn Civic Centre at Lagan Valley Island, Lisburn.
Loughshore Park, Jordanstown at the edge of Belfast Lough.
Waterfront Hall in the Laganside area of Belfast.

Distance
12 miles one way from Lisburn to Waterfront Hall, Belfast (24 miles return).
7 miles one way from

Waterfront Hall, Belfast to Loughshore Park, Jordanstown (14 miles return).

Grade
Easy.

Surface
Mainly tarmac surface throughout with a short section of cobbles.

Roads, traffic, suitability for children
Whilst the route is almost totally traffic-free there are two sections which are ideal for young children:
1. Lisburn Civic Centre to Clarendon Dock, Belfast.
2. Loughshore Park, Jordanstown to Dargan Road in North Belfast.

Hills
None.

Refreshments
Plenty of choice in Lisburn.
Cafe at Lisburn Civic Centre.
Tap Room, Hilden Brewery.
Cutters Wharf, Stranmillis.
The Stables Tea Room in Sir
Thomas and Lady Dixon Park
(just off the route at Drumbeg).
Malone House Restaurant in
Barnett Demesne (just off the
route at Shaw's Bridge).
Lots of choice in Belfast.
Ice cream shops and tea shops
in Whiteabbey and
Jordanstown.

Nearest Railway stations
1. The route goes right past
Central Station and close to
Botanic and Yorkgate stations.
2. The best connection to
Lisburn station takes you
through Castle Gardens; or use
Hilden station close to the
route.
3. Jordanstown (1 mile) or

Whiteabbey (half mile) stations
to join the route after crossing
the busy A2.

**The National Cycle Network
in the area**
1. From Lisburn, Route 9
continues west over the
Horseback Bridge at Union
Locks towards Lough Neagh at
Oxford Island and on to
Portadown to follow the Newry
Canal towpath.
2. In due course Route 93 will
run east after crossing the River
Lagan at the Queen Elizabeth
Bridge and past the Odyssey
complex before joining the
Comber Greenway at
Ballymacarrett. A second spur
will head to Holywood and
Bangor
3. Route 93 will also continue
northwards via the
Newtownabbey Way to the
Newtownabbey Council Offices
at Mossley Mill before
continuing to Carrickfergus and
Larne.

▲ *Avoid heavy traffic down by the
River Lagan at Governor's Bridge.*

▼ *The 'Big Fish' by John Kindness
dominates the waterfront area of
Belfast's Laganside.*

▲ The 'Painter's Easel' by Brian Connolly at Lisburn's Arts Centre could inspire some.

▶ Overlooking the River Lagan on Donegall Quay, Belfast.

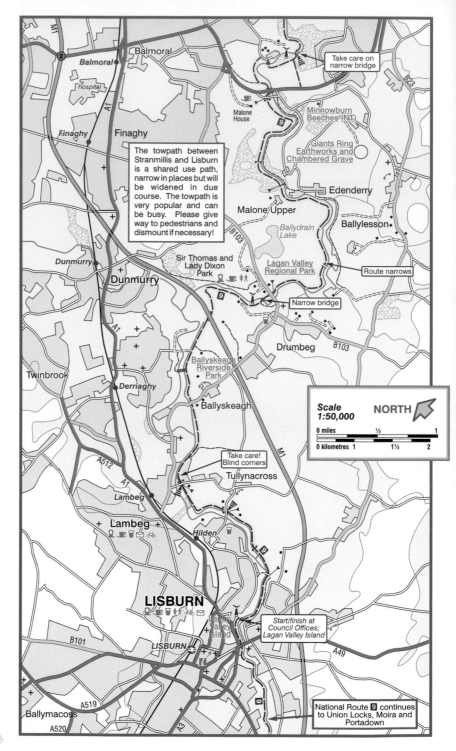

LAGAN AND LOUGH CYCLE ROUTE

The towpath between Stranmillis and Lisburn is a shared use path, narrow in places but will be widened in due course. The towpath is very popular and can be busy. Please give way to pedestrians and dismount if necessary!

Take care on narrow bridge

Minnowburn Beeches (N.T.)

Giants Ring Earthworks and Chambered Grave

Edenderry

Ballylesson

Ballydrain Lake

Lagan Valley Regional Park

Route narrows

Narrow bridge

Drumbeg

Malone Upper

Malone House

Balmoral

Finaghy

Dunmurry

Sir Thomas and Lady Dixon Park

Twinbrook

Ballyskeagh Riverside Park

Derriaghy

Ballyskeagh

Take care! Blind corners

Tullynacross

Lambeg

Hilden

LISBURN

Lagan Valley Island

Start/finish at Council Offices; Lagan Valley Island

Ballymacoss

National Route 9 continues to Union Locks, Moira and Portadown

Scale 1:50,000

NORTH

0 miles ½ 1
0 kilometres 1 1½ 2

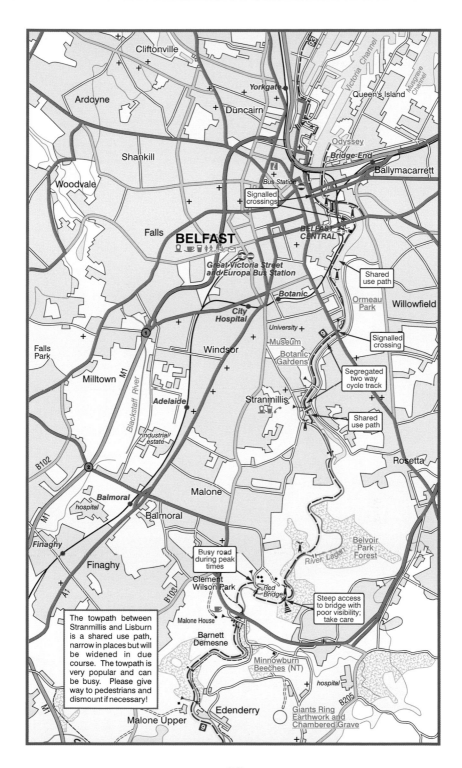

The towpath between Stranmillis and Lisburn is a shared use path, narrow in places but will be widened in due course. The towpath is very popular and can be busy. Please give way to pedestrians and dismount if necessary!

263

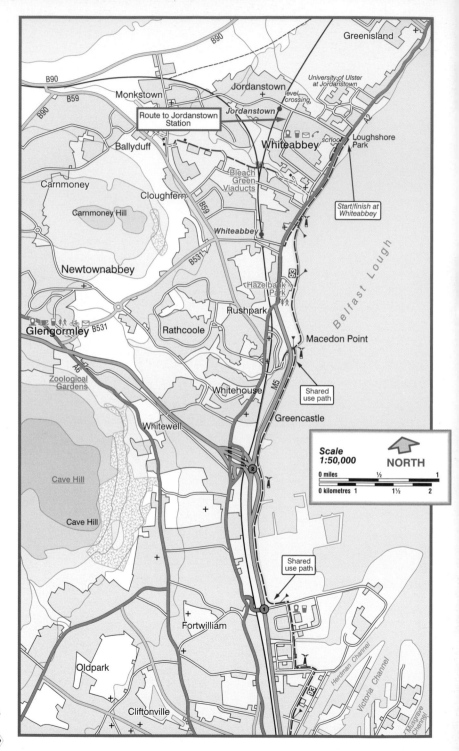

▼ *Cycling along Belfast Lough near Whiteabbey is easy!*

HOLIDAY ROUTES

Longer distance sections of the National Cycle Network offer great opportunities for touring holidays or short breaks.

Spend a long weekend with a difference cycling through Devon from north to south, coasts or leaving London for Oxford on the Thames Valley cycle route.

Escape to ride alongside remote and beautiful Northumberland beaches on the Coast and Castles route, or through the Highlands of Scotland on the Lochs and Glens.

Visit sites such as the Giant's Causeway, Shakespeare's birthplace or the Eden Project. Or test your limits on one of the challenge rides, such as the famous C2C route from west to east coast through the Lake District and over the Pennines, and Lôn Las Cymru stretching the length of Wales.

Here we profile some of the best longer distance routes, giving details of mileages and grading the routes to help you choose.

Sustrans has published a series of high-quality maps covering these and other routes. To order or for details of the full range, visit www.sustrans.org.uk or call 0845 113 0065.

The website also gives details of companies running holidays on sections of the National Cycle Network.

Cornish Way (Land's End - Bude) 123 miles + 52 miles of options
Moderate/challenging

The Cornish Way reveals historic towns and fishing villages, distinctive landscapes and friendly pubs, as well as a colourful tradition of arts and crafts, festivals and legends.

Beginning at the world-renowned Land's End, a network of routes passes through the ancient landscape of Penwith with its standing stones and magnificent Mount's Bay. The island of St. Michael's Mount forms a backdrop as you turn north to Hayle and head inland to the towns and mineral tramways of Cornwall's tin mining heritage.

At the modern city of Truro you have the choice to either head for the rugged north coast or turn south towards the beautiful scenery and milder climate of the Roseland Peninsula.

The northern route passes through quiet countryside and small villages as it makes its way to the north coast's renowned sandy beaches, popular with families and surfers, joining the popular Camel Trail at Padstow. The southern route runs through lush river valleys, meandering back and forth to the coast before reaching the contrasting lunar landscape of mid-Cornwall. You can also use this route to visit the Lost Gardens of Heligan and the Eden Project.

The routes converge at Bodmin and head towards the 'roof of Cornwall', with its remote moorland, granite tors and sweeping vistas. On leaving the moors there is a more challenging route past some of Cornwall's highest cliffs, or a gentler inland option to the holiday resort of Bude.

West Country Way (Padstow - Bristol and Bath) 252 miles
Moderate/challenging

From the commanding heights of Exmoor and the Mendip Hills to the strange solitude of the Somerset Levels and the lush river valleys of Devon, cycling from Cornwall to the River Avon is surely the best way to experience the varied landscapes of the West Country.

The route starts and ends with two classic sections of traffic-free path, the Camel Trail between Bodmin and Padstow and the Bristol and Bath Railway Path. Between these lie the delights of the Tarka Trail in North Devon, peaceful stretches of canal towpath and miles of quiet rural roads. Although the climbs onto Bodmin Moor, Exmoor and the Mendips are certainly demanding, your exertions will be rewarded by an indelible portrait of the contours and contrasts of this part of the world.

Along the way, you'll get the chance to visit Glastonbury Tor and Wells Cathedral, or explore the attractions of Bristol and Bath. You can even pop into the National Cycle Network Centre in Bristol.

Devon Coast to Coast (Ilfracombe - Plymouth) 102 miles
Moderate/challenging

The Devon Coast to Coast Route is one of the most spectacular and memorable elements of the National Cycle Network. Starting at the attractive coastal town of Ilfracombe and ending in the city of Plymouth, this route takes in the best of the varied Devonshire countryside. It combines the beaches and superb estuaries of North Devon with the green valleys of the Torridge, the Tavy and the Walkham. Its crowning glory is the tremendous traffic-free Granite Way, giving spectacular views from the north-west flanks of Dartmoor. Other traffic-free sections include the Plym Valley Trail and the famous Tarka Trail between Braunton and Meeth.

Largely tracing the course of former railway lines, the route takes you through tunnels and across breathtaking viaducts and bridges bequeathed by Victorian railway engineers. Whether you are planning a long trip across Devon, or a day's outing from Plymouth, Okehampton or Barnstaple, the Devon Coast to Coast Route is the best way to explore this varied countryside without relying on the car.

▼ *Cycling past Glastonbury Tor on the West Country Way.*

 Downs & Weald (London - Hastings or Brighton, via Eastbourne) 105 miles or 65 miles

Easy/moderate

From the banks of the Thames in Greenwich, you'll weave through parks, along riversides and on traffic-free paths, over the North and South Downs to the sea.

This route takes mainly traffic-free paths and minor roads through South London and over the North Downs. It then turns towards Gatwick Airport, running under the South

Terminal with a lift direct to the airport concourse. After Crawley, the main route follows the Worth Way railway path to East Grinstead, with an alternative via the A23 cycle track to Brighton.

At East Grinstead, the main route crosses the Greenwich Meridian Line, then joins the Forest Way, past Ashdown Forest - the home of Christopher Robin and Pooh Bear - and follows minor roads through the historic villages of the Weald. Heathfield Tunnel marks the start of the 11-mile Cuckoo Trail, running to the foot of the South Downs at Polegate.

The alternative route reaches Brighton and Hove and travels along the seafront to the Palace Pier and

To find out about other cycle routes in this area visit www.sustrans.org.uk

Brighton Marina. It passes Rottingdean and Peacehaven, with lovely views along the coast, before descending into Newhaven and the ferry port. It then heads inland, crosses the South Downs along the River Cuckmere and rejoins the main route at Polegate which continues to Eastbourne, then up the coast to Hastings.

Thames Valley (London - Oxford) 97 miles
Easy/Moderate

The perfect escape from London. Leave the hubbub of Putney Bridge for Richmond Park, the Thames at Teddington Lock and the riverside tracks past Hampton Court Palace.

At Cooper's Hill you can visit the RAF war memorial with a view of

Runnymeade, where the Magna Carta was signed, and in Windsor Great Park the route offers tremendous views of Windsor Castle. Crossing the river, the route heads westwards towards Maidenhead and Reading, passing Eton College's rowing lake.

After Reading, you follow the rural roads of the Chilterns, visiting quiet country pubs and travelling through ancient beech woods. Historic Wallingford, where the route crosses the Thames again, was once one of the most influential towns in England at the junction of two medieval trading routes. The route passes Didcot main line railway station and power station, then continues to Sutton Courtenay.

Next stop is Abingdon, once

the capital of Berkshire, and claimed to be the oldest inhabited town in England; and journey's end is Oxford, one of the most cycle friendly cities in England.

Garden of England (Dover to London and Hastings) 114 miles or 54 miles
Easy/moderate

Dover, with its famous white cliffs and ancient fortifications, marks the start of the Garden of England Cycle Route. On a clear day, before you start off, you might even see the coast of France from Dover Castle.

The route to London follows the coast to the medieval Cinque Port of Sandwich, Ramsgate and Ebbsfleet, ancient point of entry to Britain

for the Vikings, Saxons and St. Augustine. At Fordwich, Britain's smallest town, a traffic-free path takes you to the cathedral city of Canterbury.

The mainly traffic-free Crab & Winkle Way leads to Whitstable, famous for its oysters, and further on lies Faversham and the malty aroma from the Shepherd Neame brewery. The route reaches the Thames Medway Canal and passes Tilbury Ferry (which could take you to routes north of the river). At Dartford you follow the river along traffic-free paths, past the Thames Barrier, to Greenwich, ending under the bow of the Cutty Sark.

West of Dover, the alternative

ride to Hastings, starts by climbing to the entrance of Samphire Hoe Country Park: a new piece of England created from the excavated spoil of the Channel Tunnel. The cliff-top path descends to Folkestone Harbour and Hythe, before crossing the Romney Marsh into Sussex. The route passes two other Cinque Ports: Rye, with its history of smuggling, and Winchelsea. The descent into

Hastings is on minor roads with grand views over the old town and the English Channel.

1 🚲 Hull - Harwich
369 miles

Easy/moderate

A perfect introduction to longer-distance cycling, travelling through the mostly flat, open landscape of the Fens and East Anglia on minor roads and traffic-free sections. It is covered by two maps - Hull to Fakenham (206 miles) and Fakenham to Harwich (163 miles).

Highlights of the route include crossing the Humber Bridge, until 1998 the world's longest single span suspension bridge, offering fantastic views, and the cathedral cities of Lincoln and Norwich.

You'll also pass through

beautiful, coastal countryside offering magnificent wildlife. Other points of interest include the ancient port of King's Lynn and the Queen's country home of Sandringham Estate

The southern section of the route includes the traffic-free Marriott's Way from Reepham to Norwich, where you can visit the 900-year-old castle and which has more medieval churches than London, Bristol and York put together.

The Hull to Harwich route is part of the North Sea Cycle Route - the world's longest signed international cycle route running through the Netherlands, Germany, Denmark, Sweden, Scotland and England. The Harwich to Aberdeen part of the National Cycle Network makes up almost 1500 miles of the total 3700-mile route.

 West Midlands (Oxford - Derby, via Birmingham) 163 miles

Moderate

This route links many of the towns and cities of the West Midlands with beautiful countryside and places of interest.

Take a trip through history as you leave the dreaming spires of Oxford to visit Blenheim Palace, birthplace of Winston Churchill; Stratford upon Avon where you can see Shakespeare's birthplace and grave; and Coughton Court, where plotters headed after failing to blow up the Houses of Parliament in 1605.

On your way from Oxford, you'll also get some outstanding views in the Cotswolds and the rolling Worcestershire countryside.

You make your way to Centenary Square in the heart of Birmingham in a really different style on riverside, canal and parkland paths. The route also connects Walsall, Lichfield and Burton-upon-Trent on its way to Derby.

Lôn Las Cymru (Chepstow/ Cardiff - Holyhead)

Challenging

The most challenging route on the National Cycle Network. Lôn Las Cymru takes in a wide variety of memorable

▼*View St Michael's Mount from the Cornish Way.*

▼*Arriving in Newbury on Route 4.*

▼*Coatbridge on the Clyde to Forth.*

landscapes from the pastoral lanes of Anglesey to the valleys of South Wales, passing through the magnificent National Parks of Snowdonia and the Brecon Beacons. This is Wales in all its natural magnificence and is a 'must ride' for any adventurous or long distance cyclist.

The route is covered by two maps. The northern half of the route connects Holyhead and Anglesey to the northern part of the Wye Valley in mid-Wales using minor roads, railway paths, forestry tracks and ancient coach roads. The route crosses the Snowdonia National Park, goes past Caernarfon Castle, Porthmadog and Harlech Castle and along the lovely Mawddach Estuary.

There are two options for the southern part of the route. The largely traffic-free Taff Trail connects Brecon to Cardiff via the valleys heritage of Merthyr Tydfil and Taff Vale. An alternative, will take you on minor roads from Hay-on-Wye to Chepstow via Abergavenny.

Celtic Trail/Lôn Geltaidd (Severn Bridge - Fishguard) 227 miles plus 140 miles of options

The Celtic Trail travels the length of South Wales, linking the 'Gateway to Wales' at the Severn Bridge to the Pembrokeshire Coast National Park. Your journey will take you through some of the most diverse scenery in Wales, from the country's industrial heartland passing right through Cardiff and Swansea to green valleys and forests.

The route is covered by two maps. The first covers from the old Severn Bridge via Newport, Cardiff, Pontypridd and Merthyr Tydfil to Swansea, with much of the route traffic-free. As well as the main route, the High Level Route from Neath to Pontypridd offers a challenging alternative and the Taff Trail provides a traffic-free escape north out of Cardiff.

The second section gives you two options from Swansea to Fishguard. One leg goes via the coast, and an inland northerly leg goes directly to Fishguard.

Highlights here include the magnificent traffic-free Millennium Coastal Park at Llanelli and the Pembrokeshire Coast National Park.

Pennine Cycleway Derby to Berwick-upon-Tweed 354 miles plus 202 miles of options

Challenging

This route offers the ultimate long distance route or a series of escapes from the towns and cities along its length to beautiful countryside, including three of Britain's national parks.

The route is broken down into sections and covered by three maps: Derby to Holmfirth; Holmfirth to Appleby; and Appleby or Penrith to Berwick-upon-Tweed.

The first section includes the popular and accessible Tissington, High Peak and Longdendale Trails whilst highlighting routes to get you into the Peak District without a car. It also includes a return loop to Derby via Sherwood Forest and Nottingham which can equally start from Stockport, Sheffield, Penistone, Worksop or Ashbourne.

The second part of the ride offers a wide variety of scenery, including splendid examples of textile mills, delightful market towns, pastoral farmland and high open moorland. It passes through the South Pennines, close to the famous Pendle Hill (look out for witches!) before entering the Yorkshire Dales at Gargrave with its popular cyclists cafe. Steep climbs and rapid descents lead to cobbled Dent and onto the Howgill Fells with fine views over the Lune Gorge towards the Lakeland Fells.

The final leg takes in some of the most spectacular landscapes and unspoilt countryside that England has to offer, including the Eden Valley, the dramatic North Pennines, Hadrian's Wall World Heritage Site, the Northumberland National Park and the Cheviots. The journey ends at the border town of Berwick-upon-Tweed on the spectacular Northumberland coast.

C2C (Whitehaven/ Workington - Newcastle/ Sunderland) 136 miles plus 62 miles of options

Moderate/challenging

The UK's most popular 'challenge' cycle route, this one will give you a real sense of achievement.

Linking the Irish Sea with the North Sea, the route starts in either Whitehaven or Workington. Running through the northern Lake District, the route climbs the Pennines, 'the roof of England', to the highest point on the National Cycle Network at Black Hill (2,000 feet). Several sections of the route offer an off-road alternative to test the best mountain bike.

▼*Speyside Way on the Lochs & Glens.*

▼ *Moorland cycling on the Pennine Cycle Way.*

On the eastern side of the Pennines, you can choose to make your way to Sunderland or to Newcastle-upon-Tyne. One route travels along the Consett-Sunderland railway path and sculpture trail passing through towns and villages with lingering reminders that this was once one of Britain's major industrial heartlands. The other follows the River Tyne past the Gateshead Millennium Bridge to the end at Tynemouth.

☐ 🚲〉 Coast & Castles (Newcastle - Edinburgh) 200 miles
Easy/moderate
This links the Tyne and the Forth estuaries, taking in some of Britain's best built and natural heritage.

From the vibrant city of Newcastle upon Tyne, the route starts by taking you through Tynemouth, Whitley Bay and the former coalfields of south-east Northumberland, where the industrial heritage still dominates the landscape. Soon you reach the fabulous unspoiled Northumberland coastline, passing fishing villages, castles and fortresses, such as Warkworth, Bamburgh and Lindisfarne (accessed by the longest tidal road on the National Cycle Network).

At Berwick-upon-Tweed, the route moves inland along the Tweed Valley. Quiet lanes take you through the Borders via Coldstream, Kelso, Galashiels and Innerleithen, and a relatively easy climb over the Moorfoot Hills into Midlothian affords a breathtaking view of Edinburgh and the Firth of Forth.

Through the busy medieval town of Dalkeith, you follow disused railway paths that once ferried coal to Edinburgh.

Continuing along the Innocent Railway Path into Edinburgh, under the imposing volcanic cliffs of Salisbury Crags and through the long railway tunnel, you arrive at The Mound in the heart of the city.

75 🚲〉 Clyde to Forth (Gourock - Edinburgh) 91 miles plus 171 miles of options
Easy/moderate
The route starts (or finishes) at Gourock on the Clyde, one of the main ferry ports to the West Coast. It offers fine views of the Highlands and an excellent traffic-free path, which leads you almost to the centre of Glasgow. Following the Clyde cast out of the city, you get an intriguing taste of the industrial east end of Glasgow; the legacy of disused railways and canals forms the backbone of the route through Coatbridge and Airdrie.

The Hillend Loch Railway Path, a 13-mile traffic-free route across the central plateau, is a remarkable setting for a much admired sculpture trail, then the excellent network of landscaped paths through Livingston leads you to Almondell and Calderwood Country Park. The approach to Edinburgh is virtually traffic-free, along the Water of Leith and Union Canal paths.

The map covering this route also shows links to Loch Lomond, Musselburgh, Ardrossan & Kilmarnock and the Forth Bridge.

7 🚲〉 Lochs & Glens (Inverness - Glasgow - Carlisle) 407 miles
Moderate/challenging
A magnificent ride through the Highlands and Grampian mountains, this route is divided into two sections at Glasgow.

Starting from the historic city

▼ *Descent from Gospel Pass near Abergavenny on Lôn Las Cymru.*

of Inverness and heading south, the route climbs steadily to the open moors of Strathspey. Here lie the ancient remains of the Caledonian pine forest and wide open views of the snow (or cloud!) covered Cairngorm Mountains. A specially constructed cycle path enables you to cross the Drumochter Pass, avoiding the busy trunk road. The route then descends into the wooded hillsides and rich farmlands of Perthshire and Stirlingshire. Scotland's lochs are among its most famous features, and the route takes in the lochs of Tay, Earn, Lubnaig and Venachar, in their dramatic forest settings. This section takes you through Glen Ogle and over the famous viaduct on a traffic-free and scenic cycle route above a busy road. It then crosses the beautiful Queen Elizabeth Forest Park before reaching the southern end of Loch Lomond and heading down to Glasgow.

The route heads south from Glasgow along a railway path and into the rolling hills and pastures of Ayrshire, with sweeping views towards Arran and the Clyde Coast.

The dominant feature of this route is the huge Galloway Forest Park offering a complete mixture of wildlife habitats, landscapes and recreational opportunities including 300 miles of rivers and over 150 lochs.

You then take a descent to the Solway Coast - a haven for bird life - and a final leg through Dumfries and Galloway. Despite its turbulent history, the 'Gateway to Scotland' is now a peaceful area of farms and quiet country towns. Ruined castles are the only reminder of the centuries of cross-border raids.

◄ *Dunnattor Castle, near Stonehaven - Edinburgh to Aberdeen.*

94 🚲 Loughshore Trail (circuit of Lough Neagh) 113 miles
Easy/moderate

This is a mostly level circuit of Lough Neagh, the biggest freshwater lake in the UK and Ireland. The Loughshore Trail can be followed in either direction, and consists of quiet, virtually traffic-free minor roads and lanes with short stretches of traffic-free track. Touching the lough shore at several points, cyclists pass small beaches overlooking the vast expanse of the water.

From Antrim, the route heads west through the beautifully kept grounds of Clotworthy House to Randalstown, with its spectacular railway viaduct. Going close to Cranfield Bay, it enters Toome and after crossing the Lower River Bann, it runs towards the historic village of Ballyronan and past the magnificent 1,000 year old Celtic high cross at Ardboe.

Passing through tracks of ancient bogland where peat is still extracted, the route crosses the River Blackwater and continues south to Portadown. It then returns via Charlestown back towards Lough Neagh.

The route then follows the coastline close to the towns of Glenavy and Crumlin and Belfast International Airport before arriving in Antrim via Reas Wood with its abundance of bluebells in springtime.

91 🚲 Kingfisher Trail (Fermanagh and the Leitrim Lakeland) 230 miles
Moderate

The cross-border Kingfisher Cycle Trail loops around lakes and islands, along rivers and streams, through forest and country parks, down village streets, circling historic monuments and attractive landmarks.

The trail was the first long distance cycle trail in Ireland and takes minor country roads through the border counties of Fermanagh, Leitrim, Cavan, Donegal and Monaghan.

It follows a figure of eight, starting from Enniskillen Visitor Centre, and crosses the border into Southern Ireland, with the main link via Carrick-on-Shannon. Attractions include the Lough Scur Dolmen, Castle Coole and the Marble Arch caves.

The trail can be divided to create shorter loops.

OTHER LONG DISTANCE ROUTES

 South Midlands (Oxford - Derby, via Leicester) 148 miles + 40 miles of options
Easy/moderate
A route through the heart of England, undulating farmlands and market towns, linking major cities of Derby, Leicester, historic Oxford and modern Milton Keynes. Cycle without traffic along the Brampton Valley Way between Northampton and Market Harborough, into and out of the city centre of Leicester and from Worthington up to Derby. Points of interest include the National Bowl at Milton Keynes, the National Space & Science Centre in Leicester and Foxton Locks & Canal Museum.

 Derby - York 154 miles + 28 miles of options
Moderate
Nottingham, Sheffield, Doncaster, Rotherham and Barnsley are among the key urban connections on this route. Explore the legend of Robin Hood in Nottinghamshire's famous ancient woodlands, visit Conisbrough Castle or enjoy the country parks that have transformed much of this historically industrial land.

 Round the Forth 91 miles
Moderate
A route linking Edinburgh with Stirling, Alloa and Queensferry along both sides of the Firth of Forth. There is plenty to see along the way with numerous historic houses and towns and the two Forth bridges. Some of the route runs alongside the coast, while another part takes you up to an escarpment where you can get a panoramic view of the river.

 Edinburgh to Aberdeen 170 miles + 23 miles of options
Easy/moderate
This route crosses the Firth of Forth into the Kingdom of Fife with its beautiful countryside. It then follows the coast north passing through fishing villages and historic sites such as Dunnottar Castle on its way to Aberdeen.

1 🚲 **Aberdeen to John o'Groats**

320 miles + 181 miles of options

Moderate/challenging

This route is one of contrasts. It starts in Aberdeen - the third largest city in Scotland - and travels northwards into a rural landscape of coast and castles leading to the spectacular and remote scenery of the Highlands, the ancient peatlands of the Flow Country and John o'Groats, before crossing the Pentland Firth to the islands of Orkney and Shetland by ferry. Both are great cycling destinations, especially if the wind is behind you!

9 🚲 **Belfast - Ballyshannon - Ballycastle**

91 🚲

92 🚲 **467 miles + 20 miles of options**

93 🚲 *Moderate*

95 🚲 Divided into two legs, the first section from Belfast to Ballyshannon takes in the Sperrins Mountains, the lakes of Fermanagh, the Lagan Valley Cycle Route through Belfast and the beautiful sandy beaches of County Donegal.

The second leg links Pettigo, Derry/Londonderry, Omagh and Coleraine and includes the Foyle Valley Cycle Route and a link to the Giant's Causeway.

Use the on-line mapping at www.sustrans.org.uk to find other National Cycle Network routes near you.

▼ *Celtic Trail in South Wales.*

▼ *Cullen viaduct and the North Sea framing this view of the Aberdeen to John o'Groats long distance route.*

PRACTICAL ADVICE

The good news is, almost everything related to cycling is simple, straightforward and rooted firmly in common sense! If you're new to cycling, a bit rusty, or have never fixed a puncture, this section is for you. Experienced cyclists may well want to skip this chapter and get straight on with the riding.

Your bike
A few simple adjustments to your bike can make all the difference in terms of comfort. Don't be put off by hype about bikes with 30 gears, full suspension and frames made of exotic metals. Enjoying cycling is in the mind, not in the equipment.

▲ *A good bike shop will help you to adjust your bike.*

Don't worry if you think that riding a bike looks uncomfortable. It's true that some people complain of a mildly sore bottom after their first long bike ride, but it doesn't last - and doesn't happen at all if you use your bike reasonably often. Well designed, gender specific saddles are now widely available, so if you're not comfortable on yours, don't give up. Try out other people's bikes and see if you prefer the saddle/riding position/feel of the bike.

Getting the height and tilt of your saddle and handlebars right can transform how you feel. It's common to see cyclists riding with their saddle set too low, which makes it much harder work to pedal - as a rule, your knee should be only slightly bent when your foot/pedal reaches its lowest point.

The surfaces on the Network are not all sealed and may vary, so it's wise to use a bike with strong wheels (ie not a lightweight racing bike!) for traffic-free sections. Children's bikes tend to be robust enough anyway, but adults should opt for a touring bike, a so-called hybrid bike, or a mountain bike (preferably fitted with smooth tyres).

What to wear
You don't need lots of expensive, specialist clothing in order to cycle. Several thin layers of ordinary clothing will normally do, giving you the ability to remove or add layers as your body temperature changes. That said, once you use a bike regularly you may well want to invest in a few key items.

Cycling shorts are padded and make longer rides more comfortable. As well as the lycra variety, more casual style padded cycling shorts are available, as are padded gloves. Leggings on top of cycling shorts are best for keeping your legs warm, and won't rub against the chain. Tight, non-stretch jeans are about the worst thing to wear.

For your upper body, t-shirts, thermal vests, shirts or fleeces should be long enough to cover your back when you're stretched forward. The ideal outer layer is a windproof/showerproof top with zips to help adjust for changes in temperature. Your extremities are much more susceptible to cold on a bike than when you are out walking, so take gloves and a hat.

Helmets
Wearing a cycle helmet is not compulsory in the UK, so it's up to you to decide if or when to use one. If you're cycling with youngsters, see the Helmets section in Cycling With Children on page 292.

Punctures
Contrary to many people's fears, punctures are relatively rare. However, when they do happen they can ruin a day out, if you're not prepared. It's pretty easy and quick to repair a puncture when you know how and have the necessary equipment - a pump, tyre levers (to get the tyre off the wheel rim), spare inner tube and puncture repair kit are the only indispensable accessories you need.

If you don't know how to mend a puncture, it's worth learning. Below are some easy to follow instructions, but the best way to learn is to get an experienced cyclist to show you what to do.

▲ *Mending a puncture is quick and easy when you have the know-how.*

Bike maintenance

There are only a few things you need to do regularly to keep your bike running smoothly. The following checklist covers the main tasks;
• Daily: general check, tyres.
• Weekly: lubricate moving parts, gears, brakes, levers, chain.
• Monthly: check tyres & wheels, brakes, gears, steering, pedals and frame.

Some bike shops, cycle groups and local authorities run courses on bicycle maintenance. Alternatively, you can teach yourself using a good book.

Recommended are:

The Bike Book by Fred Milson (Haynes)
ISBN 1-85960323-8
Includes step-by-step guidance on all aspects of bike care.

Richard's 21st Century Bike Book
by Richard Ballantine (Pan)
ISBN 0-33037717-5
A definitive guide to all aspects of cycling.

TO MEND A PUNCTURE:

1. Release brake callipers and remove the wheel.

2. Use tyre levers (readily available from bike shops) to remove the tyre, then remove the inner tube, carefully feeding the valve back through the wheel rim.

3. Carefully run your fingers around the inside of the tyre to check for sharp objects, such as nails, glass splinters or thorns. Remove the cause of the puncture and check that there are no more spikes in the tyre.

4. Find the hole in the inner tube. Pump it up and either feel and listen for escaping air, or hold it underwater to look for bubbles.

5. Mark the hole with a pen or chalk. Use sandpaper or the scratcher from the puncture repair kit to scuff the area around the hole to help the glue stick to the tube.

6. Spread glue thinly and evenly over and around the hole and wait for it to dry until it feels tacky to touch. Place a patch over the marked hole and apply pressure. (A faster alternative is to use the new glueless patches now available.)

7. Lightly pump up the tube. Place one edge of the tyre around the wheel rim and push the tube's valve back into the rim's hole. Starting from the valve, push the rest of the tube into the tyre and onto the wheel. Ensure the valve stem is perpendicular to the rim and that the tube isn't twisted. Once the tube is inside the tyre, begin to place the second edge of the tyre onto the rim. About 75% of the tyre will go on easily - the rest will need strong fingers or tyre levers to coax it back onto the rim. Take care not to pinch and damage the tube. When complete, pump a little more air into the tube and check that it isn't caught between the rim and the tyre.

8. Slide the wheel back into place on the bike and tighten the bolts gradually, ensuring that the wheel remains aligned straight to the frame. Reconnect the brakes.

9. If you are happy with it, fully pump up the tyre. Take the bike on a short ride, and test that the brakes are still set up correctly.

Tip: save time on journeys by carrying a spare inner tube with you, so that you can simply replace the tube if a puncture happens, mending the damaged one when you get home. But do remember to remove the glass or thorn from your tyre before you put it back on.

◀ *It is a good idea to get your bike serviced once or twice a year.*

group gets split up. This allows slower riders to catch up, or for the faster ones to take a longer route to the meeting point. The thought of getting to a good cafe, teashop or pub can do wonders in terms of encouraging people up hills, but check the opening times of planned refreshment points in advance.

More experienced cyclists can help the group they're with by checking novices' bikes, mending punctures or making minor bike adjustments where necessary, as well as generally giving encouragement or advice when needed. A more experienced cyclist should always bring up the rear of a group to prevent a novice from being stranded at the back with a problem beyond his/her ability to fix. In strong headwinds you can help a weaker cyclist by getting them to follow closely behind you in your slipstream, but don't try this on unsurfaced routes - you need to keep an eye out for any rough patches!

What else to take?

Besides pump and puncture repair kit, consider the following (depending on conditions on the day):

- map/guidebook
- energy snacks and water
- spare clothes (especially hat and gloves)
- waterproofs
- bike lock
- bike lights & reflective belt
- sun protection and sunglasses

Carrying equipment

There are various ways to carry equipment on a bike. For absolute minimalists, a water bottle and pump will fit on the frame, whilst tools, keys and money will fit into a small bumbag. A larger bumbag will also carry a thin waterproof.

If you have more than this, having a rear luggage rack fitted to your bike can be very useful, so that you can either attach a bag to the rack using elasticated bungee cords, or hook-on proper luggage panniers if you have them. You'll find it's less comfortable wearing a rucksack whilst riding, and it tends to make your back a bit sweaty, too.

When using panniers, make sure they're evenly loaded - and line them with plastic bags if there's a chance of rain. Handlebar bags are an increasingly popular carrying accessory for cyclists. Most are easily removable from the bike and are useful for easy access, however they're not suitable for carrying heavy loads.

Cycling in a group

If you're cycling in a mixed ability group, it's a good idea to arrange rendezvous points for coffee/lunch/tea/ in case the

GOOD CYCLING CODE

The National Cycle Network is 10,000 miles of cycle routes, running right through urban centres and reaching all parts of the UK. It is designed to encourage people to start cycling again and to be a safe and attractive resource for families, novices and experienced cyclists. One-third of the National Cycle Network is on traffic-free paths providing a major new amenity for walkers and, in many places, people with disabilities.

On all routes:
Please be courteous. Always cycle with respect for others, whether other cyclists, pedestrians, people in wheelchairs, horse riders or drivers, and acknowledge those who give way to you.

On shared use paths:
One-third of the National Cycle Network is on traffic-free paths, such as disused railway routes. These are designed for shared use by cyclists and walkers. They are often suitable for wheelchairs and sometimes for horse riders.

Experience in the UK and abroad shows that such paths can benefit everyone and that they can be comfortably and safely shared if we show respect for others.

When cycling on shared use paths please:
- give way to pedestrians, leaving them plenty of room
- keep to your side of any dividing line
- be prepared to slow down or stop if necessary
- don't expect to cycle at high speeds
- be careful at junctions, bends and entrances
- **Remember that many people are hard of hearing or visually impaired – don't assume that they can see or hear you**
- **Ensure you have a bell on the handlebars of your bike and use it – don't surprise people**

- give way where there are wheelchair users and horse riders.

On roads:
Much of the National Cycle Network is on traffic-calmed or minor roads through towns and the countryside.

When cycling on roads:
- always follow the Highway Code
- be seen – most accidents to cyclists happen at junctions
- fit lights and use them in poor visibility
- consider wearing a helmet and conspicuous clothing
- keep your bike roadworthy
- don't cycle on pavements except where designated – pavements are for pedestrians
- use your bell – not all pedestrians can see you.

And in the countryside:
- follow the Country Code
- respect other land management activities such as farming or forestry and take litter home
- keep erosion to a minimum if offroad
- be self-sufficient – in remote areas carry food, repair kit, map and waterproofs
- try to cycle or use public transport to travel to and from the start and finish of your ride
- cycle within your capabilities
- match your speed to the surface and your skills.

Thank you for cycling!
The bicycle does not cause pollution or contribute to climate change.

Thank you for choosing this environmentally-friendly form of transport.

CYCLING WITH CHILDREN

Learning to ride a bike is a vital part of childhood, promoting health and fitness and allowing children to develop their sense of independence. The National Cycle Network provides wonderful opportunities all over the UK for families to safely enjoy cycling trips together. Elsewhere in this guide you'll find over 100 suggested routes, specifically selected as suitable for family outings.

There are a number of ingredients that make for a good, safe trip and that will encourage children to cycle from an early age. The two most important factors for your peace of mind, as well as for the child's enjoyment, are safety and comfort.

Children and bikes

Depending on their age, ability, and the nature of the intended route, a child can be included in a bike trip in a number of ways. Options include carrying them in a child seat attached to your bike, pulling them along in a trailer behind your bike, putting them on a bike that attaches to your bike, allowing them to ride on the back of a tandem with you, or putting them on their own bike.

Looking at the options for kids of different ages:

- 0-9 months: until babies can hold their heads up by themselves, they should not be carried on bikes. This may happen between six months and a year. It is a good idea to get the baby used to the bike seat as early as possible so that they are quite happy in it. You'll also get used to carrying the increasing weight, and learn how this affects the handling of the bike.
- 9 months – 4 years: the child can be carried in a specially designed seat fitted to the back or the middle of the bike. There are many different bike seats and means of attachment. Look out for reviews in cycling magazines and ask friends and cycle shops for advice.
- 18 months+: a toddler graduates happily from a push-along tractor/car without pedals to a tricycle or bike with stabilisers and eventually to a bike without stabilisers. A child interested in cycling will probably be able to ride without stabilisers by the age of 4-6.

The child seat

When choosing a child seat you need to think carefully about safety and comfort. Ask whether the seat can be adapted for different sized toddlers and children. Is there adequate padding, and is the child firmly held in place by straps and safety bars in case they fall asleep and nod forward, or in case you have to brake suddenly? Some seats recline, allowing the child to sleep comfortably and helping to stop their head lolling forwards. Other things to consider are how easily or frequently you may wish to remove the seat entirely and if the seat can be used in conjunction with panniers.

There are some saddles that can be fitted to the crossbar. These give the child a much better view and allow conversation to take place, but obviously offer much less protection both from a safety aspect and from the wind and cold.

Trailers

Trailers are a wonderful way to

▼ *Trailers are a wonderful way to carry babies and children who are too small to contribute pedal power.*

292

▲ *A bike seat on the crossbar gives a better view.*

carry babies and children who are still too small to contribute pedal power. Even babies younger than 9 months old can sometimes be carried safely in a cycle trailer (by fastening them in a small baby's car seat and then strapping that into the trailer), though we recommend that you seek detailed advice on this.

Children in trailers can sleep when they wish, and take a toy or a book with them. Trailers usually have accessible side pockets – children will enjoy disorganising their bits and pieces into them.

You'll find that towing a trailer affects bike handling far less than a child seat which can make it less tiring than cycling with a child seat. They are also extremely conspicuous on the road and motorists tend to be overwhelmingly considerate. From a safety standpoint, trailers are designed for stability – you can drop your bike horizontally,

without the trailer tipping over.

There are also some drawbacks to trailer use, particularly in built-up areas. The extra length a trailer adds to your bike is obviously not helpful at busy junctions, and if you stop and take the whole thing off the road, you block the pavement! However, on country lanes trailers are fine though, it's worth avoiding twisting little lanes through dark woodland, where drivers' vision is inevitably restricted.

Bought new, trailers are not cheap, but there is a good availability of second-hand ones (try bike hire outlets selling stock at the end of summer).

Trailer bikes
By five years old, your child is going to be quite a weight to carry either on a seat or in a trailer - yet is likely to have abundant energy! A trailer bike allows your child to contribute some pedal power, without the responsibility for steering or braking. In effect, the back half

of a child's bike is attached to the adult's machine.

There are various versions of trailer bike available; the best are purpose-built units that attach to a special bracket bolted to your own bike. This type adjusts with the growth of your child so that a single trailer bike will last them from around five years old to around nine. The worst are systems that encourage you to remove the front wheel from your child's bike and then clamp around its headset to attach it to your bike. These can wobble alarmingly – definitely try before you buy.

Helmets
Whether or not you choose to wear a helmet, children should be encouraged to wear one for several reasons. Until adolescence, children are less able than adults to judge traffic speeds and distances, and are thus more likely to suffer a mishap when they are on their bikes in the presence of traffic (even if this is on quiet back

streets or lanes). Youngsters are more likely to try out stunts and tricks which may end in a fall, too, and in the event of an accident when children are being carried on the back of a bike, they will not be able to prepare themselves for a fall in the same way as the adult rider.

Be careful when you secure a helmet on a child, as it's easy to put them off wearing one if you accidentally pinch the sensitive skin under their chin while securing the clips on the helmet straps. To avoid doing this, insert your forefinger between the clip and the chin so that your finger may be pinched, but not the child's skin. Encourage children to put on the helmet themselves – they should be able to do this from about the age of three. A helmet which is not done up is no use whatsoever: it will be thrown off in the event of a fall, exposing the head to injury.

It's important that the child's helmet is the right size and a good cycle shop will help you. As with bikes, children are likely to grow out of several helmets between birth and adolescence. If a helmet has been involved in a serious accident or fall, replace it.

Children's bikes

Having the right size bike is important, but it's a common mistake to buy a child a bike that's too large, for them to grow into. Riding a bike that's too big is not only dangerous, but is likely to put the child off cycling. Similarly, once a child has outgrown a bike, it becomes dangerous for them to ride, so think of passing it down to another child, or selling it second-hand.

A child's first bike is better if it has no crossbar; that way, the child falls through the bike and not off it. From the age a child can first cycle, he/she will

typically use and outgrow three bikes before being ready for an adult sized bike.

Hire bikes

At many of the more popular trails you can hire adult and children's bikes, childrens seats, trailers and helmets. Look in Yellow Pages, call the nearest tourist information centre or view the on-line mapping section of the National Cycle Network website at www.sustrans.org.uk for details of hire centres. Ring in advance to book equipment, particularly on fine summer weekends. The hire centre staff are often the best people to ask about safe routes in the area.

Planning a family ride: checking the bikes, what to take

It's really not difficult to prepare for a family ride on the Network, but a few simple checks the night before make the day itself a lot easier. Check bikes for punctures and that the brakes work properly, lubricate chains and ensure that all the nuts on carrier racks and child carriers are tightly done up. Pack some food and drink (water or well-diluted squash is best) - little and often is better than one big midday meal.

You don't need a pannier full of tools, but you should have the equipment to mend a puncture (tyre levers, spare inner tube, puncture repair kit, pump). If you want to play it safe, take a small adjustable spanner, a reversible screwdriver and Allen keys.

A child on the back of a bike generates no heat, so is much more likely to get cold quickly; even on a fine day, take extra clothes (hat, gloves and socks) and something waterproof. There are waterproof covers available for children's seats that will keep the child dry.

Planning a ride: when to go, where to go

Country lanes can often be quieter during the week than at weekends. Traffic-free routes are fine at any time, although you will be sharing the path with more cyclists and walkers at the weekend.

The options for where to go are much greater if the child is being carried in a bike seat or trailer (ie you are in complete control of their safety and the limits are when you get tired and /or the child gets bored). If the child is cycling rather than being carried, National Cycle Network routes on dismantled railways are ideal places for them to learn to ride and to gain confidence and stamina – the routes tend to be broad, flat, with a good quality surface and most importantly, traffic-free.

Forestry Commission tracks are traffic-free but may be steeper and slightly rougher than railway paths. Certain Forestry Commission holdings have waymarked trails, some of which are promoted as suitable for families. Some canal towpaths are appropriate for family cycling, and some reservoirs have a cycle path around their edge.

How far to go?

Don't be too ambitious! It's better that everyone has a good time and wants to go out cycling again, rather than coming back home exhausted and tearful and permanently put off cycling. If the children are on their own bikes, the ride should be designed around them and not you. If there are things to look forward to such as a picnic, a playground, a castle, a sculpture, a stream or river, or a field full of animals, then the children will be happier. On a still day, on good, flat surfaces, cycling 3-4 miles is equivalent to walking one mile, though hills, rough surfaces, wind and heavy loads all make cycling considerably slower and harder. 5-10 miles is about the right length trip for young children on their own bikes. 10-30 miles makes for a good day out for older children or for adults carrying children.

Getting to the start of the ride
The best rides are often those that start from home: children will recognise familiar places and there is far less hassle about getting everything organised. Catching a train with bikes and children is also possible, but you will need to do some research to find out which trains carry bikes, and perhaps make a booking in advance. Some trains only take one or two bikes, making a family trip with adults and children impossible. Call National Rail Enquiries on 08457 484950 for information.

Cycling on roads with young children
Children must learn about road safety whilst gaining confidence and stamina as they go out on longer rides. On the first few trips on quiet lanes, it's worth teaching children to stop and pull in to the side whenever a vehicle is heard. Teaching a child how to look behind them without wobbling or veering into the middle of the road is one of the most important skills of safe cycling.

The best configuration when riding with children, is to have adults at both the front and rear of the group. If there's only one adult, it's best to stay at the back, to keep an eye on the children

ahead - always keep them in sight. If you're carrying a child on the back of your bike, it's better to push up steep hills that you might have tried to cycle up if you were on your own, because it can be very difficult to dismount safely on a steep hill, with the weight of a child on the back.

The road manoeuvre needing most care is the right turn from a main road on to a side road. The recommended approach is to look behind you, wait for a gap in the traffic, indicate and then turn. However if the road's busy, pull in to the left and wait for a break in both flows of traffic.

Cycling proficiency training
Cycle training for children is offered by many local authorities in the UK. For information and advice, contact CTC on 0870 873 0060 or via www.ctc.org.uk

▲ *Trailer bikes are a good way to share the pedal power.*

THE NATIONAL CYCLE NETWORK AND SUSTRANS

The National Cycle Network is a fantastic resource, giving you more freedom to choose how you travel. It passes through all the UK's major cities, linking them with over 10,000 miles of traffic-free routes, quiet lanes and traffic-calmed city streets. This comprehensive, nationwide network gives everyone the opportunity to cycle and walk more in their daily lives.

The National Cycle Network has been created by hundreds of organisations working together, co-ordinated by the charity Sustrans. Those involved include local authorities, utility companies, landowners, heritage and wildlife bodies, rail operators and central government.

Making cycling a real alternative

Changing the way we travel now by increasing the amount people walk and cycle, will improve the way we live in the future. Clearer roads, cleaner air and a healthier environment, improved personal wellbeing and better quality of life - they're all achievable.

Currently, the popularity of cycling in Britain is way below the levels of many of our European neighbours. Proportionately, far more people cycle in Sweden, a country which is much colder; in Germany, which has higher car ownership; and in Switzerland, which is considerably more hilly. By playing a leading role in creating the National Cycle Network, and through a raft of other imaginative and practical projects, Sustrans is putting cycling back in the public domain in the UK.

Encouraging cycling

If we are to see cycling levels increase, it is essential that people have safe routes on road and on traffic-free paths, so they can rediscover the sheer pleasure and value of riding a bike. To encourage this, Sustrans has aimed to make the Network as attractive, memorable and useful as possible, and an imaginative programme of sculpture has been adopted to further add to users' enjoyment.

In creating the Network, significant use of recycled materials has been made in the construction process: bridges have been made from old concrete railway sleepers, sculptures created from old JCBs, and seats from wooden sleepers. Attractive features have been incorporated in

▲ *Bristol & Bath Path at Easton before the cycle path was created*

including John Grimshaw, set up a group to promote cycling to help combat climate change. Within two years the group started a programme of building cycle routes, a process which has continued - although now on a vastly expanded scale - to the present day.

A section of the dismantled railway line running between Bristol and Bath was the first railway path the charity converted for use by cyclists and walkers. Since that modest beginning, what started as a vision of a single five-mile route has become the first 10,000 miles of the National Cycle Network. Today, the National Cycle Network is just one of the many practical projects run by Sustrans to promote walking, cycling and use of public transport to benefit people's health and the environment.

other ways too: causeways through cuttings allow ponds to be formed adjacent to the path, curves break up the monotony of dead straight lines and routes weave their way through mature trees.

History of Sustrans and the National Cycle Network

Sustrans is a charity dedicated to developing practical solutions to make it easy for people to get around using more sustainable forms of transport. The origins of the charity can be traced back to 1977 when a number of people in Bristol,

Over the years, hundreds of people have helped to build sections of the National Cycle Network, extending it into dozens of cities. As well as making use of disused railway lines, Sustrans identified the potential offered by old canal towpaths. Following negotiations with British

Waterways, the Kennet & Avon Canal near Bath became Sustrans' first towpath project, and between 1984 and 1988 the path was rebuilt from Bath all the way to Devizes. It's now tremendously popular as both a walking and cycling route.

The aim of the National Cycle Network is to provide at least one quality route in every major UK city, enabling as many people as possible to enjoy the fun, freedom and independence which cycling offers. The Network is already demonstrating that the creation of attractive, safe cycle routes can generate thousands of bike journeys that might otherwise have been made by car. In 2003, 126 million trips were made on the National Cycle Network, and nearly one third of these replaced a car trip, meaning that 38 million car trips were avoided.

Funding Sustrans' work

The National Cycle Network has only been made possible through the inspiration and financial support of our Supporters. From 1994 to 2004, the number of Supporters rose from 200 to 35,000 and they have provided the essential match-funding for other sources of funding including the Millennium Commission grant in 1995.

In 1995 Sustrans put in a successful Lottery bid for Millennium funds for the National Cycle Network, originally proposing to create a 6,500 mile nationwide network of safe cycle routes by the year 2005.

Sustrans was awarded £43.5 million of Lottery money, and supplemented this with further funding from a variety of sources including local authorities, development

▲ *The route through Castle Park in Bristol is used for everyday trips to the shops and work.*

agencies, the European Union, the Highways Agency, the cycle trade and industry, and from generous contributions from Sustrans Supporters. Such has been the enthusiasm for the project shown by local authorities that 10,000 miles of these routes are already in place.

Economic value
Local economies have benefited enormously from the creation of Sustrans' long distance routes. The first of these was the C2C (or Sea to Sea, from the Cumbrian Coast to the North Sea) which led the way in featuring a mixture of traffic-free paths and on-road sections. Within a year of its opening, 10,000 people had cycled the trail and spent over £1 million in bed & breakfasts, Youth Hostels, pubs, cafes and shops

along the way. In 1995, the C2C was the Global Winner of the British Airways 'Tourism for Tomorrow' awards. Since then numerous other long distance routes have been opened, attracting many people to the idea of a cycling holiday for the first time in their lives, and supporting local business.

Sustrans' work
The National Cycle Network consists of many traffic-free paths which connect (ideally) traffic-calmed urban roads with a network of routes through the countryside using quiet rural roads. In cities, the main thrust of Sustrans' work is to increase the profile and status of cyclists by re-allocating road space to favour bikes over cars, for example in the provision of advanced stop

▲ *Cardiff.*

▼ *Rangers on the Bristol & Bath Path.*

lines at traffic lights. Lower speed limits in cities could lead to a drastic reduction in deaths and injuries to cyclists and pedestrians.

The Safe Routes to Schools project aims to radically improve one of Britain's most shameful statistics: only 2% of journeys to school are made by bike (compared to 60% in Denmark). Sustrans continues to combine practical and educational measures to give children more travel options and help them to develop good travel habits for the future. The Safe Routes to Schools programme enables hundreds of thousands of children to walk or cycle to school, promotes health and fitness and helps to develop that vital sense of independence.

Sustrans' TravelSmart scheme offers tailor-made help and information to people looking to change how they travel. TravelSmart is helping thousands of people to walk, cycle and use public transport instead of their cars.

The way we travel has a big impact on our overall health, too. Sustrans' Active Travel project is at the forefront of work promoting cycling and walking as an effective and practical way to improve health. An active lifestyle helps to prevent and reduce the risk of heart disease, obesity and other health problems.

The charity's work with communities to encourage sustainable transport extends to a surprising array of projects. For example, the

▶ *School children use the National Cycle Network in Northern Ireland.*

Liveable Neighbourhoods project puts pedestrians on a more equal footing with cars, transforming streets into social spaces where people can enjoy their local environment.

Sculpture has come to be synonymous with the building of new sections of the National Cycle Network. Works of art have been incorporated on routes all over the country, carved from wood, sculpted from stone, welded from steel or built of brick. The Royal Bank of Scotland generously donated 1,000 mileposts with different designs created by English, Scottish, Welsh and Irish sculptors.

Sustrans also runs an award winning Volunteer Ranger programme. Volunteers make a difference to their communities, looking after local cycling and walking routes, and helping people appreciate the outdoors in the process. It's an enjoyable and rewarding role, and Sustrans is always keen to hear from people interested in contributing in this way. To find out more, visit www.sustrans.org.uk or call 0117 915 0110.

In addition to its many practical projects evident at a local level, Sustrans collaborates with leading European cities on transport policy, creating pedestrian and cycling access to public transport, shops, healthcare and schools. It's also active in promoting EuroVelo, the European cycle route network, which aims to link countries throughout Europe and bring their best practice into

Britain. The first of these European routes to open was the North Sea Cycle Route taking in Norway, Sweden, Denmark, Germany, Holland and the east coast of England and Scotland.

Supporting Sustrans

As a charity, Sustrans funds its work through the contributions of Supporters, sponsors and partners, also using public monies where available. If you're interested in making cycling safer and more enjoyable, while discovering new and exciting places for you and your family to walk and cycle, please become a Sustrans Supporter.

Find out more by visiting www.sustrans.org.uk or calling 0845 113 0065.

▼ *Sleeper Seat on the Hanson Way near Didcot.*

ACKNOWLEDGEMENTS

The National Cycle Network has been made possible by a huge co-operative effort over a period of years by hundreds of organisations and thousands of individuals. It is impossible to list all of them here. However, particular thanks are due to:

Nearly 500 local authorities who have developed local sections of route and who manage and maintain much of the Network. In particular to Cambridgeshire and Lancashire County Councils who agreed to be the principal hosts for the 2005 ten year celebration rides.

The Millennium Commission for its visionary lead grant of £43.5 million.

Government departments including the Department for Transport; the Scottish Executive; the Welsh Assembly Government; the Department of Regional Development (NI); and the Highways Agency; the Department of Education and Skills; the Ministry of Defence.

The Heritage Lottery; Big Lottery Fund; and Sport England.

Numerous landowners who have agreed to links and sections of route on their land including: Alcan; All Souls Cottage, Oxford; BP Oil UK Ltd; Catholic Church; Church Commissioners; Cooperative Society; Crest Homes; Duchy of Cornwall; Duke of Beaufort Estate; Duke of Northumberland; Earl of Chichester; Earl of Mexborough; Everard Guarries; Gonville & Calus College, Cambridge; Hansons; Holkham Estate; Imerys; London & Maudsley NHS Trust; Maristow Estates; Milford Haven Docks; National Grid; Northern Electric; Oxford Preservation Trust; Oxford University; Pfizer; RJB Mining; Safeways (now Morrisons); Seaton Delaval Estate; Shoreham Port Authority; Sir Ewen Cameron; Sir Richard Branson; South West Water; Sussex Archaeology Society; Tarmac; Tesco; The Channel Tunnel Group; Trinity College, Cambridge; Trustees of Earl Spencer settlement; University of Wales; West Dean Estate; Whitbreads; Wimpey (Scotland); Yorkshire Healthcare Trust.

Utility and statutory bodies including British Waterways; Forest Enterprise and Forest Service; English Regional Development Agencies (formerly English Partnerships); the Environment Agency; Ordnance Survey and Ordnance Survey of Northern Ireland.

Countryside and regeneration bodies including the National Trust; English Heritage; the Countryside Agency; Countryside Council for Wales; Scottish Natural Heritage; the Groundwork Trusts; the Woodland Trust; English Nature; the Royal Parks and many national parks; countryside and heritage sites; tourism bodies; and wildlife trusts and groups.

Network Rail; BRB (residuary) Ltd formerly known as Rail Property Ltd; British Railways Board; the Railway Heritage Trust; the Severn Valley Railway; the Dartmoor Railway; EWS and Railway Paths Ltd.

Landfill operators participating in the Landfill Tax Credit Scheme; including: The Norlands Foundation; Grundon's; RMC Community Fund; Hanson Environment Fund; Innogy; LWS Lancashire Environmental Fund; WREN; Cleanaway; Fife Environment Trust; Suffolk Environment Trust; Essex Environment Trust; Cory Environmental Trust; CDENT; SITA Environmental Trust; Norfolk Environmental Waste Services; Northumbrian Water Environmental Trust; EB Cambrian (Shanks First).

Partner bodies representing cyclists, walkers, people with disabilities, horseriders, anglers and other users of the routes.

Many local CTC and cycle campaign groups; the London Cycling Campaign; Spokes Edinburgh and Spokes East Kent.

Charitable trusts, in particular: The 29th May 1961 Trust; The Aim Fdn; Bridge House Estates Trust; A J Burton Charitable Settlement; C H K Charities Ltd; GW Cadbury C.T.; J Anthony Clark C.T.; The Ernest Cook Trust; The Freshfield Fdn; The Gannochy Trust; The Glass-House Trust; Calouste Gulbenkian Fdn; Gunter C.T.; H.C.D. Memorial Fund; The J J C.T.; Rees Jeffreys Road Fund; The Mark Leonard Trust; The Lyndhurst Settlement; The Manifold Trust; The Henry Moore Fdn; The Network For Social Change; The Northern Rock Fdn; Peacock C.T.; The Sigrid Rausing Trust; The Rowan C.T.; The Serve All Trust; The Sheepdrove Trust; The L.J. Skaggs & Mary C. Skaggs Fdn; RH Southern Trust; The Staples Trust; The Steel C.T.; The Summerfield C.T.; The Tubney C.T.; The Underwood Trust; Vodafone UK Fdn.

In addition to some of the above, we would also like to thank the following for contributing to our Arts Projects: Arts and Business; Arts Council England; Arts Council Northern Ireland; Scottish Arts Council; Eurotunnel; Interreg; Countryside Agency; Ercol Furniture; Rycotewood College; Seed Programme; RSA - Art for Architecture; NOF; SWERDA - South West England Regional Development; Northern Ireland Department of Culture, Arts and Leisure (DCAL); Community at Heart (Bristol New Deal); Creative Partnerships; South Oxfordshire Community Fund; Marsh Farm New Deal; South Lough Neagh Regeneration Association.

The cycle trade and industry, in particular the Bicycle Association and Association of Cycle Traders, and all the contributors to the Bike Hub Fund.

**A Millennium Commission
Lottery Project**

Sister Millennium projects that have created routes including the Trans Pennine Trail; the Kingdom of Fife Millennium Cycleways; Peterborough Green Wheel; the Millennium Coastal Park at Llanelli; the Earth Centre; Mile End Park; Changing Places; Turning the Tide; and others.

For corporate sponsorship particular gratitude is due to The Royal Bank of Scotland as well as to Halfords, Madison and Ordnance Survey.

Thanks to Bike in Bristol for their help with props for the front cover photograph.

And Sustrans' 40,000+ Supporters, 1,500 Rangers, volunteers, trailblazers, route developers and letter writers who have kept up the positive momentum throughout the period.

Sustrans would also like to extend thanks to all those who have generously contributed to the creation of the Network who we have not been able to list here.

Maps

Maps based on Ordnance Survey Strategi and OSCAR digital data with permission of the Controller of Her Majesty's Stationery Office © Crown copyright. All rights reserved Sustrans. Licence number GD 03181G0001.

Maps on pages 256, 257, 262, 263, 264 are based upon the 1984 Ordnance Survey of Northern Ireland 1:50 000 maps and maps on pages 248, 249, 252 and 253 are based upon the 1997 Ordnance Survey of Northern Ireland 1:50 000 maps with the permission of the Controller of Her Majesty's Stationery Office, © Crown Copyright 2005. Permit number 40526.

Further details about OSNI products and services can be found at http://www.osni.gov.uk

Text & Research

Nick Cotton & John Grimshaw
With Bill Vallis and Sustrans

Cartography

Stirling Surveys
CycleCity Guides
Sustrans

Project Co-ordination

Julian Holland
Sustrans

Design

Nigel White

Photographs

Front cover and spine Karni Morris

Other photographs
Shirley Acreman
Tony Ambrose
Alexandra Allen
Robert Ashby
Julia Bayne
Jon Bewley
Andy Blanshard
Nigel Brigham
David Buchanan
Nick Cotton
Anja Dalton
Lorcan Doherty
Glyn Evans
Fife Council
Richard Forest
John Grimshaw
Ian Chamberland Photography
GL Jones
Nicola Jones
Jonathan Kibble
Bob McQueen
Steve Morgan
Ken Nice
John Palmer
Julie Parker
Kai Paulden
Jan and David Parsons
Peterborough Photographic Society
Philip Lane Photography
Paul Rea
Toby Smedley
Tim Snowdon
Pat Strachan
Mark Strong
Ted Giffords Photography
Nick Turner
Jez Toogood
Vincent Walsh
David Young

Join Sustrans

Supporters provide the 'foundation' income for all our activity

Sustrans often takes on the role of a catalyst, bringing many partners together to create new and higher quality routes and transport solutions. To do this we need a source of funding that allows us to retain our independence.

What do Sustrans' Supporters do? Well on one level it's quite simple - they fund our core costs. Without this financial support, Sustrans and the National Cycle Network would, quite probably, not exist.

You can become a Supporter by completing this form. You will receive a welcome pack with information about our work as well as regular newsletters updating you with progress during the year.

Give a donation of £3 or join by standing order and receive a voucher for a FREE National Cycle Network Route map worth £5.99 (30 to choose from).

1. YES I would like to support Sustrans

NAME

ADDRESS

POSTCODE

TELEPHONE   E-MAIL

2. YES I'll support Sustrans with a donation

£15 ☐   £25 ☐   £50 ☐   £100 ☐   £ other ☐   *(please tick)*   If other   ☐   Please send me a pack on
(£15 is the minimum rate)   please state _____   leaving a legacy to Sustrans.

Please EITHER enclose a cheque/PO/charity voucher payable to Sustrans OR
complete your Mastercard/Visa/CAFCard /Switch number here and sign: _____

SWITCH ISSUE NUMBER   CARD EXPIRY DATE

SIGNATURE   DATE

POCKB3

or YES I'll support Sustrans with a standing order

Your monthly standing order will provide us with vital regular income to help us complete the   **REMEMBER:** You can
National Cycle Network and enable us to keep our administration costs to a minimum.   cancel this standing order
                                                                                                     at any time by informing
£3 ☐   £5 ☐   £10 ☐   £15 ☐   £25 ☐   £ other ☐   *(please tick)*   us and your bank
                                             If other please state _____

NAME OF MY BANK

ADDRESS OF MY BANK

ACCOUNT NO   BANK SORT CODE __/__/ – /__/__/ – /__/__/

MY NAME   DATE

SIGNATURE

BANK INSTRUCTIONS: Please pay the above sum on the 8th next and **monthly** thereafter to **SUSTRANS**, Account number 01400978,
Lloyds TSB Bank, 55 Corn St, Bristol BS99 7LE, Sort Code 30-00-01. **BANK PLEASE QUOTE REF:**

3. - *gift aid it* Make your support go further for FREE

Use GIFT AID and you can make your donation worth more. For every pound you give us we get an extra 28p from the Inland Revenue.
Just tick here ☐ it's that simple.

DEC18

4. Please return this coupon with your payment to Sustrans, PO Box 21, Bristol, BS99 2HA.